Industrial Buildings

Conservation and

Regeneration

Industrial Buildings

Conservation and Regeneration

Edited by

Michael Stratton

First published 2000
by E & FN Spon
11 New Fetter Lane, London EC4P 4EE

Simultaneously published in the USA and Canada
by E & FN Spon
29 West 35th Street, New York, NY 10001

E & FN Spon is an imprint of the Taylor & Francis Group

Designed and typeset in 9.3/12.5pt Palatino by Gavin Ward Design Associates
Printed in the United Kingdom at the University Press, Cambridge

British Library Cataloguing in Publication Data
A catalogue record for this book is available from the British Library

Library of Congress Cataloguing in Publication Data
A catalogue record for this book has been requested

ISBN 0-419-23630-9

Contents

Part 3 International Initiatives

Part 4 Looking to the Future

Part 5 Regeneration Through Heritage Database

Dedicated to the memory of
Michael Stratton 1953–99

Michael Stratton died in April 1999 before this book was completed. When he was first diagnosed with myeloma, only three months earlier, he wrote to me from hospital to say that he was determined to carry on working and, above all, to finish the book. During the brief period of his illness the publication of the book was a milestone to which he looked forward. Only ten days before he died he was still commenting on drafts and chasing the last elusive contributor.

I had known Michael for some time – through work at the Institute of Advanced Architectural Studies, the University of York – but it was not until 1998 that I came to work closely with him, on the Regeneration Through Heritage database. In our first discussions about the project he said that he wanted it to be 'fun'. And so it was. I was quickly inspired by Michael's wealth of knowledge when he drew up the initial list of buildings for the database without so much as reference to a book. He carried a vast bibliography around in his head and his list of contacts was endless. He was always keen to visit buildings that he had not seen before and made a point of travelling by train whenever possible. On these journeys he gave a commentary of all the significant structures en route, whilst at the same time telling amusing anecdotes, astutely observing the latest trends in popular culture, and talking affectionately about his wife, Annabel and children, Andrew and Timothy.

The highlight of our project was when HRH The Prince of Wales launched the Regeneration Through Heritage website at Highgrove in September 1998. After an exciting but exhausting day I waved goodbye to Michael on Swindon railway station and he travelled back to York via Cardiff so that he could take photographs of Cardiff Bay for this book. He never missed an opportunity and always dashed around at great speed carrying several cameras. Many of the photographs here are evidence of this interest in which he excelled. His enthusiasm was infectious and anyone who knew him could not fail to be enriched by his energy and depth of knowledge.

Michael Stratton was one of the pioneers and unsung heroes of industrial archaeology, to which his chapters in this book bear testament. It is a great sadness that he did not live to see the book in print. It marks the turning-point in attitudes towards the conservation and regeneration of industrial buildings and the renaissance of a building type to which he devoted his career.

Sue Taylor
York, September 1999

Preface and acknowledgements

These essays bring together a wealth of experience from contributors who have made in their individual ways a significant impact on the conservation and regeneration of industrial buildings.

The book was first conceived at a conference 'Conserving and Using Industrial Buildings', held at the University of York in 1997. This event was organized by Michael Stratton in collaboration with Fred Taggart, Director of HRH The Prince of Wales's initiative Regeneration Through Heritage. Since then, the regeneration of industrial buildings and use of 'brownfield' sites have appeared on the Government agenda and the momentum to secure the best possible use of these resources has increased.

Two years after the York event, in April 1999 at the Great Western Railway Works, Swindon, the 'Making Heritage Industrial Buildings Work' conference proved a further landmark in the changing fortunes of the industrial heritage. HRH The Prince of Wales opened the conference with a résumé of some of the work that has been done so far to ensure the future of the rich industrial heritage of Britain, and a plea that those with power, including the Government, should recognize the re-use of heritage industrial buildings as an essential component of national regeneration programmes. His Royal Highness has kindly contributed an edited version of his speech as an Introduction to the book.

As well as many examples of regeneration projects in the United Kingdom, the book also contains case studies from Germany and Sweden, and throughout the book exemplars are cited from many countries in Europe and as far afield as the USA and Australia.

Michael Stratton had done most of the hard work in bringing together this book before he asked me to complete it for him. This has been a great honour. I should like to thank all the contributors, the publisher and Annabel Stratton, who have been ever-patient in awaiting its publication. I am indebted to Barrie Trinder who has very kindly commented on the text. Thanks are also due to Mark Beech who designed and developed the Regeneration Through Heritage website and Gavin Ward Design Associates for designing the book, turning the manuscripts into camera ready copy while skillfully keeping an eye on the text. I should also like to thank Pam Hodgson and Priscilla Roxburgh at the University of York for their endless support.

The jacket photograph of Rose Wharf, Leeds, is reproduced by kind permission of Carey Jones Architects and Caddick Development. Other photographs and drawings were provided by the author of the relevant chapter except where a specific credit is given.

Sue Taylor
York, September 1999

It is a great pleasure to contribute to this book as it signals a changing attitude towards a unique part of our heritage that has been until recently in danger of disappearing from towns and cities throughout Britain. Over the last thirty-five years or so, I have watched in despair as one remarkable historic industrial building after another has been systematically demolished to make way for what is sometimes described as 'comprehensive redevelopment'. The many buildings that remain as a legacy from our industrial past are often vacant, underused or derelict. They stand as icons at the core of the communities that grew up around them. But of course the world has moved on and, with their original purpose gone, all we are left with is the buildings, which are just as much part of our national heritage as cathedrals, palaces or country houses. Many were built to the highest architectural standards of their day and, despite the passage of time, remain in remarkably good condition.

Over the past decade there have been some trailblazing regeneration schemes such as Salts Mill at Saltaire (*see Plates 3 & 4*), Dean Clough Mills, Halifax and the Great Western Railway Works, Swindon, which all have been successful due to vision and willingness to take risks on the part of great entrepreneurs operating in the real world of business. Aside from a few magnificent projects such as these, until recently there has been little success in persuading policy makers to see the enormous

Making heritage industrial buildings work

HRH The Prince of Wales ▮

0.1
Dean Clough Mills, Halifax, converted by Sir Ernest Hall into a highly successful business park.

(Photo: Dean Clough Ltd)

0.2
Great Western Railway
Works, Swindon,
converted by McArthur
Glen into one of the
most successful designer
retail outlets in Britain
(*see Plate 1*).

(*Photo: Rawls & Company*)

value in converting these unique buildings to new uses. Now, at long last, and before the dwindling numbers of our unique heritage buildings are finally expunged from our towns and cities, it seems that common sense has begun to appear. Some efforts now are being made to revitalize these buildings with new uses that are appropriate for the twenty-first century.

Three years ago I established two initiatives concerned with the conservation and re-use of heritage industrial buildings, the Phoenix Trust – a charity that acquires and develops historic buildings for sale and then re-uses the income for further schemes – and Regeneration Through Heritage – to promote awareness of the opportunities offered by heritage industrial buildings and to assist community-based partnerships develop proposals for them. In view of the Government's commitment to 'brownfield' and to environmentally friendly development they are initiatives that I hope will have something to offer for the future. Indeed, the recent publication of figures on the amount of land needed for new house construction has concentrated minds wonderfully. People are looking seriously at the issues and the implications of an inexorable march onto the landscape of Britain.

This debate is not new – it has been a central and unresolved issue in regional development and urban renewal for many years. A careful look at regeneration initiatives over the past decade reveals the large amount of vacant land and blight left behind. Indeed the number of

vacant factories, warehouses, mills and depots in our towns and cities is still enormous. To these can be added a huge number of empty shops, flats and houses; and acres of empty land – often in the ownership of health authorities, Railtrack and government departments.

We hear a great deal about 'joined-up' government – I think it is time to talk about 'joined-up' regeneration strategies. Too many regeneration initiatives have been undermined by short-term rather than long-term considerations, which have favoured low-cost new-build schemes and produced lots of breeze-block and tin factories or business-parks, even in the heart of our most glorious Victorian

0.3
Stanley Mills, Perth,
the first project of the
Phoenix Trust initiative
(*see Plate 11*).

(*Photo: Louis Flood*)

cities. They have not taken sufficient account of the opportunities offered by heritage industrial buildings, nor really come to grips with the complications of ownership patterns for inner-city land and buildings that require longer-term solutions. This causes developers to configure illogical development sites if they are to meet the requirements of their brief. Policy makers and developers too often make a presumption that 'brownfield' sites mean 'cleared and vacant sites'. In reality they frequently contain many buildings often of striking architectural importance, which are a re-usable resource and should be part of our drive to give practical expression to the commitment to sustainability. I also think it fair to say that few regeneration agencies really have any understanding of how to adapt these buildings to meet present-day needs, particularly those of business. On the other side of the equation, business tends to see these buildings as presenting problems rather than opportunities. All this plays into the hands of those whose first option is wholesale clearance.

Given the fundamental shifts that we have seen in our traditional economy it is tempting for policy makers to argue for the demolition of the old factories and communities. Then what? Are we to recreate the suburbs in the heart of our cities? Or perhaps whole cities are expected to move away to more prosperous areas in order to find work? Surely a better way forward is to promote the process of re-inventing communities where people already live, and recognize the value of the investment both in people and the built environment which already exists rather than abandon it. I therefore believe the time is right for a new philosophy to direct our approach to the regeneration of our towns and cities, one that recognizes these complexities and opportunities – one that people can understand.

After the last war and until the 1970s governments carried through an ambitious programme to build new towns. Millions of people were moved from congested cities to new and expanded towns with good facilities, modern houses and workplaces. Lives were transformed for the better, but at a price. It took years for communities to become established and we had the phenomenon of 'new town blues' where people felt they were living on building sites. But, crucially, everyone understood that the policy was to move people away from appalling conditions in the cities to good conditions in the new towns. The challenge now is to catch the popular imagination in the same way with a policy to conserve our precious countryside, use the resources in our town and cities which now stand idle, and create new and exciting communities in the places where people already live. We can then focus public and private sector effort to achieve this.

If we are to give meaning to any strategy of favouring brownfield development there has to be an explicit recognition that much of the built environment, and especially heritage industrial buildings, represents a sustainable resource from past generations which is capable of being 'recycled' for new uses. We are accustomed to thinking of cities like Bath or Edinburgh as places with a great architectural heritage, but visitors to Manchester, Glasgow and Newcastle are now, at last, beginning to recognize the beauty and value of our heritage from the industrial age. It is significant that the resident population of the city core in Manchester has risen from 400 to 6,000 in eight years – almost all living in converted warehouses and mills. Where a choice exists in favour of living in an exciting urban community, people are willing to make it.

Regeneration strategies in the new millennium will be operating in new economic circumstances. The world has moved into a new economic order which is knowledge-based.

0.4
Mistley Maltings, Essex, where a local partnership has been created which has put together a package of new uses for this building.

(Photo: Michael Stratton)

We need to create new kinds of communities where this can flourish – places where people will want to live and work, will want simply to *be*. Given a choice, I doubt if many people actually want to live in isolated, soulless housing estates; or to endure long journeys to workplaces which are often on characterless industrial estates or business parks at motorway junctions. I rather suspect that the majority would prefer to be part of living communities characterized by a built environment that reflects something of humanity's gift for artistry. It is time public policy makers started to pay attention to an aspiration which has long been suppressed by a fashionable, 'progressive' ideology. Industry is becoming harder and more expensive to attract to areas of high unemployment. Increasingly, communities will have to create more of their own jobs and enterprises, and so the quality of our urban environments will be a central determinant of the levels of economic activities which communities will be able to generate.

In the past, cities and towns were shaped by the needs of the industrial economy, but at the same time the people who built them never quite forgot that the inhabitants were sentient beings and not machines – hence the industrial buildings reflected something of the natural world and of the innate urge to beautify our surroundings through human craftsmanship. With the move towards the knowledge-based economy, individuals and small groups of people can take control. In a world of smaller scale, high value businesses – often dependent on new technology – people have choices. I hope this will lead to a fundamental shift in our value system and the way we perceive the places where we live and work. Britain's legacy of heritage industrial building offers an ideal place to start the process of rediscovering the essential characteristics of communities for the next century.

Over the years I have been associated with a number of projects to bring redundant industrial buildings of architectural or historic value back into contemporary use. I have also visited many more both in Britain and abroad. I am not talking about the restoration of these buildings just because of their architecture, nor the creation of 'Heritage Theme-Park Britain' where we repackage our heritage as a pastiche for the benefit of tourists. But there is no doubt that these buildings, and the environment in which they stand, can provide a uniquely attractive atmosphere for modern living and working. Above all, we need to rediscover the ingredients for such an atmosphere and try to emulate them in the future. Heritage industrial buildings need to be used and to be adapted. I established Regeneration Through Heritage and the Phoenix Trust precisely because the emphasis should be on identifying contemporary economic, residential and cultural uses for these buildings.

0.5
Sir Richard Arkwright's
Cromford Mills,
Derbyshire,
a community-based
project which created
workspaces for much
needed new jobs in a
rural community.

(Photo:
Crown copyright. NMR)

0.6
Sowerby Bridge, West Yorkshire, one of the Regeneration Through Heritage pilot projects (*see Plate 2*).

(Photo: Michael Stratton)

In case I am instantly accused of arguing that we should seek to recreate these buildings as we think they originally were, I am not actually suggesting that we try to build a better yesterday. On the contrary, we should encourage and welcome appropriate new additions and adaptations to our heritage industrial buildings. Sensitive contemporary design can bring new vitality, add to the value of an old mill or warehouse, and open up opportunities for the future.

In September 1998 I launched the Regeneration Through Heritage website (*see Chapter eleven*). It gives some wonderful examples in the United Kingdom and abroad of the successful conversion of heritage industrial

0.7
Smithfield Buildings, Manchester, a former warehouse converted by architects Stephenson Bell into retail and residential units for Urban Splash developers (*see Plate 7*).

(Photo: David Grandorge)

buildings, and draws attention to vacant buildings in need of regeneration. These projects demonstrate that you can do most of the things required of a modern economy in a heritage industrial building. They also reflect the shift in our economic base. In addition to conventional jobs we now see housing, culture, leisure and small-scale, high skill enterprises emerging as key drivers of regeneration. What is more – people *like* heritage industrial buildings. They are usually accessible by public transport and instead of swallowing precious greenfield land are helping the wider regeneration of existing communities. Above all, they give back pride to communities because people's spirits are raised by the sheer quality and elegance of these surroundings.

Of course all of this costs money. We as a nation therefore have to make choices. Community groups seeking to regenerate mills and warehouses are frequently told by public funding agencies that their projects are too expensive and public resources can be better applied elsewhere. Regrettably, funding agencies tend to see costs in a very limited way. Heritage buildings can cost more to refurbish than new-build. Yet if some of the non-attributed or unaccounted costs associated with greenfield building were included, things might look different. If you add in the provision of infrastructure costs – roads, services and so on – needed to get to greenfield sites, which are met from separate public budgets, and the costs for people to commute from home to work in these locations, then I think the picture would look more balanced in favour of regenerating existing buildings, even with the existing rules. The House of Commons Select Committee on the Environment's 1998 report on housing specifically recommended a presumption in favour of the re-use of such buildings and Government accepted this recommendation in its response. There is little doubt that once these buildings have been brought back into use they acquire an important character and value in excess of many of the alternatives on industrial estates and business parks.

I very much hope the new Regional Development Agencies and the Heritage Lottery Fund will recognize that heritage industrial buildings, because of their intrinsic attractiveness and location, have a real merit in the regeneration strategies being developed for

the country. As in examples such as Salts Mill and Dean Clough it is possible to develop a design vision for the entirety and yet undertake it in incremental stages. You don't have to have grand plans and big architectural teams to tackle these buildings. Small sums of money can provide enormous leverage and, once a project gets underway, new opportunities arise. Growth can be organic.

In an initiative to promote a more integrated form of theory and practice about urban planning, design, architecture and development, I have created the new Prince's Foundation for Architecture and the Urban Environment. The Foundation brings together practitioners and theorists, students and professionals from different backgrounds in order to help us all better understand how to create more liveable urban environments. It acts as an umbrella for all the existing initiatives that I have established in this area – including Regeneration Through Heritage and the Phoenix Trust. I am especially delighted that the Foundation is operating from a converted nineteenth-century warehouse in East London, where an ambitious programme of activity is in progress. I want it to be the crucible for a more humane and holistic approach to the way in which we plan and build in the twenty-first century. The Foundation will give a very practical application to the idea of linking the best of the past with the needs of the future and will, I hope, make a real contribution towards creating better places in which to live and work.

It was the great American urban historian, Lewis Mumford, who wrote that 'If we would lay the foundation for a new urban life, we must first understand the historic nature of the city'. As we wrestle with the regeneration of so many of our urban communities, finding successful new uses for remarkable old buildings is a very tangible way of retaining just such an understanding. And, when all is said and done, I believe we owe something to those craftsmen who built these buildings with such skill and pride.

Adapted from a speech at the Making Heritage Industrial Buildings Work conference held at the Great Western Railway Works, Swindon on 26 April 1999.

Part 1

Conservation
and Regeneration

1.1
The iron-framed
structure of Ditherington
Flax Mill, Shrewsbury,
by Charles Bage, 1796–7.
Photographed when
used as a maltings but
now empty.

Chapter one

Introduction: balancing preservation and change

Reviving

industrial buildings:

an overview of

conservation and

commercial interests

Michael Stratton

The University of York

Britain was the world's first industrial nation. It was also one of the earliest to experience the full trauma of decline in traditional manufacturing and dock handling, and has pioneered the conservation and re-use of redundant factories and warehouses.

The key challenge, from the very first initiatives just before and after the Second World War to current Millennium-linked projects, has been to find the right balance between preservation and change. Conservation, almost by definition, involves reconciling a desire for continuity with the introduction of new uses, and purist preservation with needs to update the structure and image of a building. Project directors also have to achieve a balance in terms of appropriate and complementary uses and in gaining the right mix of public and private funding.

Adaptive re-use for industrial buildings embraces both projects promoted largely through public initiatives and dominated by cultural uses, and conversions undertaken by private developers motivated more by profit-seeking than any altruistic concern. A key issue in either case, and throughout this book, is the relationship between building conservation and the revitalization of run-down urban areas. How can projects have an invigorating effect across towns and cities – involving and inspiring whole communities and promoting long-term employment?

A principle that runs through several chapters is that regeneration works best if it is based on broad principles of conservation, building incrementally on surviving resources in terms of buildings, landscape and people. Typically, in an inner-urban context, this involves taking stock, devising integrated strategies and bringing a cocktail of agencies, skills and funding to bear – not in one grand-slam scheme, but over several years.[1]

Much can be learnt from history. The first, introductory moral is that the re-use and physical adaptation of industrial buildings is as old as the Industrial Revolution itself. The furnace where iron was first successfully smelted with coke in 1709 is revered as a shrine at the birthplace of the Industrial Revolution;

but there is little that is heroic about this structure. Abraham Darby had taken over a derelict furnace incorporating beams fabricated in the mid-seventeenth century for his experiments. Nearby in Shrewsbury, the world's first iron-framed building, the Ditherington Flax Mill[www] of 1796–7, spent almost as much of its working life as a maltings than a textile mill (*see Figure 1.1, page 7*), and is now awaiting a third and this time non-industrial use.[2]

The process of evolution and adaptation has been largely pragmatic, motivated as much by the need to save money and time, as any considerations of preservation or cultural enrichment. Redundant mills have provided cheap workspace for pioneering car manufacturers while roller-skating rinks were once used to build some of Britain's first aircraft. One might argue that the key to success in conservation and regeneration is to combine the economic pragmatism of re-use in the past with the inspirational qualities and community benefits of successful modern projects.

Decline and dereliction

British towns and cities gained an intricate network of factories, workshops and housing during the Industrial Revolution. A particular trade – whether textiles, ceramics, metalworking or brewing – might predominate but different types of firm were often grouped in the same street or locality. Not only were mills dependent on dye works and breweries on maltings, but most towns would have foundries to supply machinery, warehouses for storage and stabling for horses. Businesses were clustered together, surrounded by housing. Walking and horse and cart were the key modes of transport across towns, and industrialists needed easy access to banks, exchanges, canal basins and railway stations.

During the inter-war period the constraints that had tied most industry to a central urban location loosened. Factories became powered by electricity rather than coal. Materials and products could be delivered and collected by motor lorry rather than narrow boat and steam train. Workers could commute by tram and trolley bus, and managers and customers would arrive by car. At the same time industrialists sought a fresh, modernistic image, partly drawn from modern American complexes, and as divorced as possible from the congested, warren-like complexes and belching chimneys portrayed on many Victorian letterheads.[3]

From renewal to regeneration

Progressive architects and left-wing writers shared a disaffection with the traditional industrial city, as caricatured by Charles Dickens' Coketown in his novel *Hard Times*.[4] Documentary films of the 1930s portrayed a working class struggling to maintain respectability within slums and unsafe working conditions. Most industrial areas remained fundamentally unaltered, long-established metal-working businesses staying in their old inner-city factories. New firms, such as those producing electrical and other consumer goods, often opted for greenfield sites on the urban fringe or within garden cities. The contrast between these old and new worlds, brilliantly portrayed in J.B. Priestley's *English Journey*, was exacerbated by the Blitz during the Second World War.[5] The industrial inner areas of London, Birmingham, Coventry and Bristol were left battered and increasingly tawdry while suburban areas with their modern by-pass factories suffered only localized damage.

Politicians and designers were encouraged to think boldly, with the aim of creating crisp modern working and living environments. Industrialists were willing allies, some having managed new purpose-built plant erected for the mass production of guns and aircraft. Such shadow factories (so named because one factory shadowed the production of another) were huge single-storey sheds located on the urban fringe – offering uncongested access for motor vehicles and being easy to adapt and extend for peacetime production.[6] Some of the vast shell-filling factories of the Second World War were quickly adapted as industrial estates, and those at Wrexham, Hereford and Bridgend have become major centres of industrial growth within their regions.

Job losses and site clearance

Britain's post-war planning system, influenced by the ideals of the Garden City movement, was dead-set against the mixture of factories, workshops and densely-packed housing inherited from the previous century. Local plans defined precise zones for industry so excluding new factories from largely residential areas, while slum clearance further undermined the physical and social interrelationships of inner-city neighbourhoods.[7] Looking back, it is remarkable how resilient the mixed industrial and housing inner-areas of most cities proved to be. Bombing razed individual buildings rather than whole complexes or industrial areas, and firms successfully adapted to peacetime markets if not to new manufacturing technologies. Most Midland cities still have streets combining terraces and workshops. The old docks and shipyards of Glasgow and Newcastle survived on the Clyde and Tyne until the 1970s.

The Oil Crisis of 1973 marked the end of the post-war boom. The de-industrialization that followed had a catastrophic effect across many areas of Britain, though its impact can also be seen across the Ruhr in Germany or the 'rust belt' of Pennsylvania in the United States. The statistics are frightening, even in retrospect – Greater Manchester lost 73,000 or 51 per cent of its manufacturing jobs over the decade of 1971–81. In Tyne and Wear (the industrial area focusing on Newcastle and Sunderland) unemployment rose to 20 per cent in 1985.[8] Cutbacks and mergers did not always lead directly to plant closures and clearance. The acres of car factories in Coventry or of railway workshops in Crewe, Derby or Swindon survived, albeit under-utilized until rationalization over the last decade. A similar chronology can be seen overseas, Berlin retaining much of its industrial plant through the Second World War and partition – the strongest pressures for rationalization and redevelopment coming only with re-unification.

The rapid growth of the tertiary sector with booms in retail and office construction promoted the decentralization of many conurbations, leading to what planners gastronomically describe as the donut effect. Developers avoided inner-city areas with their confused and congested layouts, to focus on out-of-town retail and office parks. The main exceptions, such as the shopping malls of Merry Hill at Dudley, Meadow Hall at Sheffield and the Metro Centre at Gateshead, are based on brownfield sites cleared of any industrial remains.[9]

Death of the traditional city?

British culture has long shown an ambivalence towards urbanization and a near hostility as regards industry and technology. These deeply entrenched prejudices are manifest in the nation's seemingly insatiable appetite for visiting country houses, and the popularity of life-style magazines such as *Country Living*. Meanwhile, the broad concept of the integrated city has been eroded. Social differentiation through wealth and class – already well-entrenched in modern society – was reinforced by the boom in house prices and the cult of consumerism during the 1970s and 80s. Ready mortgages and share issues following privatizations made the well-offs even better off while unemployment made the poor relatively poorer, so exacerbating feelings of segregation. Major cities became carved up into a series of enclaves, middle classes and the new home-owning groups defending their territory against the decay and crime of the inner city and 'sump' housing estates.[10]

Jane Jacobs, writing in 1962, was one of the first to recognize and defend the subtle intricacies of traditional urbanism: 'This ubiquitous principle is the need of cities for a most intricate and close-grained diversity of uses that give each other mutual support, both economically and socially'.[11] In the following decade, urban historians extolled the rich complexity of market centres and Victorian suburbs while critics and conservationists pleaded for the end of comprehensive redevelopment that was ripping through many towns and cities.

Public policy
and the industrial heritage

Disused or even under-used industrial buildings quickly take on an aura of decay, although their structure may be still relatively sound. Professionals and public alike – whether in the Staffordshire Potteries or the South Wales valleys – assumed they were worthless and condemned them as agents of neighbourhood decay. To many, clearance was a solution in itself.

Pioneering preservationists seemed to reinforce such prejudice. Even industrial archaeologists were slow in recognizing and rising to the challenge presented by factories, warehouses and their surrounding landscape. Industrial preservation evolved primarily through concern for Britain's canals and for early wind and water-powered mills. L.T.C. Rolt had an ambivalent attitude to the factories that he passed on his way through industrial cities.[12] Pioneering preservationists focused their efforts on compact and enclosed complexes such as the Abbeydale Industrial Hamlet in Sheffield. The key open-air industrial museums – Ironbridge^www and Beamish – were established in the late 1960s in semi-rural settings, though, at the former, part of the Coalbrookdale ironworks and two ceramics factories were successfully restored and interpreted.

Industrial museums that were developed within towns and cities were likely to be housed in redundant factories, so providing a nucleus for the conservation of surrounding workshops. Birmingham Museum of Science and Industry was housed in an empty electroplating works in the Jewellery Quarter^www and the Gladstone Pottery Museum^www was established to preserve a cluster of ceramic workshops and bottle ovens in Longton, Staffordshire.

Recognition of the value of re-use was paralleled by the protection of industrial buildings by listing. In the wake of some shameful losses – most notably the Propyleum at Euston Station and the Coal Exchange in the City of London, both demolished during 1961–2, the conservation lobby strove for protection of important Victorian buildings. St Pancras Station and Hotel, also in London, were listed Grade I in 1967.[13] The net spread

wider when English Heritage embarked on a national re-survey, undertaken from 1969 to 1990. The emphasis is now on thematic surveys, detailed attention being given to textile mills, breweries, corn mills and gas works.

The criteria for protecting factories and warehouses has broadened out from a pre-occupation with architectural and constructional innovation. English Heritage's listing branch is now also interested in the completeness of the complex and evidence of evolutionary change. A parallel initiative, the Monuments Protection Programme, was launched in 1986 primarily to enhance the protection of ancient monuments through scheduling. Non-ferrous metals, ironworking and electricity generation are among the themes studied to date.[14] Parallel progress has been made by Historic Scotland and by Cadw in Wales. The status of industrial archaeology has been advanced by the designation of World Heritage Sites. Ironbridge, inscribed in 1986, looks set to be joined by further key monuments to the Industrial Revolution, such as the Forth Railway Bridge, Blaenavon ironworks, and the Great Western Railway between Paddington and Bristol. Despite this intensity of survey and protection, innumerable industrial buildings remain vulnerable to decay, vandalism and demolition. Several councils have commissioned studies of local factories and workshops to identify those that have potential for re-use, even though they may not be of sufficient architectural merit to justify being listed.

Area protection

Conservation areas were introduced by the Civic Amenities Act of 1967; they helped to stem the tide of comprehensive redevelopment, especially after 1974 when it became necessary to gain permission to demolish unlisted buildings within the designated areas. But parallel conservation studies could do more to damage than protect inner city areas. A report entitled *Traffic in Towns* had promoted policies of ringing central conservation areas by roads cut through the inner-city zone of workshops and terraced housing, the formula being given conservation credibility by the studies of Bath, Chester, Chichester and York commissioned in 1968. They urged the designation of large conservation areas in city centres embracing the key listed buildings with cars and car parking being channelled via ring roads, or in the case of Bath, a tunnel. Reports conciding with Architectural Heritage Year, 1975, served to highlight the folly of destroying one sector of the town to protect the other. A book by Colin Amery and Dan Cruickshank, *The Rape of Britain*, took thirty cases, from Bath to Newcastle, to show how inner relief roads and major shopping and office proposals were threatening all but the prime listed high points of so many historic towns and cities.[15] SAVE Britain's Heritage was established in the same year and quickly emerged as the key pressure group in fighting for industrial and commercial buildings, especially where planners and councillors were still committed to major road schemes and redevelopment.

During the next few years outrage and good intentions led to action, aided by grants for outstanding listed buildings and for conservation areas. Town schemes involved a combination of central government and local authority funds to finance structural repairs on groups of buildings. Further provisions encouraged councils to upgrade traditional terraces rather than clear them for tower blocks. The designation of General Improvement Areas (GIAs) from 1969 focused on groups of houses that were fundamentally sound though shabby and lacking facilities and insulation. From 1974, Housing Action Areas were established to help improve the homes of vulnerable groups – whether pensioners or the long-term unemployed.[16]

The Civic Trust, established back in 1957, found that the principles and provisions of conservation areas and general improvement areas could be combined to promote rehabilitation across historic industrial towns. Wirksworth is a Derbyshire town that grew from the wealth created by the Derbyshire lead, textile and quarrying industries. By the late 1970s it was depressed and decaying. The Civic Trust was the catalyst for change by providing a small team to show the potential of conservation area and GIA designation, and of the small grants that they could bring. The

community was brought together through exhibitions and meetings and motivated through examples of good and successful practice in the form of pilot conservation projects. Wirksworth and subsequent Civic Trust initiatives have provided a series of ground rules for subsequent regeneration projects, such as the importance of legal protection, mixed funding, exemplar projects and public participation.

Inner city industrial quarters

Several local authorities applied the provisions of conservation areas and GIAs to the more promising parts of their inner cities. The Jewellery Quarter in Birmingham[www] was built up from the late eighteenth century to have a dense cluster of workshops, factories and houses. After the Second World War the Quarter was blighted by road and land-use zoning proposals. Following a change of bureaucratic heart it was designated as a conservation area, the local authority using Industrial Improvement Area (a variant of GIAs) status to give £4.5 million to building conservation projects, another £6 million coming from private investment. The Jewellery Quarter now has refurbished workshops and

1.2
Russell & Co Warehouse in Little Germany, Bradford, by Lockwood & Mawson, 1874.

jewellery shops, newly created offices and flats and a jewellery centre based in an old factory. Part is now the subject of an Urban Villages Forum initiative to encourage the provision of housing in the area.

Nottingham's Lace Market[www] suffered rapid decline after the First World War. In 1969 it was designated as one of city's first conservation areas, later becoming the subject of a town scheme and then an Industrial Improvement Area. Conservation work has progressed incrementally but to a high standard. Part of Rochdale in Lancashire and Little Germany[www] in Bradford, West Yorkshire have been the subject of similar provisions. The warehouse district of Bradford is now separated from the core of the city by an inner ring road, and progress has proved fitful with some firms moving elsewhere.

Early prestige regeneration projects – lessons from America

Conservationists have learnt a crucial lesson from America – that not just modest Victorian workshops but huge redundant factories and warehouses could have a future and that they could be powerful forces for area regeneration.

The historic harbours of America's great coastal cities had been in decline from the 1950s, as larger ships, bulk cargoes and containerization resulted in new facilities being provided downstream in deep water channels. Local politicians and developers quickly saw the potential of these redundant docks and warehouses, and managed to bring in huge sums of federal and city funding to encourage new construction, conservation and public access in the historic core. Boston was one of the first American ports to go into decline and a Redevelopment Authority was founded as early as 1957. During the 1970s, Quincy Market, a fine classical complex, was restored for speciality retailing by Benjamin Thompson Associates working with the Company, commercial developers from Maryland. Walkways provided links to the harbour and other refurbished buildings.

Further down the East Coast, revitalization of Baltimore's harbour started in 1962, aided by $180 million of federal moneys. New-build has predominated over conservation. Rouse and Thompson provided pavilions for tourists drawn in huge numbers to the science centre, marina and by a plethora of opportunities for shopping and eating. The harbour now attracts some 18 million visitors a year.[17] Other projects such as Fulton Market, New York and Fisherman's Wharf, San Francisco have provided a generic inspiration for waterfront regeneration across Europe and now Africa and Asia. In simplest terms the formula consists of a mixture of new land uses, including offices, housing, retail and recreation. Businesses tend

1.3
Inner Harbor,
Baltimore, USA,
transformed following a
waterfront plan drafted
in 1964. To the left is the
restored power station.

to be 'high-tech', housing for the young and well-off, and shops of the 'festival market' *genre* to complement a variety of leisure attractions. Selective or even pragmatic conservation is combined with bright and breezy post-modern architecture.

Conservationists and industrial archaeologists have taken careful note of another major American project – conserving the New England cotton conurbation of Lowell,^{www} Massachusetts. Most of Lowell's huge nineteenth-century cotton mills were empty by the 1970s. The town was designated a National Historic Site to bring in federal money for preservation and commercial re-use of the mills, and for a museum and network of trails involving streetcars, boats and costumed interpreters. Computer firms and heritage tourism have proved to be compatible with high standards of conservation and the rekindling of community identity among the town's inhabitants. Further reference is made to Lowell in Chapters two and seven.

Regeneration and conservation: docks and waterfronts

Boston and Baltimore taught British preservationists how to attract mixed funding and large numbers of visitors, but most have taken a more purist line in terms of architectural preservation.[18] Covent Garden offers an early exemplar of the 'British way'. After years when the whole area was earmarked for redevelopment, the Greater London Council led the meticulous conservation of the iron-roofed market hall in the late 1970s. Covent Garden quickly became a major visitor attraction resulting in the resurgence of the whole quarter and the opening of such 'draws' as the London Transport Museum and the Theatre Museum. During the same period Camden Lock, on the Regent's Canal in London, became a highly popular destination for Londoners and tourists through a more ad hoc project, three developers using warehouses and their courtyards for stalls, craft workshops and restaurants.

1.4
Camden Lock, Regent's Canal, London. Developed incrementally by three developers from 1971 with crafts shops and restaurants.

The growth of the Ironbridge Gorge Museum in Shropshire, established in 1967, had already shown the merits of closely integrating industrial conservation and area regeneration – with a museum working closely with a development corporation. The formula was applied to a major city in response to pressure far more forceful than any preservationist campaign – namely the riots in Liverpool during 1981. The government was rudely awakened to the depths and volatility of the inner-city problem and more specifically of unemployment and racial tensions. Merseyside Development Corporation was founded to bring new uses to land and buildings isolated from the rest of the city and no longer needed for industry and merchant shipping. The directors of the Development Corporation, drawn largely from the world of business, sought to promote the status of the city through new commercial, retailing and cultural activities and many of the 2,700 acres of the Corporation's six areas were allocated to offices and housing. Their flagship project was Albert Dock,^{www} applying £8 million of pump priming to save the complex built during 1841–6 to designs by Jesse Hartley. Some £2.25 million was spent on the conversion and a further £2 million to create the Tate Gallery of the North in one of the warehouses. The Tall Ships Race came in 1984 bringing wide publicity to the complex. The complete development has cost some £120 million, initially some 80 per cent of the funding being from public sources but now the great bulk being commercial investment. Albert Dock became an optimistic symbol of national hope for the future of beleaguered industrial cities and of the potential of industrial conservation projects. For further information on the Merseyside Maritime Museum, created at Albert Dock, see Chapter seven.[19]

Other urban development corporations and dock projects have built on the successful example of Liverpool and Albert Dock, typically with one or two warehouses being restored as an example to encourage subsequent private investment. At Gloucester[www] the City Council moved into the dockside North Warehouse in 1986 while the Llanthony Warehouse was renovated as the National Waterways Museum so providing an ideal base for the interpretation of the port. At Bristol the Bush Warehouse was converted to house the Arnolfini Gallery in the early 1980s, while one transit shed became the Watershed Arts Centre and another the industrial museum. Both cities were fortunate enough to retain coherent docks within walking distance of the city centre.

Elsewhere, geographical remoteness, bomb damage and clearance have made it more difficult to realize the potential of these redundant dock areas. At Hull the oldest dock basin was cleared and filled-in, leaving only basins and warehouses away from the city centre. Cardiff, Glasgow and Southampton are among the other ports where there are few warehouses or associated structures to conserve as a basis for regeneration. Cardiff has achieved a notability, even a notoriety, for the dramatic scale of its transformation of the coal port. The Cardiff Bay Development Corporation, established in 1987, pegged its mast on the creation of a half-mile long barrier to transform 500 acres of muddy estuary into a freshwater lake. Inland, a dual carriageway 'boulevard' will re-unite the docks with the centre of Wales' booming capital. Modern headquarters offices and leisure complexes occupy the key sites and dominate the landscape – the key adaptation project being Techniquest, a science centre housed within the frame of a marine engineering workshop. Cardiff has been the subject of much criticism, partly due to the debacle of its competition for a new opera house. Construction of the Welsh Assembly Building and completion of the barrage have brought renewed confidence; but doubts remain whether such prestigious projects will improve the housing conditions and employment prospects for those living in nearby Butetown and Tiger Bay.

Most of London's docks were also cleared. St Katharine's Dock, just downstream of Tower Bridge, lost all but one of its main warehouses and the larger downstream docks were levelled before it was decided, in 1981, to establish the London Docklands Development Corporation (LDDC). One of the few survivors within the London Group of Docks, to the east of St Katharine's, was the unique Tobacco Dock[www] at Wapping, with its stunning iron frame and wooden roof. It had been bought by two entrepreneurs in 1979 and converted into a shopping mall to designs by Terry Farrell. The £20 million 'shopping village' opened in 1989, during the recession. Remoteness from London's offices or the tourist 'beaten track' have made it even more difficult to fill the units. Conservation does not come cheap in Docklands. It has taken a contribution of £3.5 million from the LDDC and £11.5 million from the Heritage Lottery Fund to allow work to commence on creating a Museum in Docklands[www] at West India Quay, within one of the few other dock warehouses in London to survive the Blitz and post-war clearance.

The most successful group of conservation projects in London's Docklands front the river just downstream of Tower Bridge. The Anchor Brewery was reworked from 1983 to create apartments. Butler's Wharf,[www] just beyond on the south bank, was refurbished from 1988 by Conran Roche with shops and restaurants and 98 luxury flats above. These complexes were included in London Bridge Conservation Area,

1.5
Cardiff Bay with the red brick and terracotta Pierhead Building, by William Frame, 1896–7, and, beyond, a modern office block.

1.6
Shad Thames Street,
London, now a
conservation area
and with warehouses
restored by Conran Roche
and other developers.

so encouraging a sensitive approach to the
revitalization of the richly-atmospheric Shad
Thames Street. Other warehouses have been re-
used further downstream at Wapping and
Rotherhithe. Elsewhere the LDDC used its
wide-ranging powers to create large sites for
new construction and to improve transport
links. The rise in land values and boom in office
construction around Canary Wharf over 1985–8
resulted in some local firms selling up and
moving out of the Corporation's area. The
property slump that followed over 1989–95
highlighted the risks of pursuing policies that
were so market-led and hence so dependent on
the state of national and even global economies.

Several European projects have proved more
successful in reconciling commercial
development of offices, hotels and up-market

housing with integrated planning and with
addressing the needs of the typically less
affluent indigenous population. At Rotterdam,
the *Kop van Zuid* (City of Tomorrow) project has
been led by a city authority determined to
exploit the potential of the waterfront for a
broad community. When the eastern docks in
Amsterdam closed in the 1960s, many of the
warehouses were taken over by squatters. The
council accepted their initiative, designating the
area for high-density housing, above ground-
floor offices and restaurants. In Italy, Renzo
Piano has developed a public project for a
bonded warehouse and a group of cotton
warehouses in the port of Genoa. His aim is to
create a multifunctional environment typical of
an urban centre, combining 'utilities, culture,
services, housing, universities, craft, trade'.[20]

Looking beyond Europe, plans for restoring the major series of quays at Walsh Bay, adjacent to the Harbour Bridge in Sydney, have been challenged for not only involving partial demolition, but for turning a focal part of the city over to prestige hotel and apartment developments. The Victoria and Alfred Waterfront scheme in Cape Town has been phenomenally successful in commercial terms. Initiated in 1990 with the creation of a hotel, 'quayside taverns', a theatre and a museum, it now attracts 17.9 million visitors a year. But many conservationists are critical of its Disney-like atmosphere and concerned that demand for more 'themed' shops and restaurants will result in the clearance of historic structures, including an impressive grain elevator. Enthusiasm for waterfront regeneration has spread to a wide range of economies, a recent initiative examining the relationship between the Saigon River and the Vietnamese cities on its banks, including Ho Chi Minh.

1.7
Model of Walsh Bay, Sydney, showing its four wharves and its proximity to the Harbour Bridge.

(Photo: New South Wales Ministry for the Arts)

Naval dockyards

Naval bases remained secure in their original use for several centuries until modern cut-backs, especially those that followed the reunification of Germany over 1989–91 and the end of the Cold War. Chatham,ʷʷʷ established in the seventeenth century, closed earlier in 1981. Fortunately, the government accepted, on the example of successful open-air museums and Liverpool, that new uses could be found for its historic core while the more modern area could

be adapted largely to new industrial purposes. Established in 1984, the Chatham Historic Dockyard Trust, endowed with £11 million from the government, has conserved an 80 acre core of the 600 acre complex. Preservation and interpretation is combined with continued manufacture of flags and natural ropes for the Navy.

Portsmouthʷʷʷ continues to be one of the Navy's two key bases. The Trust, established in 1985, not only looks after a 12 acre site but seeks to market three historic ships – the *Victory*, *Warrior* and *Mary Rose* – and the museum collections as a co-ordinated attraction and enterprise. Much has been achieved in repairing buildings but there is an underlying tension in that the separate trusts – one for each ship and museum – can end up competing against each other for custom, so detracting from any appreciation of the complex as a whole. Some of the finest structures, such as the Block Factory, complete with Marc Brunel's equipment, and the Steam Factory, are, however, made accessible to special groups. These commercial and operational pressures are even more apparent at Plymouth. One of the finest groups of buildings, the abattoir, bakery and brewery in the Royal William Yard,ʷʷʷ has been the subject of a proposal, backed by Plymouth Council, to make it into a factory-outlet shopping mall complete with multi-storey car parks and new canopies, much to the ire of most conservationists.[21] Meanwhile impressive covered slips survive within the nearby but still operational Devonport Dockyard.

More naval dockyards are being made redundant in most European countries as a result of the thaw in international tension. Some governments bow to a commercially-led re-use while others seek to involve local authorities and councils from the outset. Sweden has one of the best-conserved complexes at Karlskrona, which passed to the city in 1989, and museums have been established at Amsterdam, Barcelona and Rochefort. The canal-side base of New Holland in St Petersburg dating back to the eighteenth century is currently the subject of a scheme for a shipbuilding museum, a 'techno-park' and housing. The Arsenale at Venice represents the greatest challenge of all, founded as early as 1104 and retaining a sixteenth-century ropeworks, Renaissance boat sheds, Napoleonic fortifications and a huge, British-

1.8
Entrance gateway
to New Holland,
St Petersburg, developed
by the Admiralty from
1732 with a series of
warehouses being built
1765–80s. New Holland
is currently the subject
of plans for conversion
to house a hotel, offices
and exhibition hall.

1.9
Arsenale, Venice, with its
covered boat stores and
one of its nineteenth-
century cranes.

built hydraulic crane.[22] Conservation schemes for naval bases are so large that they can be held up or derailed by the vagaries of the property market. In the case of Copenhagen the two main challenges have been agreeing a way of achieving closer physical links with the city centre, and persuading the Ministry of Defence to accept a more conservation-angled but less profitable mixture of uses.[23]

One major tranche of the military estate has been sold on and re-occupied with great speed and with little input from conservationists. Houses from several Ministry of Defence barracks and air bases became redundant with successive rationalizations of regiments and squadrons. The entire stock of married quarters was bought by Annington Homes in 1996, and are now being sold to developers, housing associations or the public at a rate of around 700 a year. Annington has adopted a policy of undertaking only basic upgrading work before selling at bargain prices.[24]

Textile mills

Many of the great cotton and woollen mills of the Industrial Revolution also became redundant in the 1980s. Some of the finest woollen mills are situated by canals or pools; such settings and their grand proportions can make them attractive to both commerce and visitors, without the need for massive public inputs of money and the provision of new public infrastructure as in the case of most docks. One of the largest is Salts Mill,www Saltaire, on the western edge of Bradford, built 1853 as the focus of Titus Salt's model community (*see Plates 3 & 4*). After the mill closed SAVE organized a conference to publicize its plight and in 1987 the complex was bought by the late Jonathan Silver, who had already been involved, four years earlier, in purchasing another great West Riding mill complex, Dean Cloughwww in Halifax which has become a thriving industrial and business estate.

Gloucestershire was another centre for the woollen industry, but virtually all the mills had shut down by the mid-1980s. Local pressure groups and URBED collaborated to convince the local council to study the successful project at Wirksworth and to develop their own project, aiming to combine conservation and the re-use of redundant buildings with a renaissance in local pride and new employment opportunites. The council itself decided to set an example, designating a conservation area running through the valley in 1987 and by relocating, three years later, into Ebley Mill,www with its landmark tower and chimney. Dunkirk Mill has been converted into apartments and Egypt Mill into a restaurant. A parallel initiative has been the work of the Cotswold Canal Trust in using volunteers and job creation teams to re-open the waterway that runs through the Stroud valley.

Textile mills have been widely re-used in many countries, and most have one or more still working, if sporadically, as museums. A mill at Brede to the north of Copenhagen is used as a base for interpreting the industrial and agrarian economies of Denmark. The Jannink Mill at Enschedé in the Netherlands is large enough to combine a textile museum with apartments in the upper floors.

1.10
Dunkirk Mill, near Nailsworth, Gloucestershire, before being converted into up-market apartments.

Conservation and regeneration

Renewal has given way to regeneration, at least in the rhetoric of urban planning and politics. Regeneration is now an international cause that should combine the conservation of buildings with improvement to living conditions. In some projects, it can also offer exciting new architecture, cultural provision and improved public transport. There is a flip side to this glistening coin – tacky conversion schemes, 'jobs for the boys', a squandering of public monies and a disregard for local people and their aspirations.[25]

The underlying philosophy of regeneration is that cities have rich resources and values that can be nurtured and revived, and that the benefits of an improved environment and of new jobs will filter down to bring lasting or sustainable benefits to the whole community. In contrast to the emphasis on physical renewal in the post-war period, regeneration implies that the existing urban form is a starting point, to be upgraded within social, economic, cultural and, where appropriate, natural contexts. Early initiatives were closely tied to the planning system developed after the Second World War and the work of civic societies and other trusts. Soon, approaches shifted to focus on ways of enabling the commercial sector to revitalize the local economy, public monies pump priming private investment.

Regeneration had its origins in the Urban Aid Programme, which was initiated in 1969 to fund social schemes in areas of multiple deprivation. Extra monies were allocated to the programme in 1977 and its remit became more comprehensive. The Liverpool initiative, led by Michael Heseltine, the local Member of Parliament, resulted in managers from twenty-five financial institutions developing ideas for the regeneration of Merseyside – the recommendations including making fuller use of redundant buildings. The key outcome was the introduction of urban development grants in 1982, aimed at attracting private investment into inner-city areas.

The Conservative Government sought more dramatic transformations through Urban Development Corporations, already mentioned above in the context of waterfront initiatives. The role of the UDCs was defined in 1980 as 'to

secure the regeneration of its area... by bringing land and buildings into effective use'.[26] They were established in four tranches. The first were Merseyside and London Docklands, the second focused on run down industrial zones such as Trafford Park, the Black Country and Cardiff Bay, while the third and fourth groups embraced the centres of major provincial cities such as Manchester, Leeds, Sheffield and relatively prosperous Bristol. The early UDCs, largely driven by business ethics, antagonized local authorities, ignoring or even contradicting their polices and in the case of Docklands making little of the listed building and other conservation powers that they took over. London Docklands Development Corporation was founded, in part, because the London boroughs could not agree on how to tackle the acres of redundant warehouses and dereliction.

Co-operation soon improved and the UDCs took greater care to respond to community as well as purely economic concerns. Most of them have or are now being wound up since they were only meant to have a life of ten years. It is perhaps too early to present a verdict on their success. They achieved major turn-arounds in terms of infrastructure and identity and have lured in new major investments, the dozen corporations claiming at least 150,000 new jobs, 27,000 new homes and 2,400 hectares of derelict land reclaimed. The cost has been around £3 billion of public money; and it has to be admitted that there are all too few examples of high quality design and planning, and of community-based regeneration.[27]

Following re-election of the Conservative Government in 1987, support for the inner city was re-shuffled – with more emphasis on City Action Teams and Urban Development Corporations and the introduction of city grants. The Prime Minister, Margaret Thatcher, encouraged the private sector to become more closely involved. 'Business in the Community', founded in 1986, seeks to encourage the involvement of commerce in regeneration while 'Investors in Industry' channels capital for schemes in the inner city. City Challenge was launched in 1991 to relate development projects more directly to the need of urban communities. Despite the huge sums of money fed into these schemes there is uncertainty as to the extent to which newly created jobs do last, and of the effect property development has on a run-down local economy. Some believe that the emphasis on inner cites is counter-productive – there is no archetypal inner city, and none operates as a dicreet economy – the key is to identify the forces of unemployment, congestion, blight and social tension across particular cities and then concentrate efforts on these problems.

English Heritage has focused its energies on neighbourhood renewal through Conservation Area Partnerships. Since 1994, 357 schemes have been developed, with funding from English Heritage being matched by commitments from local authorities and other sources – especially the Single Regeneration Budget and the European Union. The schemes tackle areas where repair and restoration of key buildings can stimulate commercial investment and hence address underlying causes of urban decay. The old harbour and warehouse areas of Whitehaven and Hull have been included and many of the CAP schemes are set in deprived inner-city areas. A CAP programme was agreed with the Heritage Lottery Fund in 1998 and a total of £50.8 million has now been offered in grants.

CAP schemes and other projects have benefited from the Government's Single Regeneration Budget which should rise in expenditure from £16 million in 1995–6 to £625 million in 1999–2000. Projects with SRB funding have achieved good results – during the first three years with eleven authorities running projects, it is estimated that around £1.3 billion of private sector investment was levered in and 53,510 jobs preserved or created. The Private Finance Initiative is another, though controversial, way in which business may be involved, whether for retail schemes or new roadways.

The latest regeneration initiative is concerned with housing and combines refurbishment with clearance and new homes. The 'New Deal for Communities' programme commits £800 million to England's most deprived neighbourhoods. Improved security and local services are to be provided but the worst estates are to be to be written off as architectural failures and targeted for redevelopment, guided by close consultation with community groups.[28]

Sustainability and new design

Regeneration now embraces a broad range of aspirations and angles. Many see it as a means to build on the qualities of urban living (about which only the British seem to remain ambivalent), to integrate work, home and recreation, and to counter rapid and traumatic change and wastage of assets.

Within this broadly ecological philosophy, the aim is not simply to preserve buildings largely unchanged but to bring back into use the energy and materials invested in them. If conservation is the minimum intervention to protect the structure from change, recycling is the minimum expenditure of effort to make best use of such resources. This principle is now encapsulated by the term sustainability, with its worthy 'connotations of building a solid future and achieving prolonged, lasting, worthwhile progress'.[29] Sustainable planning purports to achieve a balance between development and conservation. Westwood Mill Development Trust[www] is seeking to apply these principles at Linthwaite, Huddersfield by restoring the eighteenth-century complex as an environment/community centre, according to the principles of permaculture and sustainability as defined by Agenda 21 from the Rio summit.

The potential and difficulties of community-led regeneration are highlighted by the example of London's south bank, downstream of Waterloo Bridge. This section of London's river frontage became dominated by industry and working class housing, partially due to its susceptibility to flooding. It slid into dereliction as river traffic retreated downstream, and then became the subject of commercial redevelopment proposals including a skyscraper hotel. The remaining occupants (the population had fallen from 50,000 around 1900 to just 4,000) rallied and formed Coin Street Action Group in 1977. After winning Greater London Council to their cause, they formed Coin Street Community Builders (CSCB) in 1984 to develop social housing. Some derelict industrial buildings were cleared for a park and other ramshackle buildings were given temporary community uses. The visual focus of Coin Street project is the Art Deco Oxo Tower,[www] built in the 1920s on top of a turn-of-the-century power station (*see Plate 17*). Redundant and un-listed, the power station and its tower were highly vulnerable; but from 1988 CSCB embarked on a £20 million project to convert the building into seventy-eight low-rent flats, retail design studios, a bistro and a restaurant. The Tower is now flanked by a garden, and linked to other cultural centres such as the Globe Theatre and the Royal Festival Hall by the riverside walkway, now dubbed the Millennium Mile.[30]

A report produced by SAVE Britain's Heritage links government policy on sustainability to the conservation agenda. The study encourages a holistic approach that recognizes the importance of the historic environment to quality of life. SAVE urges that conservation should be more positively integrated into government strategies for environment, transport and regeneration, and that funding channels should be simplified with the reduced rate of VAT for works of repair and alteration on historic buildings.[31]

Conservation purism versus architectural evolution

Through the British system of conservation, specific values are given to individual buildings. In crude terms the best architecture – defined by aesthetic qualities, structural innovation and historic associaitons – is given the highest value through its grade of listing. Such protection should guard, through the need for listed building consent against drastic, unsympathetic alterations – what Neil Cossons has derided as 'rampant rehabilitation'.[32] This purist approach, developed and applied by conservationists, historians and industrial archaeologists, is now being undermined as much from within the preservationist movement as by its critics. The boat has been rocked though not yet capsized by the commitment to public participation, and more specifically the study and protection of twentieth-century commercial and industrial buildings. These are often large structures that need commercial uses to fund their maintenance and have steel or concrete frames

that can rust and spall from within. Specialists are evaluating tower blocks and power stations with great zeal, but the broad public can only be expected to share such enthusiasms if these buildings are made attractive and usable. Andrew Saint has argued that listing must be seen more of a 'marker' than an 'objective standard of excellence ...We must become more open to debates about preference, manipulation and personal aspiration and taking on board the attitudes of local people'.[33] English Heritage is also exploring these issues through the concept of 'environmental capital'. A group are analysing the extent to which conservationists can be less dogmatic, embracing local attitudes to buildings and sites and especially those not deemed to be 'nationally significant' , looking forward as well as back and accepting fundamental change.[34] All involved in such debates accept that conservation must build on the distinctive social and cultural qualities of an area.

There is great value in seeing industrial buildings and industrialized inner-city areas in this dynamic context. Large robust buildings have already had long, chequered histories and most are undergoing dramatic functional change when they are being re-used. Stewart Brand, author of the highly influential book, *How Buildings Learn*, would argue that such change can augment, rather than dilute the historical significance of a complex – most buildings are born to evolve and often perform better after they have been through a period of adaptation. But how should such evolutionary change be marked, if at all, in terms of fabric and image?[35]

This issue is considered further in the following chapter and re-emerges in some of the case-studies. Approaches to conservation and industrial archaeology will be seen to differ from one country to the next. The British have shown a particular commitment to identifying and preserving key monuments to the Industrial Revolution, as judged by advances in technology, engineering virtuosity, architectural style and entrepreneurship. By way of contrast, Italians perceive many of their industrial monuments as symbols of the *Risorgimento* (the creation of the Italian nation) and ripe for dramatic and stylish conversions. Scandinavians tend to pursue an ethno-graphical approach, focusing on the lives and conditions of the workforce rather than any heroic leaps in technology, and retaining as much historic fabric and atmosphere as possible. In larger countries, and above all in Canada and the United States, interests and policies differ widely between provinces or states. Each seems to have a highly individual group of specialists, devoted to the protection of mining sites, hydro-electric plant, grain silos or even fish-canning plant.

Current practice

Planning 'control' measures are, in themselves, no more than a means of responding to the symptoms of conservation problems; they cannot be expected to tackle underlying causes such as economic or social decline. The injection of public funds through grant aiding is just a form of alleviation, a short-term answer and, at best, a starting point for drawing in other forms of investment and support. The scale of most industrial conservation projects is so large that public grant aid is simply not sufficient. For a good thirty years charitable trusts proved successful in raising monies for industrial projects through appeals, and in funding their upkeep through admissions and sales. Increasingly they have found it difficult to generate enough revenue to maintain their stock of monuments and, at Chatham and Ironbridge for example, government endowments have been provided to fund such crucial repairs.

Conservation must be linked to other policies, to raise the necessary funds, to achieve a viable and sustainable scheme that relates to the surrounding economy and community. Industrial regeneration is a collaborative process and it is important to be aware of the key organizations involved. This is a major and continual challenge in itself, as names, addresses and budgets change continuously. The following is presented as no more than a starting point:

Government regeneration agencies and funds

❚ European Commission

The European Regional Development Fund provided £1.25 billion for designated English Regions over 1994–6.

❚ Department of the Environment, Transport and the Regions

Assistance in the form of grants is available for businesses in Assisted Areas.

❚ Enterprise Zones

Areas where tax burdens and controls are eased to encourage private investment. Examples relating to the industrial heritage include Chatham, Sunderland, Tyne and Wear and areas around closed coal mines.

❚ Urban Development Corporations

Twelve were established to spearhead regeneration in inner-city districts. They could acquire and develop land. £3 billion public expenditure brought in £12.6 million private investment by the end of 1996.

❚ City Challenge.

Launched in 1991. Local authorities gained support for initiatives to improve urban areas in partnership with private business and voluntary organizations. Thirty-one schemes were approved. Now absorbed into Single Regeneration Budgets.

❚ City Pride

London, Birmingham & Manchester projects involving governmental regional offices.

❚ English Heritage

Their Conservation Area Partnership schemes (detailed above) will have given grants of £71.8 million by 2001, resulting in a total of £430 million invested over a period of seven years. The successor schemes to CAPs were announced in November 1998 as Heritage Economic Regeneration Areas, with English Heritage committing £15 million over three years for area regeneration.[36]

▌ English Partnerships

Established 1994 to encourage job creation, inward investment and environmental improvement by reclaiming and developing derelict or under-used land. It has its own investment fund and can act as a developer. English Partnerships's work is being absorbed by the new Regional Development Agencies.

▌ Single Regeneration Budget

A single source of public money to provide support for regeneration projects. Replacing twenty separate programmes, £1.3 billion was available in the 1995–6 budget.

▌ Private Finance Initiative (Public-Private Partnerships)

A Conservative initiative to encourage joint public and private ventures.

▌ Local Government

Draw in national and EU funds and have Economic Development Units to encourage commercial investment.

Business practices

▌ Property and management consultants

▌ Architectural and planning practices

▌ Developers

▌ Land use consultants.

Amenity societies

▌ Urban Design Group, formed 1978 to promote an understanding of key issues and best practice.

▌ British Urban Regeneration Association, formed 1990 to promote best practice in regeneration.

▌ Civic Trust Regeneration Unit promoting community led initiatives.

▌ Urban Villages Group formed in 1992 to promote sustainable mixed-use developments.

▌ Community groups.

National Lottery

▌ Launched in November 1994. Funded projects embrace the heritage and ventures to celebrate the Millennium. There is now a shift away from architectural conservation and heritage work. Funds are administered through the National Heritage Lottery Fund.[37]

It has often been difficult to coordinate different bodies, such as central government, local authorities and regeneration agencies – due partly to entrenched allegiancies, and hostilities in particular between elected councils and non-democratic corporations. Local authorities may establish cross-departmental forums, with officers from planning, housing, leisure and economic development, to pool resources and skills and work with specially formulated committees of councillors.

Most can agree that the major challenge is to find a group of compatible and sustainable new uses just as much as funding and managing any physical works on a complex of run-down buildings. There is a small group of entrepreneurs who have made a speciality of seeking out redundant buildings that have hidden merits and then exploiting such potential through finding appropriate, though sometimes unlikely, uses and users. Drawing on the cult of 'loft living' in the United States many warehouses can provide wide, well-lit plans for apartments in central urban locations. Tom Bloxham of Urban Splash has proved especially successful in this field converting redundant stores and workshops in Manchester and Liverpool, that will appeal to young professionals keen to live as well as work in the city (*see Figure 1.11*). Another developer, Bennie Gray of the SPACE Organisation has filled empty warehouses and factories with offices and studios – giving hard-worked buildings a new, brighter image with modest outlay. His approach to re-use is considered in Chapter six.

Regeneration Through Heritage projects

The need to bring the resources of the private sector to bear on buildings and areas apparently at major disadvantage resulted in the formation of Regeneration Through Heritage (RTH) in

1.11
Smithfield Buildings,
Oldham Street,
Manchester; a Victorian
department store vacant
from the 1970s and now
converted by Urban
Splash and Stephenson
Bell (architects) into
eighty-one apartments,
thirty-one shops and a
fitness centre
(*see Plate 7*).

February 1997 on the request of HRH The
Prince of Wales. A steering group and its
officers work with councils, businesses and
local groups. The aim, considered more fully by
Fred Taggart in Chapter four, is to help local
groups re-use redundant industrial buildings
and hence create new economic and social
opportunities and, above all, jobs.

Action planning

Public participation is a key factor in the work
of RTH. The aim is not to garner public support
for policies devised by planners and architects
but to gain an understanding of problems,
generate ideas, resolve conflicts and aid
successful implementation. Action planning is a
much favoured element of most regeneration
projects. Professionals visit an area and conduct
a brainstorming seminar or weekend, working
with as wide a range as possible of local
interests. The report must have support from
both groups and be followed by both
implementation and further dialogue.[38]
Action planning sessions have the following
agenda:

▌ Identify short and long term strategies

▌ Devise the means to implement those
strategies

▌ Increase public awareness

▌ Form a steering group

▌ Prepare a briefing paper.

They should include in their programme:

▌ Briefing discussion

▌ Public meeting

▌ Workshops and design time

▌ Presentations of the workshops and
discussions.

Regenerating the complete city: Manchester

Few would deny that industrial conservation
projects must relate closely to area regeneration
and broader urban planning policies. In several
cities the industrial heritage seems to be a key
to unlocking their potential in both economics
and culture. Manchester was heralded as

1.12
Victoria Mill, Miles Platting, Manchester, before being restored as a community centre.

Britain's first industrial city by Friedrich Engels for the close relationship between its cotton mills, warehouses and canals. This inheritance became a liability in post-war Britain, decaying buildings and unusable canals symbolizing a series of drastic problems:

▎ Decline in manufacturing.

▎ Only growth has been in service sector, and especially part-time work.

▎ Poor housing. In 1994, 14 per cent of private sector stock statutorily unfit, and over 5,000 homes empty.

▎ Manchester men have 58 per cent greater chance of dying prematurely in relation to the national average.

▎ Problems with drug trade, burglaries, property and vehicle crime.

In the 1980s, Manchester recognized the architectural potential of its industrial heritage and then discovered a means to turn this inheritance to good value. The Council led the restoration of Liverpool Road Station for the Museum of Science and Industry, the first phase opening in 1983. It was also a prime mover in the restoration of the Central Railway Station as a major exhibition centre – G-Mex. During the 1980s, private developers and businesses took up the council's example by re-using historic buildings for shop developments, offices, housing as well as museums.[39]

The area of Central Manchester Development Corporation, established 1988, embraced 1,187 hectares from Piccadilly in the centre of the city westwards to Pomona Docks on the Manchester Ship Canal. By December 1995 it had brought in £440 million in investment. The parallel City Pride project was launched in 1993 to encourage investment across an area covering the city centre and much of Salford and Trafford. The city centre is being partly rebuilt, following damage due to a bomb blast, a £20 million Lottery grant being allocated in July 1998 to create the new civic Exchange Square in the Millennium Quarter. Castlefields[www] is now a major tourist centre and, to the east, Ancoats[www] and Miles Platting are the focus of initiatives in community-based regeneration with support from the Urban Villages Forum. This latter area of decay and social distress is a true test of the effectiveness of industrial regeneration. There are fine mills fronting a historic canal but an action planning seminar presented a vulnerable community excluded from the nearby vibrant city centre. A Development Trust has rejuvenated Victoria Mill. Single Regeneration Budget funds are now being applied across the district to 'invest in people, strengthen the economic base, and improve the environment' of this area ready for the Commonwealth Games in 2002. Building conservation, improved housing and recreational facilities are intertwined with ritzy images of a '24 hour city' of clubs and recording studios. Local people are justifiably sceptical towards short-term projects and want long-term support to help realise the strengths of Ancoats in terms of its location, industrial heritage and community spirit.

Several other European cities have made industrial conservation a key element in their regeneration plans. Bilbao in northern Spain may be best known now for its titanium-clad Guggenheim Museum by Frank Gehry, but numerous other conservation projects have transformed the face and life of the city over the last decade. The market building has been restored and industrialists' mansions re-used as schools and by other institutions. The city has made a huge financial and political commitment to regeneration; it has succeeded in nurturing a sense of sociability and community, although much dereliction remains downstream on the left bank of the River Nervión.[40]

Millennium projects

The pots of gold offered via the National Lottery have permitted some huge structures to have a future and will bring a number of grand projects to Britain's run-down dockyards. Some schemes, such as the Spinnaker tower for Portsmouth, designed to symbolize the city's maritime past, have been dismissed as Millennial ego-trips. Some will create major cultural attractions, such as the Lowry Museum by the Manchester Ship Canal in Salford, Manchester. Others, such as the Centre for the Performing Arts in Bristol have fallen by the wayside.

The new Tate Gallery of Modern Art (Tate Modern) has the most conspicuous building and site of all the Millennium conservation projects – Sir Giles Gilbert Scott's Bankside Power Station^{www} built in the 1940s and 50s facing St Paul's Cathedral across the Thames (*see Plate 10*). Herzog & de Meuron are using a budget of £130 million to create three floors of galleries within the 35 metre high turbine hall with extra displays being in a glass 'conservatory' set on the roof. Southwark Council have contributed some funds in the belief that the gallery will help bring visitors and hence money and employment into their borough, still very much the poor relation to the City of London on the north bank of the Thames.

At Gateshead, over the river from Newcastle-upon-Tyne, an arts centre is to be created in a 1940s concrete flour mill. The £100 million Baltic Mills^{www} project is part-funded by the Lottery. The project design by Dominic Williams involves gutting the silos and building a lightweight construction for a restaurant and viewing platform on the roof of the mill. It will become the largest contemporary visual arts gallery outside London and, it is hoped, attract 345,000 visitors a year.[41] This dramatic venture would have been inconceivable if council initiatives and commercial investment had not already turned the banks of the Tyne from a neglected backwater into an attractive setting for offices and restaurants.

English Partnerships

English Partnerships has emerged as the largest agency involved in regeneration. No less than 2,700 projects were underway by 1998 with a programme budget of £235 million and estimated to attract £630 million of private investment, facilitate 5,200 new homes and create 910,000 square metres of commercial and industrial floorspace. These targets will only be realized by major new-build programmes; but there are also twenty city regeneration initiatives typically building on the work of Conservation Area Partnership (CAP) schemes or the UDCs. Over the next six years £25 million is being allocated to Grainger Town, linking the heart of Newcastle to the River Tyne, while other projects are underway in Bradford, Nottingham, the harbour area of Bristol and in Manchester and Salford. The intention, in each case, is to work closely with local councils and, by working through six regional offices, relate to the needs of local communities. Projects involving the re-use of industrial buildings include the rationalization and re-opening of the railway carriage works at Holgate, York; the re-opening of Sutton Harbour in Plymouth; the refurbishment of the stables close to the National Indoor Arena, Birmingham; and the transformation of the Spirella Factory, Letchworth into offices.[42]

Brownfield challenges

Inner cities and derelict industrial areas have been brought into the political limelight by the widely publicized projection that 4.4 million new homes need to be squeezed into the United Kingdom by 2016. Industrial wasteland has been targeted as the means whereby houses can be provided without undue encroachment on the countryside. However, there is concern that such brownfield development will result in the loss of redundant though sound buildings and of rich ecological sites that provide much needed havens for city dwellers and wildlife alike. Chris Baines, President of the Urban Wildlife Partnership, emphasizes that most old industrial sites are not brown but have become naturally green: 'The complex mosaic of railway land, old mineral workings, demolished factories, old waste tips, neglected allotments and canals constitutes a huge network of wildlife habitats often free from pesticide, herbicides and the intensive agriculture that has damaged much of the countryside'.[13] As yet ecologists, industrial archaeologists and conservationists have failed to share their concerns let alone create any framework to guide regeneration agencies and developers as they move in on the ripe and politically favoured potential of brownfield land.

Conclusions

Already some of the great Millennium projects seem shaky in terms of basic economics due to the problems of gaining matching funding and the realization that there will not be enough visitors to go round during the heritage hangover that will follow the year 2000. Public disquiet over the allocation of lottery money is matched by debate as to the long-term value and even the political morality of grand ecological and cultural centres.

As Lottery and European Union grant money is trimmed if not slashed, the key lessons for the new century are likely to be those learnt from the more modest projects rooted in conservation and area regeneration. In summary:

▮ Projects should be related to broad regeneration strategies.

▮ Public and private agencies must work in new forms of partnership.

▮ Uses should be balanced to achieve viability and help local communities.

▮ Public participation and action planning should be part of an early stage in any regeneration programme.

▮ Incremental approaches are most likely to result in sustainable success.

Notes and references

1 These principles were discussed at the conference held at the University of York in 1997, especially in the papers presented by Nicholas Falk, Fred Taggart and contributions by John Worthington.

2 The extent to which industrial buildings take on new uses is considered in Stratton, M. & Trinder, B. (1997) *Book of Industrial England*, Batsford/English Heritage, London.

3 See Skinner, J. (1997) *Form and Fancy: the Architecture of Wallis, Gilbert & Partners*, University of Liverpool.

4 Dickens, C. (1854, 1967 ed.) *Hard Times*, Dent, London.

5 Priestley, J.B. (1934) *English Journey*, Heinemann, London.

6 The architecture of shadow factories is analysed in Collins, P. & Stratton, M. (1993) *British Car Factories from 1896*, Veloce, Godmanstone.

7 For an overview of British post-war planning see Esher, L. (1981) *A Broken Wave*, Allen Lane, London.

8 Usher, D. & Davoudi, S. (1992) 'The Rise and Fall of the Property Market in Tyne and Wear', in Healey, P. et al, *Rebuilding the City: Property Led Urban Regeneration*, E & F.N. Spon, London, 77–99.

9 See Clark, D. (1989) *Urban Decline*, Routledge, London.

10 Cowan, R. (1997) *The Connected City*, Urban Initiatives, London.

11 Jacobs, J. (1962) *The Death and Life of Great American Cities*, Penguin, Harmondsworth.

12 Rolt, L.T.C. (1944) *Narrow Boat*, Eyre & Spottiswoode, London.

13 Stamp, G. (1996) 'The Art of Keeping One Jump Ahead: Conservation Societies in the Twentieth Century', in Hunter, M., *Preserving the Past*, Alan Sutton, Stroud, 77–8 (90–1).

14 Stocker, D. (1995) 'Industrial Archaeology and the Monuments Protection Programme in England', in Palmer, M & Neaverson, P. eds., *Managing the Industrial Heritage*, School of Archaeological Studies, Leicester University.

15 Amery, C. & Cruickshank, D. (1975) *The Rape of Britain*, Paul Elek, London.

16 Cullingworth, J.B. & Nadin, V. (1994) *Town and Country Planning in Britain*, Routledge, London, 196–7.

17 Colquhoun, I. (1995) *Urban Regeneration*, Batsford, London, 2.

18 Some early British projects also provided inspiration, for example the conversion of Snape Maltings,ʷʷʷ Suffolk into a concert hall after being bought by George Gooderham in 1965.

19 For an overview of such projects see Colquhoun (1995). This pioneering UDC was wound up in March 1998.

20 Andreae, C. & Trottier, L. (1994) *Conference on the Conservation of Industrial Heritage: National Reports*, TICCIH/CSIH, 32.

21 *Building Design*, 10 October 1997, 3. For more information on the politics and economics of waterfront regeneration see: Atamturk, E. (1996) *Forms of Decision Making in Waterfront Regeneration Projects in Western Europe*, MSc Thesis, Bartlett School of Architecture and Planning, London.

22 For further information see Clark, C. (1994) *Conservation, Community and Economic Aspects of the Transition of Naval and Military Sites to Civilian Uses in Four Former Dockyard Towns*, MA thesis, Oxford Brookes University.

23 For a detailed consideration of the re-use of dockyards see: Middleton, J. & Walker, A. (1998) *Rendoc 98: the redevelopment and regeneration of former naval dockyards*, Chatham Historic Dockyard Trust.

24 *The Times*, 4 July 1998, weekend section, 16.

25 There are several useful studies of urban regeneration, for example: Berry, J.N., Deddis, B. & McGreal, S. eds. (1993) *Urban Regeneration: Property Investment and Development*, E & F.N. Spon, London; and Central Office of Information, *Urban Regeneration*, HMSO, London. See also Pearce, G. (1994) 'Conservation as a Component of Urban Regeneration', in *Journal of Regional Studies*, 28 (1), 88–93; and Healey, P. (1991) 'Urban Regeneration and the Development Industry', *Regional Studies*, 25, 97–110.

26 Cullingworth & Nadin (1994) op cit, 211–19.

27 *The Independent*, 2 April 1998, 18.

28 *The Times*, 16 September 1998, 9.

29 Steele, J. (1997) *Sustainable Architecture*, McGraw-Hill, New York, ix.

30 Coin Street Community Builders (nd) *Coin Street: There is Another Way*, CSCB, London.

31 SAVE (1998) *Catalytic Conversion: Revive Historic Buildings to Regenerate Communities*, SAVE, London, 6, 9.

32 Cossons, N. (1987) *The BP Book of Industrial Archaeology*, David & Charles, Newton Abbot, 19.

33 Saint, A. (1997) 'A Case for Reforming Architectural Values', in Stratton, M. *Structure and Style: Conserving Twentieth Century Buildings*, E & F.N. Spon, London, (34–6) 43.

34 (1998) *Conservation Bulletin*, March, 8–10.

35 Miller, G. (1996) *Urban Regeneration: Opportunities for Architects?* Miller, Leeds.

36 English Heritage (1998) *Conservation-Led Regeneration*, English Heritage, London.

37 Contact: Heritage Lottery Fund, 7 Holbein Place, London SW1W 8NR.

38 Wates, N. (1996) *Action Planning*, The Prince of Wales' Institute of Architecture, London.

39 Butler, S. (1992) *Science and Technology Museums*, Leicester University Press, 65–9.

40 (1998) *The Times*, 1 August, weekend section, 28.

41 (1998) *The Architects' Journal*, 206, 6, 20–21.

42 English Partnerships (1997) *Annual Report*, English Partnerships, London.

43 (1998) *The Times*, 1 August, weekend section, 18.

Chapter two

Understanding

the potential:

location, configuration

and conversion options

Michael Stratton

The University of York

Introduction

This chapter sets out some principles concerning the nature of industrial buildings and their potential for re-use. Such an approach is, one hopes, of value, given that most of the literature on this subject was written over a decade ago, and recent years have seen many advances in terms of research, policy-making and practice.

Devising a strategy: the value of feasibility studies

There are two ways of devising strategies for the adaptation of industrial buildings: 'sixth sense' intuition or meticulous feasibility studies. Some developers claim to gain their ideas spontaneously when visiting buildings. But even those with the greatest bravura will test their first thoughts – with capacity studies examining leasable space and possible revenue, and marketing studies which may be undertaken by commercial agents. Terence Conran was described as having a 'gut feeling' about his London projects, when relating vacant buildings to one or more niche markets. His perception has proved generally sound, judging by the success of the Michelin Building[www] and the Bluebird Garage[www] in west London in their new life as restaurants and shops (*see Plate 22*). His experience with Butler's Wharf[www] by the Tower Bridge was a little more bruising. The first conversion scheme hinged on a major company taking much of the space as its headquarters. This prospect evaporated due to delays and the recession, resulting in insolvency and the need to devise a strategy again, virtually from scratch.[1]

Re-use is a risk business, but the chance of failure can be reduced by a feasibility study. This research method was first propounded in the 1980s as a key, preliminary stage in any conversion project. It is worth reviewing how they have been used to identify the optimum range of uses and to form a basis for detailed design work. Most projects need to be nurtured through four stages – incubation, negotiation, construction and management. It may be appropriate to undertake three types of feasibility study as part of the incubation stage:

▌ Taking stock of opportunities, evaluating possible strategies for development and choosing buildings for detailed study.

▌ Testing possible approaches and deciding on investment of appropriate resources.

▌ Confirming an approach and developing an implementation programme.

Eley and Worthington presented a systematic approach to feasibility studies, particularly appropriate for conversions taking relatively small buildings into multiple occupancy. In simplest terms a feasibility study might contain:

▌ Introduction to the building and its location

▌ Building condition report

▌ Financial summary

▌ Market study

▌ Architect's report and specifications

▌ Drawings with plans as existing and proposed site plan

▌ Cost report.[2]

For historic, especially listed buildings, the first two stages may now be expanded into a conservation plan. This strategic document is presented by English Heritage as the first stage in evaluating any scheme, to be prepared once 'you have an idea for a project' and before significant time and resources have been invested in a particular scheme. Built up from documentary and field study, it explains the significance of a building or site, its particular sensitivities and polices for managing and protecting what is significant. A conservation plan is a starting point for:

▌ Developing a new project for a heritage site

▌ Preparing management proposals

▌ Developing a restoration scheme

▌ Planning any conservation work.

The plan may have the following sections:

▌ *Section 1* Summary

▌ *Section 2* Background

▌ *Section 3* Understanding the site

▌ *Section 4* Assessment of significance/heritage merit

▌ *Section 5* Issues – ownership, resources, physical condition, quality of uses, public expectations.

▌ *Section 6* Conservation policies.

▌ *Section 7* Adoption and review.[3]

Such conservation factors then need to be related to studies of buildings focusing on their potential and the financial implications of differing re-use options. Some of this information will emerge through a standard business plan, but there are some particular issues – in particular location and building form – that need careful attention with redundant or under-used factories and warehouses.

Location

Industrial buildings manage to both fulfil and confound the key adage of estate agents that location is the key factor in the property market. Britain is littered with fine industrial buildings in the wrong places – Britain's greatest twentieth-century factory lies vacant in the bleak hilltop settlement of Brynmawr[www] and the world's first iron-framed building in a bland suburb just too far from the centre of Shrewsbury. While Brynmawr seems virtually a no-hoper in supporting a viable new use, there are some prospects for a unique building in Shropshire's county town. The flax mill can be seen as an asset capable of rejuvenating one of Shrewsbury's less distinguished suburbs. It is the marginal locations that offer the golden opportunities for re-use. Numerous outdated but impressive factories survive where land values were too low to justify demolition and redevelopment. As a direct consquence they can now be bought at a sufficiently modest cost for repair and conversion to be viable, whether for office, community or domestic use.

A group of entrepreneurs have demonstrated the art of understanding such marginal locations and, above all, of perceiving whether an area is still declining or, at least potentially, 'on the up'.

At Dean Clough,ʷʷʷ Halifax and Saltaireʷʷʷ near Bradford, Ernest Hall and Jonathan Silver were working on mills blessed with relatively promising locations to attract new occupants and visitors. In contrast, the most striking Yorkshire mill complex of all, Manningham,ʷʷʷ remains empty largely because of its bleak surroundings in one of Bradford's more disdvantaged inner suburbs.

2.1
Manningham Mill,
Bradford, Yorkshire.

It is worth considering the locations where historic industrial buildings are found in more detail:

Rural

Rural locations were chosen by many of the pioneers of the Industrial Revolution, whether Abraham Darby at Ironbridgeʷʷʷ or Robert Owen at New Lanark.ʷʷʷ They needed access to water power and, in some cases, local raw materials. An extra justification for a rural location, in the case of Owen or of Richard Arkwright at Cromford,ʷʷʷ Derbyshire was to create a model community away from the temptations of towns and cities.

These rural communities – embracing factories and housing – survive largely because their rural setting left them remote from pressures for redevelopment, but also because buildings could be quietly adapted to alternative low-grade uses once their original function had gone. The Coalbrookdale Company's Gothic warehouse became a tatty garage and Arkwright's mill used for making paint pigments. Many rural sites combine attributes and weaknesses for re-use projects. Their idyllic setting may attract tourists and middle-class residents, but access may be poor and many uses incompatable with the protection of the natural surroundings and the sensitivities of the newly-settled commuters or second-homers.

Some of the most problematic industrial sites are in essence rural rather than urban. Coal and metal-ore mines will have a cluster of buildings set amidst acres of spoil heaps. Only a token number can be preserved as tourist sites or stabilized as ruins. England, Wales and Scotland only seem able to sustain one coalmining museum project each, at Caphouse, West Yorkshire; Big Pit, Blaenavon; and Prestongrange and Newtongrange, Lothian. Few other complexes survive complete, though some mining workshops, generator houses and pithead baths have been re-used by small engineering firms.

Urban

British manufacturing industry became increasingly urban in location with the advent of steam power from the late eighteenth century. The archetypal image of the Industrial Revolution is the landscape of mills, chimneys and canals at Ancoatsʷʷʷ on the eastern side of Manchester, as illustrated in engravings. Other key factors encouraging industrialists to locate in cities – transport, proximity to skilled labour, suppliers and markets – are still critical issues today for adaptive re-use and regeneration projects. Many workshops and warehouses are clustered close to city centres, but densely developed sites in narrow streets have restricted car parking and lorry access.

Docks present a distinctive sub-type, standing in a detached and traditionally sealed-off world often remote from town and city centres. While Bristol's harbour is within walking distance of the cathedral and prime office and retailing areas, Cardiff Bay^www is separated from the city centre by over a mile of industry and dereliction.[4] Other countries are also seeking to overcome the problem of geographical isolation with their redundant dockyards – one of the biggest challenges being Bombay's traditional port of Mumbai, now being taken over by squatter settlement.

Suburban

The urban fringe, once rural and now suburban, became seen as an ideal location for model industries from the late nineteenth century. Factories at Bournville, Birmingham and at Port Sunlight in the Wirral were surrounded by high quality housing and wide avenues. The by-pass factories of the inter-war period were set on greenfield sites by arterial roads running out of major conurbations. Good access was and remains a prime quality of such sites. Most of these works are unprotected by listing, leaving them liable to redevelopment or insensitive reworking. However, several have recently been the subject of imaginative residential conversions, from the Luma Factory in Glasgow^www to Wills at Newcastle-upon-Tyne and Bryant & May at Speke, Liverpool. The Bryant & May match factory is being transformed by Urban Splash into a business village, Shed KM acting as architects for the £30 million conversion.

Regional location

Attitudes to, and policies for, redundant industrial buildings differ from one part of the country to another. Loft-living is a fashionable concept in London, Liverpool and Manchester but has yet to be adopted by the young professionals of many provincial cities. Some cities, Glasgow for example, clearly encourage imaginative, even radical re-use projects whereas other councils hold to a more purist, preservationist line.

The location in detail

As regards the nature of the site, built-up and open complexes each have their merits and problems. The former are more likely to have surrounding activity and hence local labour and demand but they may suffer from congestion; while the latter may have space for expansion and easier access and car parking but may be remote and unsafe. Roads are a critical factor. They can provide the ready access to make re-use possible. But in some cities, and especially Birmingham and Glasgow, ring roads have a negative influence, isolating inner city warehouses from the city centre. One of the major challenges in restoring the Navigation Warehouse^www by the River Calder in Wakefield (*see Plate 6*) is reducing the impact of the frantically busy road junction directly in front of the complex. In north America all too many waterfronts are cut off from the city centre by an elevated, urban freeway. Some specific criteria to consider are:

▮ Proximity to main road

▮ Proximity to railway station and bus routes

▮ Distance to shops and other facilities

▮ On-site car parking.

Local area surveys can clarify the merits and the problems of a particular locality. They should record:

▮ The characteristics of nearby vacant buildings, and data from estate agents.

▮ Economic activity in the area and whether current investment is primarily local authority or privately led.

▮ Potential and effective demand by studying the occupancy levels, rental and types of tenant in previous conversions; the rent and vacancy levels and shortages for particular types of accommodation.

▮ The nature of the local economy by gaining data on occupied floor space, industry-by-industry employment and size of firms.

▮ Current and planned building activity whether local authority or commercial.

▮ Development or conservation initiatives in the area – EEC objective status, enterprise zone? conservation area?[5]

The local planning office will have information on other factors, such as zoning for industrial, commercial or domestic use classes within the local plan, any special orders concerning closing or compulsory purchase, or any dangerous structure notices.

Typology of building form

Buildings and complexes should be considered in terms of their typology – to counter the pre-occupation with multi-storey mills and warehouses characteristic of most studies of adaptive re-use, and to encourage analysis of their basic form and hence understand their potential and constraints.

Multi-storey mills and warehouses

Solidly-built mills and warehouses are the staple-diet of industrial conservationists. Ever since the writings of J.M. Richards they have been lauded for their 'functionalist' architecture, the innovative use of iron and their contribution to urban landscapes.[6] Cleared of machinery they offer wide, well-lit spaces and sturdy floorloadings. However they are by no means homogenous in their form and potential. Early water-powered cotton mills were typically three or four storeys high, around 22 metres long and 9 metres wide. A turn-of-the-century Lancashire cotton mill, by way of contrast, might be six storeys high and over 60 metres in length.

The woollen mills of Yorkshire and Gloucestershire, built largely of stone and set amidst wooded hills, have long been appreciated as valuable additions to the English landscape. Cotton mills of lowland Lancashire have had a more chequered history in terms of public perception. Having been heralded as symbols of Lancashire's prosperity, they became reviled for their harsh red brickwork, flat roofs and apparent uniformity and their associations with Britain's industrial decline. It took a spate of clearances for them to become appreciated as a threatened species. Historical surveys by the Royal Commission on Historical Monuments have been complemented by selective listing. A group of flagship

conservation projects – Dean Clough,[www] Saltaire[www] and Trencherfield Mill,[www] Wigan – convinced planners, developers and businesses of their worth.

Mills and warehouses can accept a variety of internal treatments, from most simple use of the existing interior spaces to the more interventionist, as at Ebley Mill,[www] Stroud, which was converted into local authority offices. Although most have lost their water wheels, engines and machinery, there is value in retaining or at least recording any evidence of the way these huge factories worked, for example brackets for line shafting, chimneys and watercourses. Many projects restore the multi-storey block to a pristine state while clearing the surrounding low-lying sheds and workshops that were crucial for such processes as weaving, fulling and dyeing and that also created an enclosed complex of courtyards. The result of such clearance can be a bland, historically misleading monument surrounded by a car park. So saying, some sites do benefit from the removal of unsightly asbestos or corrugated iron-clad additions. A detailed survey or a full conservation plan will unravel which elements have architectural or historical significance and which are expendable.[7]

Other countries also have a number of flagship mills – *Crespi d'Adda* near Milan in Italy being a prime example. But reflecting the later date of industrialization in southern Europe there are likely to be more, simple,

2.2
Swan Lane Mills, Bolton, by Stott & Sons, 1904–5. One of the biggest group of cotton mills in Lancashire and now in multiple industrial occupancy.

concrete or steel-framed mills that are ripe for commercial conversion.

Some practical problems often emerge with mill conversions. In many textile towns there may still be a surfeit of industrial floorspace, depressing rentals below which can make any re-use viable. Upper floors may only be accessible by narrow stone staircases and rickety lifts, and tenants may dislike having to share access and security. The internal character of mills depends on leaving the interiors as open as possible, but many uses, especially residential, will necessitate subdivision. Flexibility and a little opportunism may enable even the most difficult spaces to have a new use. At Dean Clough,[www] an attic storey with low ceiling heights has been converted into an archive store for an insurance company.

Breweries and maltings have traditionally been multi-storied structures, and in some towns were combined within the same complex. High brewhouses abutted lower fermentation sheds and malting floors creating a variety of architectural forms. The potential for re-use is further enhanced by the tall central spaces created to house tanks, which will remain as voids once all the plant has been removed for scrap. The shell of the Lone Star Brewery in San Antonio, Texas now houses a municipal art museum. There have been several projects in north America exploiting the potential of brewery buildings. Recent research has highlighted both variations in the forms of maltings and in attitudes towards conversion.[8] Maltings typically combine long rectangular floors – three or more storeys high – with kilns at one end and cisterns at the other. Natural lighting may be inadequate for many new uses, due to the relatively small windows and low roof heights. New, deeper windows may be necessary or a light well or atrium cut through the core of the structure. While the cisterns typically have been removed for scrap, the kiln structure will remain, presenting a challenge to any architect and developer. The kiln is a key element of any traditional maltings, with a distinctive roof and few windows. Smaller examples are readily reworked, especially in the home counties, while the larger structures to be found at Mistley,[www] Essex; Sleaford,[www] Lincolnshire (see Plate 16) and Newark,[www] Nottinghamshire have proved more problematic. The wooden floors and roofs of

maltings prove highly attractive to arsonists. Sadly the town with the greatest inheritance of breweries and maltings – Burton-on-Trent – had until recently a particular poor reputation in terms of industrial conservation.

Daylight factories

It is worth noting a twentieth-century development of the mill type, namely the multi-storey daylight factory, typically dating to the early decades of this century, and built with a concrete frame and elevations more of glass than masonry. Their great durability and good lighting has resulted in most remaining in industrial use, though often making widely differing products than when first completed. The Arrol Johnston car factory in Dumfries, built in emulation of Ford's Highland Park in Detroit, now houses production of the Hunter wellington boot. Such daylight factories can be vulnerable to corporate redevelopment schemes. Most firms prefer to arrange their production lines in single-storey sheds, and few daylight factories are protected by listing. Bizarrely, the greatest of all daylight factories, and one of the most important industrial sites in the world, Highland Park, lies derelict. This huge complex, where Henry Ford developed the mass production of the Model T and the concept of the powered production line during 1908, lies empty and un-landmarked.[9]

2.3
Interior of Ford Factory, Highland Park, Detroit, by Albert Kahn, 1908 & 1914–5 showing the concrete structure of an American daylight factory.

Great halls

Confidence in using iron and glass allowed Victorian engineers to create huge railway sheds and erecting shops. Such buildings vary in their potential for re-use, largely according to their location. The train sheds of railway stations are normally set in central urban locations, though often, as in the case of St Pancras, London or the *Hauptbahnhof* in Frankfurt, in areas of dubious social status. The revival of Europe's railway networks will allow many to be refurbished within their original function, as will be possible, one still hopes, for St Pancras, as the London terminus for Eurostar trains from Europe. Others have been the subject of more fundamental change. The buffers may be relocated to just beyond the shed as at Atocha, Madrid where the original station is now a palm court. Germany's DB 2000 entails more dramatic changes. Rail lines at Frankfurt and Stuttgart are to be sunk to sub-terranean level, with terminii becoming through stations as lines burrow under the city centres.[10] At Frankfurt the overall roof will be kept, arching over the new, low-level platforms.

The situation is far more problematic with the dramatic erecting shops built for the final assembly of railway locomotives, ship's engines or turbines. Many have become redundant and are set in fringe locations, often cut off from city centres by railway lines or waterways. Very few are protected and they have had to stand or fall largely on the whim of the property market. One of the greatest erecting shops in Britain, that of Westinghouse, later Metropolitan Vickers, Trafford Park, Manchester, dating to 1903, has just been razed.

New uses can be found for such huge, often unlisted and largely unappreciated structures. While 'A shop', the largest erecting hall at the Great Western Works, Swindon,[www] was demolished, another workshop, is now a highly successful factory outlet shopping mall for designer goods (*see Plate 1*). Some, such as the Lancashire & Yorkshire Railway's works at Horwich, are simply re-used as industrial estates. Others can provide dramatic exhibition spaces for museums – the Coalbrookdale Company's erecting shop houses the large objects store of the Ironbridge Gorge Museum,[www] the Linthouse Boiler Shop[www] has been relocated to the maritime museum at

Irvine and, at Cardiff Bay, Techniquest[www] is housed in a marine erecting shop, reworked to provide a suitably technological backdrop for the hands-on experiments. With this scale of structure, the flexibility of the internal space is the key asset for any re-use. By way of contrast, two roundhouses – in effect engine sheds set round a turntable – at Camden, London and Derby, are protected but await full restoration, largely because of the restrictions that their form imposes on adaptation. After many years of lying derelict, the roundhouse and the crescent-shaped repair shop in Leeds, built by the Leeds and Thirsk Railway, are now in new uses, the former for a commercial vehicle firm and the latter as part of a business park.

The turbine halls of power stations are generically similar to erecting shops, with their steel frames, wide, open spaces, and overhead cranes. With the exception of Bankside, London,[www] they have proved difficult to adapt, as witnessed by the prolonged saga concerning Battersea, also in London, and the clearance of most coal-fired power stations soon after their closure. Many are surrounded by conveyors, rail sidings and spoil heaps, and pollutants will have seeped into the walls and foundations. Ironbridge A, one of the 'super-stations' of the inter-war period, was offered to the Ironbridge Gorge Museum for just £1 but the cost of removing asbestos and the scale of any preservation project proved too daunting.[11] A smaller Edwardian power station in Dublin is currently the subject of plans for a technology centre, but its location beyond the south docks may make this impracticable.

Aircraft hangars are the greatest of the great halls. They have proved incredibly useful and adaptable by virtue of their completely open interiors, their fire resistance, and due to the prosperity of civil aviation, and the ease with which they can be relocated. The largest are still used to house jumbo jets or military transports. The 319 metre long Brabazon hangar at Filton, Bristol was built in 1947 for the production of a new eight-engine airliner; it now accommodates refurbishment work on airbuses. Airship hangars have a particularly dramatic impact on the landscape due to their height. Two rise above the Bedfordshire lowlands at Cardington, and one is used for experiments by the Building Research Establishment. The 358 metre long airship dock built in 1929 at Akron,

Ohio has survived to return to its original function. Many more modest hangars, built as part of military airfields, now house workshops, warehouses and grain stores, as well as aviation museums.

Single-storey sheds

The humble single-storey shed is the most successful of virtually all industrial building forms and, as a result, is the least understood and appreciated. Derived from agriculture, used for iron making in the eighteenth century and for cloth and brick production from the nineteenth, it has evolved into the modern metal-framed and metal-clad factory. Industrial archaeologists now recognize the importance of the single-storey shed in accommodating weaving machinery, vehicle production and many other types of assembly. Some have analysed the transition from wooden to iron and then steel construction, and the development of north-lit and then monitor roofing.

Very few sheds are protected by listing and all too often re-use schemes, as at the Clement-Talbot plant, Notting Hill; the Argyll car factory at Alexandria[www] near Glasgow; and the Hoover Factory in Perivale, London involve the demolition of the production sheds with only the fronting office block being preserved. Industrial sheds are readily adaptable to almost any form of industrial use; but there is prejudice against their re-use for offices, community facilities or homes, partly due to the lack of conventional windows and partitions but also as a result of their low architectural status. There are more stylish forms of north-lit shed in southern Europe, some with ornate gables and curved roof profiles that attract the eye of conservationists and curators. A curvaceous, brick-vaulted weaving shed of 1907–8 at Terrassa near Barcelona now provides a stunning backdrop for collections of the *Museu Nacional de la Ciència i de la Tècnica de Catalunya*.

Non buildings

Industrial archaeologists devote much of their energy to process-specific industrial structures as opposed to conventional buildings. British conservation legislation tends to separate the

2.4
Weaving shed with wave-profile, brick-vaulted roof, 1907–8 Terrassa, near Barcelona, Spain. Now restored as the *Museu Nacional de la Ciència i de la Tècnica de Catalunya*.

two, with a small number of blast furnaces, bottle ovens and lime kilns being protected as monuments through scheduling. They are typically preserved shorn of accretions, inert, and tidied up as far as funds will permit. The sheds around the Darby furnace in Coalbrookdale were cleared, as have been the buildings surrounding most glass cones. A number of kilns and cones exist as no more than sculptural set pieces or talking points, the remains of one such cone forming the walls of a restaurant in Bristol. A few projects do manage to achieve an integrated relationship between such structures and the sheds and warehouses with which they were operationally dependent: for example the Gladstone Pottery Museum[www] in the Potteries, Staffordshire with its bottle ovens, workshops, offices and showroom, and Blaenavon ironworks in south Wales with its blast furnaces, casting floors, hoist and housing.

Over the last decade there has been much systematic research evaluating these archaeological structures. English Heritage's Monuments Protection Programme, introduced in the preceding chapter, has evaluated monuments of the iron, lead, tin and glass industries leading to recommendations as to which justify protection as monuments through scheduling, even though most will have no viable future use. The Cornwall Archaeology Unit has undertaken detailed studies of the surviving Cornish engine houses, formulating typologies, again to guide decisions as to which should be protected and consolidated.[12]

Of the non-buildings steelworks have proved the greatest challenge, due to their scale and the susceptability to rust of metal structures and pipework. It is difficult to imagine a directly commercial or domestic re-use for furnaces and coke ovens. There are no significant conserved monuments to large-scale steel production in Britain, beyond a Bessemer converter set on a plinth outside Kelham Island Industrial Museum in Sheffield and embryonic plans for converting the Templeborough Steel Plant at Rotherham[www] into the Magna visitor attraction and educational centre. Some see this as a sign of faintheartedness among British preservationists. Others consider that Britain has enough monuments to focus on from the Industrial Revolution of the period 1750–1850. They believe that, due to the scale of these unconventional structures, measured or

photographic survey has to be accepted as a more practicable, alternative form of record for future generations.

In contrast, a number of steelworks have been conserved abroad. Most are stabilized and interpreted as monuments. America provided an inspirational example with the Sloss Furnaces in Birmingham, Alabama which were preserved on closure in 1970 and opened as a National Historic Landmark in 1983. More radically, part of Völklingen steelworks in Saarland, Germany has become a venue for public events including rock concerts. A second German steelworks has been saved at Emscher Park within the Ruhr. The *Internationale Bauaustelling* (literally translated as the International Building Exhibition) was launched in 1989 as a subsidiary project of the *Land* North-Rhine/Westphalia to co-ordinate regeneration initiatives. The Exhibition uses the old Rheinelbe Colliery as its headquarters and is conserving a range of massive industrial structures. The disused Meiderich steelworks is the focus of the Duisburg-Nord Landscape Park (*see Plates 20 & 21*), which attracts over 500,000 visitors a year. The public can follow interpretive tours which take them to the top of No 5 Blast Furnace. A gas tank, now filled with water, is used for training divers and ore bunkers are used as climbing walls. The modernist pithead and colliery buildings at Zollverein XII Colliery are now a centre for computer design projects and

2.5
The blast furnace at Meiderich steelworks, now the focus of the Duisburg-Nord Landscape Park.

(Photo: Peter Zielske)

2.6
Gasworks, Piraeus Road, Athens, Greece. Developed from 1862, this is possibly the most complete city gasworks to survive in Europe. Part has been converted into a theatre.

for exhibitions on 'art and culture'. A 120 metre high gasometer at Oberhausen has been used as an exhibition hall since 1994.[13]

Industrial archaeologists in other countries are now working to preserve historic steel and gas plant. In Poland, Warsaw's Museum of Technology has taken over the Chlewiska Steelworks and the Opole Gas Works at Paczków is being converted into a museum of gas engineering. The Urals has been one of the world's most important centres for iron and steel production. Research by the Russian Academy of Sciences resulted in the registering of monuments; the Nizhny Tagil integrated plant is now open to visitors as a works-museum, while an early twentieth-century blast furnace at Kishva is also preserved.

The example of gasworks illustrates the problems of adapting structures into useable buildings. One of a group of gasholders in Athens, which forms part of a remarkably complete city gasworks complex, has been converted into a theatre but its utilitarian form and archaeological interest have been severely compromised. A radical design to convert four brick-clad structures at Simmering, Vienna has met with considerable opposition from

conservationists. In Britain, proposals have been developed for securing the future of the group of five Victorian gasholders at King's Cross, London. Three of these will need to be relocated to allow Eurostar trains to reach St Pancras and one or more may form the framework for a sports centre. Even so, their preservation is justified primarily through their status as monuments to an important and neglected industry and as striking visual elements of this inner-city landscape.[14]

Grain silos have proved rather easier to adapt. Again in Vienna the Handelskai Silo, one of Austria's earliest concrete structures, has been converted into a 742-bed hotel. Another hotel conversion was completed in Akron, Ohio in 1980, with a cluster of thirty-two silos being pierced with new windows to form the Quaker Square Hilton.

There is one option that often has been adopted by owners of redundant structures, but only recently recognized as a valid form of management – simply to let them decay as a natural continuum in their history. At Orford Ness, Suffolk, the National Trust has decided to allow some of the monuments to the Cold War to decay naturally, including a group of concrete 'Pagoda' structures, built 1965-6 for environmental tests on atomic bombs. They are already ruinous and trying to protect them from the ravages of the North Sea would be expensive if not impossible.

Approaches to conservation and future uses

The identification of future uses for redundant industrial buildings can be a mystical, even bizarre process pervaded by wishful thinking and gross optimism. Consultants suggest the most ludicrous combinations of science or eco centres, web cafés and IMAX theatres in almost any area of urban dereliction. They are paid to propose exciting futures for buildings that are likely to attract European and Lottery funding. Sadly, some show little responsibility towards the future of a project beyond the date of their invoice. It is hardly surprising that their ideas are sometimes far-fetched and their visitor projections over ambitious.

New uses have to be financially sustainable, whether through an adequate income or through some agency underwriting maintenance on the structure. Development costs for different types of building and conversion should be balanced with expected rentals. The costs which include purchase, legal charges, and building works, will vary from one part of the country to another and according to the sophistication of the design. Annual rental income can be set against the sum needed to pay a mortgage on the cost of buying the property and its conversion. If a mortgage is not the key issue, then a payback period for the capital expended can be worked out by a cashflow projection.[15] Eley & Worthington analysed financial viability in relation to industrial buildings. They considered that the repair and conversion cost for a warehouse might be 80 per cent of the total budget, while for a more modern factory the purchase cost may be the higher sum. The cost of repairs will depend on the condition of the building, its previous use, and the extent to which it has suffered decay and vandalism. Different new uses and levels of finish will influence the cost of conversion but the

provision of new services might be the largest expense.[16] It can be helpful to analyse conversion costs according to differing levels of intervention, from the most expensive to the simplest:

▮ Major structural alterations and additions

▮ Provision of new services

▮ General repairs and fireproofing

▮ Installation of non-structural partitions.

Other contributors will return to this complex field, but it is worth suggesting a basic categorization of uses and their compatibility with particular types and qualities of building. If one thinks in terms of a sliding scale of change – from minimal intervention to fundamental reworking – museum projects have traditionally been seen as compatible with purist preservation while commercially-driven adaptive re-use is viewed as more intrusive. As will be seen, the pattern is more complex. All too many museum conversions result in the sanitization of industrial sites while a low-budget pragmatic conversion to another industry or warehousing may retain far more of the historic fabric and atmosphere.

Commercial adaptive re-use

It still seems amazing that the long-established process of adaptive re-use, as common as individuals renovating their houses, had to be re-discovered in the late 1960s and 1970s. As mentioned in the introductory chapter, industrialists have traditionally opted to take over or adapt existing buildings rather than plan afresh. It was a valuable means of saving money, especially during periods of experimentation when no income was coming in. By adapting existing buildings, firms avoided the major interruption to work necessitated by clearance and building anew. Even in the immediate post-war period, conversions continued to take place on a purely commercial basis, munitions works becoming trading estates, and airfield runways being used as foundations for chicken sheds.

The modern age is associated with a pre-occupation with building anew and a belief that redevelopment had to be driven by narrow, short-term considerations of costs and profits.

For several decades there has been a gulf between many business owners and developers and the world of conservation. Not only are developers seen as agents of demolition, but their wish to work rapidly and within tight financial margins runs against the grain of committee schedules and site inspections by which councils and amenity societies are run.

URBED consider that re-use should be seen as a type of property development. Two approaches have been identified. The conventional path is driven by the assumption that the building will or could be bought by a financial institution and that a commercial loan or mortgage might help fund the scheme. In this case the finished building must be readily marketable and most of the details defined before work commences.[17] Numerous single use conversions will follow this pattern. Others will be undertaken by a company as an aspect of site management, for example the reworking of the chocolate factory at Noisel to form Nestlé's corporate headquarters. This project apart, most corporate adaptations gain little publicity because the buildings are likely to be less problematic in terms of their future and because the end use is unlikely to involve public access.

According to URBED, if the aim is not primarily to produce a saleable building, re-use schemes require an entrepreneurial approach. In this case, the key is to ensure a successful new use or range of uses. The key skills are identifying viable new functions, generating enthusiasm, being flexible and maintaining momentum. In contrast to the speed needed by the conventional developer, there may be every merit in phasing works to stay in tune with demand, and in feeding profits back into the next stage of the project. Mixed uses may help generate greater activity and interest, but detailed thought has to be given to the future management and maintenance of the building. Above all, entrepreneurs must have the vision to make the most of the qualities of historic buildings and their marginal locations.

Industry

This is not a study of facilities management within industry, but it is worth noting some of the approaches taken by firms to improve the performance of their ageing factories. They may install new services or, more radically, new windows and roofs. Motor manufacturers have transformed the productivity and working conditions of British plants largely dating back as far as the First World War – from Dagenham to Cowley and Coventry. Long-established firms and those making traditional products – whether furniture, jewellery or chocolates – may gain prestige from their historic complexes and especially an ornate office block. Smaller businesses have found old, multi-storey buildings suitable for a modest scale of light assembly, and ideal for promoting a team spirit and collaboration with nearby firms.

Housing

There are long traditions of people combining their workplace and their home, whether in farming or in domestic textile working. After a century when work and domestic life became increasingly segregated, there is now a trend back towards integration, as redundant factories and warehouses are converted into apartments. Such conversions gained a cachet in the SoHo district of New York, once the megalomaniac scheme for a Lower Manhattan Expressway had been abandoned in 1965. The blighted warehouses became occupied by artists wanting large areas of cheap space, and then others by galleries and restaurants. The core of SoHo, with its remarkable range of cast-iron frontages, was declared a historic district in 1973.

Domestic conversions became something of a minor cult in Britain from the 1970s, the Landmark Trust working with the most eccentric architecture imaginable – from pineapple-shaped follies to Swiss-style chicken houses. However, well-entrenched prejudices have worked against any broad acceptance of domestic re-use. Owners, developers and even councillors see housing as a second rank use, not matching the profits and employment generation associated with industry and commerce.

Demographic and social factors – especially the relative decline of the traditional family unit – have increased demand for one-bedroomed apartments. Frustration with commuting, the lure of the '24 hour city' and the chic status of minimalist loft living have all made conversions more desirable. A number of historic factories have such strong images that re-use is worthwhile even if it would have been cheaper to build anew. The Luma Light Factory at Glasgow^www^ is marketed, somewhat inappropriately, as an Art Deco masterpiece, the Argyll Motor Works^www^ at Alexandria by Glasgow for its palatial Baroque frontage. Some developers create apartments that are complete with all fitments while others offer a series of shells for purchasers to fit out as they desire. The work of the Manhattan Loft Company in London is now complemented by Urban Splash in the north-west and the Leeds Loft Company on the other side of the Pennines. At Simpson's Fold, the Leeds Loft Company is currently marketing a warehouse converted into forty-three lofts, four penthouses, a design shop and a deli/café.

At the more modest end of the market, housing associations have found old buildings to be ideal for creating apartments for a wide range of age groups, the structures being durable, adaptable and well-located for shops and recreational facilities. The Redwood Housing Co-operative has been able to provide far more desirable accommodation at Oxo Tower Wharf^www^ than in most schemes to be found in south London. There have also been many conversions to house students. They wish to live in city centres and have less need for car parking or gardens. A sensitive re-use scheme for a large dramatic building can create an atmosphere akin to a historic college at modest

cost. Recent projects in Britain include a textile mill in Huddersfield,^www^ quayside warehouses in Hull and a station hotel in Liverpool. Overseas industrial buildings have been converted not just as halls of residence but into teaching and research accommodation. Part of the silver and lead works at Lávrion in Greece has been taken over by the National Technical University of Athens to house both its own staff and enterprises wishing to apply aspects of its technological research.

Offices

Offices have been a prime re-use for industrial buildings over the last two decades. Many early conversions were on a modest scale and for firms involved in design work or the media, which seek low cost and simply-designed and serviced environments. The large uninterrupted floorspaces of factories and warehouses are ideal for open-plan office-working. The architectural practice, DEGW, has demonstrated, in its own offices, how a warehouse can provide a sophisticated working environment through carefully designed partitioning, lighting and furnishings, and the use of portable computers and telephones. Large, prestigious firms are choosy almost by definition. They need to have prime locations, buildings that reflect their corporate aspirations and that provide air-conditioned and networked workplaces.

2.7
Silver and lead works established by a French company from 1863, Lávrion, Greece, now being restored for the National Technical University of Athens.

As regards design, it has proved possible to adjust the image of high quality historic works to form highly desirable offices, widely publicized examples being the Menier chocolate factory at Noisel and the printing works of the Daily Express located on the edge of Manchester's central district. In creating an international headquarters for Nestlé at Noisel, Philippe Robert turned the most prestigious element – the iron-framed and polychromatic brick range straddling the canal – into the offices for the president and the senior staff. The new entrance building and spinal links were clad almost entirely in glass to contrast as boldly as possible with the original buildings. Meanwhile, Owen Williams' Daily Express Building of 1939 conveyed a sufficiently crisp, even contemporary image to be readily convertible into luxury offices. Michael Hyde and Associates created a new interior to complement the swish, streamlined style of the metal and glass façade. Most recently, an oversupply of commercial space in many cities has curtailed such conversions, with post-war office blocks becoming redundant themselves and likely candidates for re-use.

Mixed use

With large complexes there are many merits in mixed uses. Different forms of building can house the most appropriate functions, financial risks are spread across different markets, and several sources of funding can be tapped. Above all, complementary functions – residential,

2.8
Daily Express Building, Ancoats, Manchester, by Owen Williams, 1939; converted into offices by Michael Hyde and Associates.

office, retail and cultural – can feed off each other, making a scheme more attractive to all users and giving it a long term vitality. Salts Mill at Saltaire^{www} combines offices, workshops, shops, restaurant and an art gallery. Fiat's Lingotto^{www} plant in Turin has an exhibition space, a conference suite and a hotel. The great Stucky Mill in Venice is to house a 400-room hotel with some of the smaller buildings being an associated health and beauty centre and 140 apartments, while the adjoining pasta factory will become a 500-seat convention centre.

Cultural use

A key element of a mixed-use scheme may be a cultural centre – to attract large numbers of visitors, make best use of any wide interior spaces and, possibly, to provide a means of interpreting the building and its history. This approach emerged in the 1960s, the re-use of the maltings at Snape, Suffolk^{www} as a concert hall providing an influential example. Subsequent schemes may simply include a flexible auditorium or display space, but a number seek to exploit the qualities of the buildings and their interiors in a more direct way. Dean Clough, Halifax^{www} was a major carpet factory until the 1970s. Sir Ernest Hall worked, for several years with Jonathan Silver, to develop a highly successful business, arts and education centre. The Henry Moore Studio is a key component of the complex, allowing artists and especially sculptors to work at a large scale, within the stimulating context of the iron-framed mill.

Curators and artists continue to appreciate the potential of industrial buildings to provide more challenging display spaces than offered by the 'white boxes' of modernist galleries or the formal rooms of Victorian museums. Bankside Power Station, London^{www} will provide high, dramatically-lit spaces, when it opens as the Tate Gallery of Modern Art (Tate Modern) in 2000 (see Plate 10).

Cultural facilities, whatever their precise use, act as lead projects, drawing in visitors, restaurants, income and hence further investment. Norrköping was the key centre of the Swedish woollen industry. Once the last mill had shut down in the 1970s, the municipality sought to bring in new activity to fund conservation of the mills and associated buildings. A

conference centre was established in the Gryts Building, music and dance studios provided in a mill at the 'Islands in the Stream', and a paper mill re-used as the entrance foyer for the Louis de Geer Concert and Congress Hall. Other mills are now occupied by companies and by the university, drawn back to the riverside area by its revitalized image and economy.

Monument approach

At the opposite extreme to a commercial re-use, some types of industrial heritage, in particular structures such as furnaces or engineering features, are most likely to be conserved as monuments. The Iron Bridge, opened in 1781 at Coalbrookdale, Shropshire is listed, scheduled and closed to vehicular traffic. Saltford Brass Mill, near Bath, is a less clear-cut case. Again it is scheduled, largely because of its two brass annealing furnaces built shortly after 1769. A re-use scheme, involving a restaurant and flats, was stopped in 1987, in part due to the archaeological damage that would have been caused. Commercial re-use was clearly inappropriate for Britain's most important monument to the brass industry. The structure is now being conserved with English Heritage funding and will be presented as a very modest heritage attraction, managed by a local trust.

Some textile mills also need to be seen primarily as monuments, with any re-use having to be reconcilable with high standards of preservation and public access. Arkwright's mills at Cromford, Derbyshire^{www} are of such significance that the conversions are as simple and low key as possible, timbers being treated only where necessary and walls just limewashed. Finding the right new use for Ditherington Flax Mill, Shrewsbury^{www} has been made more difficult by the need to keep at least some of the floors, with their lines of cast iron columns and beams, open to view, rather than obscured by office or flat partitions.

Monument and process

Some industrial buildings make much sense as monuments only if they retain the equipment to demonstrate a process. Finch's Foundry at Sticklepath, Devon is such a valuable addition to

the portfolio of the National Trust because its waterwheels and 'Heath Robinson-like' transmission system, once set in motion, are so evocative of rurally-based industry.

Stott Park Bobbin Mill in Cumbria, dating from 1835, has been preserved complete with its steam engine and coppice barns. English Heritage, who administers the site, accepts that such complexes cannot be truly viable in terms of the visitors they attract, but are worth subsidizing for their uniqueness and educational potential. Historic equipment is only operated at tick-over speed, to limit wear-and-tear.

Monument and museum

There is a long tradition for saving industrial monuments by using them to house museums. Abbeydale Industrial Hamlet, Sheffield, based round a steel and scythe works of the late eighteenth century and closed in 1933, was an early example, and Gladstone Pottery Museum at Longton, Staffordshire[www] was widely lauded in the 1970s. Both were developed with the aid of funds raised from industry and of free labour through government employment schemes.

An industrial monument rightly imposes constraints on the development of a museum. The public may fail to retain their enthusiasm for an attraction that cannot be transformed to keep pace with fashions for science centres and computer interactives. Even so, there are some highly successful projects such as the

2.9
Stott Park Bobbin Mill, Cumbria dating from 1835, and now administered and operated by English Heritage.

2.10
Workshops at Coalport built in 1795.

Merseyside Maritime Museum in Albert Dock, Liverpool[www] which is considered in more detail in Chapter seven, and the Long Shop Museum at Leiston, Suffolk where Garrett's engineering works is, appropriately, filled with steam rollers and farm equipment.

Museum buildings must have high standards of environmental controls, services, and full access for the disabled. It may be difficult to reconcile these requirements with a purist approach to the conservation of a monument. Robin Wade Design Associates established virtually a model in relating displays to industrial monuments through their work at the Ironbridge Gorge Museum[www] in the late 1970s. Timber partitions, hessian wall coverings, muted paintwork and serif lettering blended with, but were also distinct in image from, the brick and ironwork of the workshops and warehouses at Coalbrookdale and Coalport. Approaches to museum design have since diversified, with modern plate glass and polished metal being used at the Museum of Science and Industry in Manchester while several open-air museums have drifted towards an industrial heritage pastiche for their reception buildings.

Looking abroad, Italians and Iberians are more likely to pursue a contemporary style that boldly juxtaposes old and new, even though some patina and historical evidence may be lost. A recent and highly stylish example is the conversion of the Montemartini Power Station in Rome to house collections from the Capitoline Museums. Classical figures are

displayed on modern plinths in front of old diesel engines while the 'furnace room' is now a conference hall with the steam boiler dating to 1950 forming a sculptural backdrop. One of the most radical schemes to use modern design to interpret a monument was undertaken in Canada, at Forges St Maurice in Quebec. Following archaeological research commenced in 1966, the Quebec Department of Cultural Affairs and the Canadian Parks Service collaborated to conserve and interpret this prime monument to ironmaking from the early eighteenth century. A modern roof protects the excavated masonry, while a new tower structure and gables, also in the form of a steel space frame, indicate the likely outline of the furnace and its associated buildings when complete.

Monument, museum and process

A three-way combination of monument, museum and process can be highly successful if the process is relatively economical to operate, produces a marketable product and is visually appealing to the visitor. Textile mills are obvious candidates, as at Helmshore Textile Museum housed in buildings dating back to 1789 and where spinning mules can be operated by the throw of a switch. There are not many other types of process that can be started and stopped as and when required. The Ironbridge Gorge Museum[www] established a wrought-iron works at the Blists Hill open-air site, but it has proved difficult to combine necessary entrepreneurship, the retention of a labourforce with specialist skills and provision of a regular, scheduled experience for visitors. After some juggling, an ideal working arrangement has been achieved in the case of the nearby Jackfield Tile Museum. Visitors progress from inspecting the museum displays to seeing tile making in action, presented not by the museum but by staff of the Decorative Tile Works who are fulfilling commercial orders for traditional encaustic and glazed tiles.

Monument, museum and commerce

Many major projects seek to combine the creation of a tourist attraction with more overtly commercial interests. Most quote Lowell,

Massachusetts as an exemplar. This major cotton town now has over a million visitors a year. Just under half that number come to Market Mill for the introductory audio-visual and then embark on tram and boat tours of the mills and waterways. Visitors can see working looms on the ground floor of Boott Mill (*see Plates 12, 13 & 14*). Local unemployment was reduced from 12.6 per cent in 1978 to 4.7 per cent in 1984 with high-tech firms coming into some of the redundant mills. Other buildings, including Massachusetts Mill, have been converted into apartments. The key to the success of Lowell was the partnership between public and private investment, starting with $21.5 million of federal money in 1978 but followed by the $300 million invested largely from commerce by 1985.

No British project has managed to match Lowell – in particular for its combination of conservation, commercial success and a challenging interpretative programme. Albert Dock, Liverpool[www] is probably the nearest analogy. The first shops opened in 1984 and the Maritime Museum, an outpost of the Tate Gallery, flats and a television studio filled the large floorspace available. The inward-looking and austere nature of the architecture made any change controversial and some critics have harked back towards the days before the tourist shops and acres of car parking arrived. Albert Dock was condemned by Peter Buchanan as 'prettified and touristed', whereas before it was 'powerfully poetic in its solidly stoic and noble forelornness'. However, few could expect such a large complex to be preserved empty and barren. It now has a vitality that is, even in the elements of tourism tackiness, honest to its new uses. Above all, Albert Dock has made a strong contribution in attracting visitors to Merseyside and to the cause of the industrial heritage.[18]

Building evaluation

Some conservationists and entrepreneurs believe they can 'read' the potential of a building or complex through the quality of its design and location – a strong architectural image and waterfront setting being key assets. Most will prefer to combine their background knowledge of industrial archaeology and completed re-use projects with a sober analysis of the nature of the site, and the plan, structure and condition of the buildings.

Site coverage

It is ideal if a building or a group of structures only cover around 60 per cent of a site, offering better natural lighting, space for on-site access, and potential for expansion. There may be pressure to demolish some ancillary buildings on congested sites, but key ranges such as engine houses and gatehouses should be protected, and on historically significant sites, the coherency of the complex retained. Linked to this, occupants usually wish to have an open view from their workplace. Buildings are easier to let or sell if they have windows on at least three elevations.

Plan and configuration

The diversity of industrial buildings makes for variety in re-use. A few schemes successfully break all the rules, but it is worth making some generalizations:

- Single-storey ranges are ideal for industrial use or associated functions such as training workshops or storage. Multi-storey (up to four floors) layouts are often desirable for office, craft and certainly for residential use.

- A total floorspace of 4,500 – 15,000 square metres is ideal for many conversion projects. Those below 1,000 and above 15,000 square metres are more challenging. Having visited the Lingotto[www] plant at Turin, an associate of Renzo Piano admitted 'the sense of emptiness in the building was terrifying at first...the most difficult aspect of the project was then conquering its scale'.[19] The *Tour et Taxis* complex of warehouses in Brussels, built 1904–7, remains largely empty despite its stylish façades and good condition. The three, huge sheds are simply too large to be readily re-useable.

- Ceiling heights of around 4.3–4.9 metres are desirable for ground floors and 3–4.3 metres for upper floors; below 2.4 metres makes many new uses uncomfortable if not impossible. But often the floor-to-ceiling height in redundant industrial buildings is no more than 2.7 metres giving little room for manoeuvre, while for maltings the space might be as little as 2 metres. Such low clearances are now rather less of a problem. While it was considered advantageous to have a void space of 0.6 metres for services, heating, lighting and computer linkages can be provided far more compactly thanks to modern technology.[20]

2.11
Tour et Taxis Freight Warehouse, Brussels by E. Van Humbeek, 1904–7. Its three massive sheds pose a major challenge for conservationists.

The Merseyside Maritime Museum, Albert Dock, Liverpool shows how, with a little architectural licence, different qualities of internal space can be achieved. Most of the galleries retain their original jack-arch ceilings, but a section of the first floor was removed to create a double-height reception area. By way of contrast, for the Tate Gallery of the North, set in the western range of the Albert Dock, Sir James Stirling also removed a floor level but then inserted a dramatically modern mezzanine.

The nature of a particular historic interior will reflect the original function of the building, and influence the appropriateness of different new uses:

Nature of space	Building type	No. of storeys	Attributes
Small single space	Chapel	Single storey	Character for specialized uses
Large single space	Warehouse	Single storey	Flexibility & easy movement
Small repeated spaces	Workshops	Up to four storeys	Small units, poor access
Large repeated spaces	Mill	Multi-storied	Flexibility, difficult to subdivide

An open internal structure gives flexibility, especially if columns are widely spaced. Internal partitions contemporary to construction of the building can add greatly to the sense of character but are all too often lost during commercial conversion projects.[21]

Lighting

Natural illumination will be adequate during daytime if the floor plan is no deeper than 15 metres, since outside light can normally reach around 7.5 metres. Such shallow buildings are ideal for uses where occupiers are pre-occupied with individual tasks. Deeper buildings can facilitate greater interaction and may be essential to accommodate large machinery or other equipment. Some

warehouses may be 50 metres deep and will need artificial lighting in daytime. Their cores may be best used for services such as kitchens or bathrooms or be given a central atrium, typically in the form of a stair well. In the case of residential conversions, such as Brandram's Wharf, in London or the Dreher Brewery in Venice, internal galleries can be created with stairs and doorways giving access to the apartments.[22] With listed buildings, there may be problems in removing most of the internal structure and roof members. There was concerted opposition in the case of the Great Northern Warehouse in Manchester, where it was proposed to cut out many of the columns and beams of Britain's earliest surviving steel-framed building, dating to 1895–8, in order to create an atrium.

While large windows are usually an asset, the curtain walls of twentieth-century factories can create major problems of solar gain, and threaten a lack of privacy for the occupants of newly-created apartments. The depth of the fenestration at the Luma Light Factory, Glasgow[www] was reduced during conversion, though, in most cases, blinds, permanent sunscreens and tinted glass can overcome such problems.

Access

Provision must be made for disabled access. Most factories will have lifts but these may be antiquated and unsightly. It may be especially difficult to achieve access for wheelchairs to clusters of workshops with ranges set at different levels and narrow, stepped doorways.

Structure and cladding

The cost of a renovation project may be fundamentally affected by the condition of the building. Most factories are robust, but vandalism and theft of leadwork and slates can quickly lead to rot and the additional expense of treating or replacing floors and rafters. Too many redundant buildings seem doomed to lie stagnant and vulnerable for several years, while their future is pondered and debated. An element of hopelessness and eleventh-hour brinkmanship seems to be necessary to focus minds, draw in grants and achieve the necessary give-and-take among developers, architects, planners and conservationists. Kit Martin, Director of the Phoenix Trust, has seen numerous hospitals and asylums turned from being in perfect condition to ruination within no more than two years. He pleads for stronger action by national and local authorities to ensure that buildings are secured and, ideally, their future addressed even before they become redundant. The Wills Factory in Newcastle and Battersea Power Station have been reduced to masonry shells, by a combination of vandalism and exposure to the elements.

Different materials have their own properties, and those used for structural support have been the subject of much debate and some prejudice about their strength or their resistance to fire:

I Timber: readily adaptable but combustible and liable to wet and dry rot if buildings are derelict.

I Cast-iron: high compressive strength and hence widely used for columns in the nineteenth century, incombustible, resistant to corrosion but brittle. May shatter in a fire.

I Wrought-iron: high tensile strength so used for beams in the nineteenth century.

I Steel: strong in compression and tension and more ductile than cast-iron. Corrodes if not protected. Used from the 1880s.

I Reinforced concrete: strong but resistant to corrosion as long as reinforcement is not exposed. Difficult to cut through or adapt. Patent systems introduced from the 1890s.

Strength can be assessed by a structural engineer and several manuals on the appraisal of historic structures have been written in recent years.[23] These studies emphasize the extent to which the strength and consistency of steel and concrete in particular have advanced since their early usage from the turn of the century. More reassuringly for conservationists, they argue that a structure is likely to continue to remain stable if it has not deteriorated and if the loading is not increased. Nevertheless the structural engineer will wish to understand how the columns and walls carry dead and live leads to the foundations. The dead-load

carrying capacity can sometimes be estimated from the standards defined by building acts in force at the time of construction. Mills and warehouses were built with great reserves of strength, while workshops and sheds may be lighter in their construction. It will be worth calculating the current, actual loads and then relating them to those associated with the proposed new use, especially if a significant increase in loading is anticipated. Office conversions can be the most problematic, with BS 6399 suggesting high loadings of 2.5kN/m² for general office use and 5.0kN/m² for storage space. English Heritage considers that the latter load is rarely needed in conversions as long as any roller storage is on the ground floor, though account will have to be taken for partitions inserted into formerly open industrial buildings.[24]

Services

Services – heating, water supply, sanitation and lifts – will typically need to be replaced, though more of the character of an old building can be retained by refurbishing fittings wherever possible. Housing conversions usually necessitate the most intrusive changes, as all plumbing and electricity provision has to be duplicated. High standards of food hygiene will be needed for restaurants, and sophisticated systems of security and environmental control for museums.

Fire safety

Fire risks have to be taken into account when converting industrial buildings, especially if meeting halls or sleeping accommodation are being created. Historic factories might have only one staircase and incorporate materials that are combustible or fail in a fire. Exposed timber members are safe only if they were over-sized, to retain structural effectiveness after a given period of combustion. Cast-iron can shatter when heated and then rapidly cooled by firehoses. Steel loses half its strength when heated to 550°C and often also needs to be protected by sprinkler systems. Intumescent paint and sprayed coating-paint provide fire resistance of one and two hours respectively.

The alternative of boxing-in columns and beams involves a loss of space and of character. The provision of escape routes and fire divisions will be dictated by BS 5588. Much angst or destructive alteration work can be avoided by considering fire safety at an early stage of any conversion project.

Design ethics and issues

There is no clear philosophy concerning the design in conservation projects and how new work – whether additional buildings or new detailing – should be incorporated. The official guidance in the government circular on conservation, PPG 15, focuses on new buildings in conservation areas: 'What is important is not that new buildings should directly imitate past styles, but that they should be designed with respect for their context. Special regard should be had for such matters as scale, height, form, massing, respect for traditional pattern of frontages, vertical or horizontal emphasis, and detailed design'.[25] Recent books on modern design in historic settings imply a division, at least in Britain, between architects and public taste. The majority of designers are keen to express new forms and materials while the public, still bruised by decades of ugly Brutalism and crass post-modernism, tend to be more happy with historic imagery and even façadism – with a new structure being inserted behind a restored façade.

Many architects or planners – apart from those taking extreme modernist or neo-classical stances – broadly agree with the guidelines presented in PPG 15. They aim to take their cue from the existing buildings in terms of scale and rhythm but using modern materials and structural forms in an honest, contemporary way. Les Sparks asserts that 'our architects must produce buildings that are recognizably of our own age but with an understanding and respect for history and context. If this involves some challenges to public taste and convention, it may not be a bad thing. At the same time we should treat our historic buildings with care and integrity, minimizing the changes they undergo to meet current needs, and maximizing their authenticity'.[26] So should a new entrance or

wing on a mill be guided by 'minimizing the changes they undergo' or be 'recognizably of our own age'? The answer is that different approaches are valid in diffferent contexts. An inspired designer may succeed with either, and a poor one fail dismally whichever approach is taken.

Industrial buildings are of particular interest in this context. Their scale, robustness and lower status in the conservation pecking order might suggest that designers can experiment with radical interventions that would be unlikely to gain acceptance with, say, cathedrals or country houses. Given this opportunity for originality, it is worth pondering why the British seem to have locked onto a heritage style for industrial areas. New elements are designed largely in traditional forms or even as replicas of existing work. Their modernity is expressed through the use of simplified detailing executed in steel section and stained softwood, in contrast to the bravura of cast iron, carved stone and moulded brick. Is such modernity with deference a sign of respect for context, or a *fin-de-siècle* compromise that panders to the nostalgic tastes of board members, councillors and the general public? The following paragraphs aim to articulate different approaches – from those seeking to minimize any change to historical character, to those keen to introduce their own and typically a more modern language. Designers may be guided by the remit of their commission, whether to simply stabilize the structure, 'conserving as found', or to adapt, upgrade or re-animate the architecture. But conservation is an art rather than a science; there will be some projects that seek to adapt a building to new uses without affecting its appearance, and others that update the appearance and image while leaving the same old structure and function buried underneath.

What makes this issue so intriguing and so fluid is that the typology and quality of industrial buildings is so varied, from Grade I listed mills to lowly and unappreciated sheds. As noted above there is also tremendous variety in future functions, from monuments through to commercial offices and apartments. Partially guided by the perceived quality of the building and the nature of its future use, designers and clients will choose either to maintain the industrial image, reinforce a particular aspect of it, or, alternatively, to suppress or adjust the industrial character for a more commercial or homely identity.

Preservation

The preservation approach will be a natural starting point with most monuments such as blast furnaces or lime kilns, but also for buildings of high quality and a strong identity. If this seems so logical, why do so many structures look so utterly different once they have been supposedly 'preserved' in their original form? Industrial archaeologists prefer to study monuments in their unrestored state not just because they like picturesque decay, but because so much historical evidence is lost once many an architect, surveyor and builder have done their work – demolishing outbuildings, replacing floors, windows and replastering walls – all supposedly in the name of preservation. Scheduled industrial monuments are still vulnerable to such dramatic make-overs, especially if they are being converted into well-funded museums or heritage centres, in a way that would be inconceivable for many other building types. Volunteers and firms with little money to spare may achieve a conversion that retains more of the original surfaces and fittings.

Commercial schemes may successfully pursue a preservationist agenda, if the building has a strong image that will attract custom in its new life as an apartment block, restaurant or in mixed use. The bulbous outline of the Michelin Building ᵂᵂᵂ in west London and its walls of decorative tilework provided a unique image for Sir Terence Conran's Oyster Bar without any significant re-working, while the lesser additions at the rear of the site could be reworked for his store, the Conran Shop.

Conservation and new design

Most would accept that the architecture of a modern building should reflect or, at least, relate to its function. But if an industrial building is given a new function, then should the transition be expressed in bricks and mortar? The right answer seems to depend on its architectural quality. With a Grade I listed building there is a presumption that its original form should be preserved as much as possible. With a building of lesser stature the guidance in PPG 15 is open-ended:

Listed buildings do vary greatly in the extent to which they can accommodate change without loss of special interest. Some may be sensitive even to slight alterations; this is especially true of buildings with important interiors and fittings – not just great houses, but also, for example, ...industrial structures with surviving machinery. ...Achieving a proper balance between the special interest of a listed building and proposals for alterations or extensions is demanding and should always be based on specialist expertise; but it is rarely impossible, if reasonable flexibility and imagination are shown by all parties involved.[27]

Apart from taking a dim view of façadism, the question of design is left to those idealistic words: 'expertise', 'flexibility' and 'imagination'. Many consider that the planning bureaucracy of development control and listed building consent does not nurture any of these qualities, but some conservation officers, inspectors and caseworkers are now proving to be far more inspired and inspirational in their approach. In most simple terms a conservation approach, as seen in many of the projects illustrated in Chapter eleven, consists of retaining as much as possible of the original fabric; new work, maybe stairs and ramps, partitions and even an additional mansard storey or wing will be in a restrained but crisply modern idiom. For success, the conservation approach requires an assured touch with modern materials and a sympathy with the subtleties of the original architecture.

Heritage vernacular

A more common way of reworking industrial buildings is to take a cue from the existing architecture, and then replicate or rework it. External hoists will be preserved but 'taking-in' doors converted into balconies. For extensions or new ranges, historic forms, such as round-headed arcading or polychromatic brickwork, may be replicated. Modern roof-vents, lucams and clock towers may be added to strengthen the flavour. Traditional design can readily drift into pastiche. Several brickmakers offer a 'heritage range', with bricks that are battered and coloured to look old and reclaimed. A new curtain wall of red, buff and blue bricks may be almost indistinguishable from the old, once the latter has been sandblasted or cleaned with chemicals. Many towns and cities end up with an amorphous jumble of new buildings made to look old, and old buildings looking too new.

Some canal basins have become a heritage nightmare of over-restored bridges, warehouses and lockhouses and retro-modern shops and offices. This unholy combination can be seen at its most gross with Brindley Place, the speciality shopping development facing a canal and the Convention Centre in Birmingham. The loss of authenticity and distinctiveness is exacerbated by the near uniform and sterile approach to landscaping around canal basins. The time-worn textures of grimy masonry and cinder towpaths are banished for fancy 'hard landscaping' littered with replica benches, bollards and bins. Sensitive landscape design can enhance the individuality of a conservation area; at worst it dilutes it and mocks the robust historic buildings to which it is supposed to be subservient.

In many re-use projects the exterior of a building may be carefully restored but the interior heavily reworked. It can be argued that internal arrangements and services have been more susceptible to change than the building structure. In most cases the public and the conservation lobby are more concerned with external appearances, while intending occupants demand the best possible working or living environment. Such justifications can become an excuse for too little care being taken with the interiors of industrial buildings – walls being gritblasted, spaces dramatically altered and any evidence of machinery removed. In the case of the Thames Tunnel Mills at Rotherhithe, London, great sensitivity was shown in conserving the exterior with the brick being left uncleaned, but the internal structure was completely replaced in modern brick and concrete.[28] There are some exceptions, such as the Verdant Works,[www] Dundee (*see Plate 25*), where the Edwardian offices were conserved complete with their wooden panelling, desks and even a telephone booth.

2.12
Brindley Place, Birmingham. The Convention Centre is to the right of the canal, the Arena can be seen in the distance.

Conservation and Regeneration

Juxtaposing old and new – modernism

Given that industrial buildings can readily take on new uses, one might assume that industrial architecture should also be adaptable to convey secondary functions and hence different meanings. Conservation philosophy and governmental guidance concur in recommending that new uses and and additions should be marked by sensitive modern design. Polished metal and plate glass, the materials of high-tech modernism, appeal widely to architectural critics due to their industrial overtones and suave minimalism. High-tech design has also gained a strong credibility in conservation through the work of Sir Norman Foster, most recently with the Cultural Centre built facing the Roman temple in the historic square of Nîmes, France.

There are few examples of such carefully-proportioned and meticulously-detailed modern design in relation to industrial archaeology, especially in Britain. Herzog & De Meuron are adding a long simple roof terrace for Banksideᵂᵂᵂ to allow visitors to enjoy the view across to St Paul's Cathedral and to express the change in function from power station to art gallery. At a more modest scale John Lyall has exposed the steelwork of his new frame for the Third White Cloth Hall, Leeds; for the First White Cloth Hall, nearby in Kirkgate, he has created a glass façade set in front of four slender steel columns. His philosophy is to 'bring out' the best qualities of historic

structures, remove those that are derelict or worthless, and introduce new architecture where appropriate that is 'of our age' but that is sympathetic, echoing proportions and patterns of fenestration.[29] Sadly even the use of steel and glass has become downgraded into a stock-in-trade of conservation, especially for retailing. A supermarket-style canopy was proposed and fortunately rejected as an addition to the bold stone elevations of the Royal William Victualling Yard in Plymouth.

Modern design is likely to be considered appropriate by many architects for major new additions to historic factories or warehouses. When the offices of the Great Western Railway at Swindonᵂᵂᵂ were converted into the headquarters for the Royal Commission on Historical Monuments, the buildings designed by Brunel and Gooch were carefully conserved. A new archive building had to provide optimum conditions for storing archives. The architects, D.Y. Davies, decided to express its contrasting function and precise operational requirements by creating a range that was overtly modern – curved in plan, with exposed steel bracing and aluminium cladding.

Designers, clients and planning agencies in other countries have proved more willing to experiment with radical juxtapositions of old and new at major industrial complexes. *Le Grand Hornu* in Belgium provided an early inspiration. This engineering complex was built in 1831 in a neo-classical style with a line of arcades set round an an elliptical courtyard.

2.13

Le Grand Hornu, near Mons, Belgium; an engineering works for a group of coal mines, designed by Bruno Renard and opened 1831. Converted into offices from 1971 with part being stabilized as ruins.

Starting in 1971, the French architect, Bruno Renard, restored part as ruins but converted the eastern range into offices by inserting glass screen walls. In Germany, Foster & Partners have designed purely modern display spaces at the Zollverein Colliery in the Ruhr for the North-Rhine Westphalia Design Centre. Their scheme draws upon the Bauhaus idiom of the Colliery buildings dating to 1930 and fully exploits the bold forms of the boiler house – even the interiors of the boilers themselves will contain works of art. The new Centre for Art and Media Technology at Karlsruhe is housed in a concrete-framed armaments factory completed in 1918. The architects, Schweger & Partner, stripped back the concrete frame of any accretions and then added new courtyard roofs and a 'Music Cube' in steel and glass. The Cube was designed as a glass box for performances and appears as though it is plugged into the eastern side of the factory, preserving its integrity but making a bold, clearly contemporary addition.

In Italy, Renzo Piano developed a philosphy for converting the Fiat Lingotto Factory[www] in Turin – one of the great icons of industrial futurism – that juxtaposed preservation and modern design. The conversion of a car factory to a conference centre and hotel was expressed by introducing unapologetically modern design where original fabric had to be replaced, and by one major and symbolic addition. The rusted window frames of this vast daylight factory were replaced by lightweight designs with a series of perforations in the mullions. More controversially Lingotto is now topped by an addition (*see Plates 8 & 9*) – a futuristic dome housing a conference room and a helipad, the combination almost parodying the aspirations of the magnates who fly in for their meetings. Modern design can be justified as a way of marking a major re-use scheme, especially if it is clearly an addition, and if it is reversible.

In France, Sarfati's conversion of the Roubaix Spinning Mill is expressed through the application of striking, bolt-on additions in white aluminium – marking the provision of lifts and staircases and, most assertively a huge window, illuminating a new reading room. Many would argue that the additions at Roubaix are self-indulgent and drastically compromise the original architecture. But in some instances a bold addition can actually highlight the nature of the original structure by way of contrast. An ironworks in Germany has been converted into a museum and exhibition

2.14
New helipad and conference room added to the Fiat Lingotto Car Factory, Turin, designed by Giacomo Matté Trucco, 1916–20. Converted into an exhibition and conference centre and a hotel by Renzo Piano.

(Photo: M. Denance)

and congress centre. The architect Günther Domenig expressed this fundamental change by adding a suspended walkway in the form of a rectangular girder reaching the full length of the structure – the harsh angles and lightweight form of the steelwork contrast with the solid masonry ruins while also linking the structures into the immediate landscape.[30] In Los Angeles, Eric Owen Moss took a mundane warehouse and converted it into offices. Rather than just re-working the warehouse, he set a new structure above it on dramatic pilotis – so creating an eye-catching complex that stands out amidst a district of scruffy sheds and parking lots.[31]

Old and new – post-modernism

An alternative is to pursue a broadly post-modern agenda, giving a factory new detailing that adjusts its imagery towards its new function and the expectations of its new clientele. In most simple terms, gaunt warehouses are given additional trim in the form of pediments, brightly coloured balconies and jazzed-up interiors. New cornices were added to Butler's Wharf, London[www] to create a more sophisticated identity for the 98 luxury flats being created by the CD Partnership. Over the Atlantic, a simple, daylight warehouse on Boston's waterfront was given a classical doorway and a huge cornice pediment to express its new status as a design centre while the interior was lined with polished marble.[32] One of the British architects most closely associated with post-modernism, Terry Farrell, created an Egyptian style entrance and brightly-coloured shopfronts and staircases for the Tobacco Warehouse in London's docks[www] to help draw visitors into the complex. The commercial failure of the project has not helped to justify such gaudy interventions on historic buildings of the highest rank.

Post-modernism has a valid philosphical justification in terms of adding historical layers and articulating the changed role of historic buildings, but has been sold short by many of its advocates and even more so by commercial plagiarists. There are all too many buildings where green woodstains and pink renders are fading, while their loosely classical motifs seem more suited to housing estates than to the

industrial heritage. The visual strength of a mill or warehouse may have become diluted through a dressing-up that seems contrived and, all too quickly, outdated.

There are other more subtle design philosophies, rarely tried and never discussed. One is to rework the architecture to enrich the original industrial image, even though the new function will not involve manufacture or storage. Philosophically controversial to say the least, this approach has been applied to great success in the case of the Luma Light Factory on the edge of Glasgow. The streamlined, modernistic style of the factory has been made even crisper and more characteristic of the new industries of the inter-war period through the complete replacement of the external walls and fenestration, even though the factory now houses homes rather than production lines. This is not conservation but an exceptional case of architectural reworking that successfully breaks the rules.

Another approach is to design new additions not in a replication of the original form or a style of our time, but to take an intermediate point – such as adopting the stripped classicism of the 1920s, or the render and metal windows of early British modernism. If undertaken with sensitivity and to a high standard, the designer may succeed in creating a secondary, enriching layer that will not be pastiche and that will date more satisfactorily than either high-tech steel and glass or the latest brand of post-modernism.

Once a design is draughted, agreed and approved then the project can be taken towards implementation. Particular care must to be taken in protecting surviving historic features and machinery. Archaeologists may need to be on site with a watching brief, first to record the structure and then to study the foundations of old buildings and watercourses as they are uncovered. With some industries, such as dyeing, chemicals and military sites, it may be necessary to remove toxic wastes. Finally, an appropriate management structure will have to be devised if the building is not to be sold on, and especially if multiple uses are planned. Such management issues will be considered further in the chapters by Fred Taggart and Bo Öhström and will re-emerge in many of the exemplar case studies.

Notes and references

1 Paul Zara, pers comm, August 1998.

2 Eley, P. & Worthington, J. (1984) *Industrial Rehabilitation*, Architectural Press, London, 43–65.

3 Clark, K. (1998) *Conservation Plans*, English Heritage, London, 4.

4 A broad study of the locations and landscapes of factories and docks is provided by: Trinder, B. (1982) *The Making of the Industrial Landscape*, Dent, London.

5 See Eley & Worthington (1984) op cit, 55–6.

6 Richards, J.M. (1958) *The Functional Tradition in Early Industrial Buildings*, Architectural Press, London.

7 English Heritage (1995) *Industrial Archaeology: A Policy Statement*, English Heritage, London

8 Patrick, A. (1996) 'Establishing a Typology for the Buildings of the Floor Malting Industry', *Industrial Archaeology Review*, 18, no 2, 180–200.

9 Collins & Stratton (1993) *British Car Factories from 1896*, Veloce, Godmanstone, 44–6.

10 On the changing fortunes of terminii see: Parrisien, S. (1998) *Station to Station*, Phaidon, Oxford.

11 Stratton, M. (1994) *Ironbridge and the Electric Revolution*, John Murray, London, 87.

12 Sharpe, A., Lewis, R. & Massie, C. (1991) *Engine House Survey: The Mineral Tramways Project*, Cornwall Archaeology Unit, Truro.

13 IBA (1996) *Emscher Park*, IBA, Gelsenkirchen.

14 Hunter, M. & Thorne, R. (1990) *Change at King's Cross*, Historical Publications, London, 45.

15 Green, H. & Foley, P. (1986) *Redundant Space: A Productive Asset*, Harper & Row, London, 31-2.

16 Eley & Worthington (1984) op. cit., 66.

17 Department of the Environment (1987) *Re-Using Redundant Buildings*, HMSO, London, 7.

18 Quoted in Pearce, D. (1989) *Conservation Today*, Routledge, London, 85.

19 Pearson, C. (1997) 'Project Diary: Lingotto Factory', *Architectural Record*, March, 44.

20 Boeckx, S. (1998) *The Re-Use of Redundant Buildings*, MA in Conservation Studies thesis, University of York, 32.

21 Eley & Worthington (1984) op. cit., 25.

22 Catalano, A. (1998) *The Conversion of Redundant Industrial Buildings*, MA in Architecture by research thesis, University of York, 121.

23 Institution of Structural Engineers (1996) *Appraisal of Existing Structures*, Institution of Structural Engineers, London.

24 English Heritage (1996) *Office Floor Loadings in Historic Buildings*, English Heritage, London.

25 Department of the Environment (1994) op. cit., 18.

26 Sparks, L. 'Historicism and Public Perception' in Warren, J, Worthington, J. & Taylor, S. (1998) *Context: New Buildings in Historic Settings*, Architectural Press, London 61–70, 70.

27 Department of the Environment (1994) op. cit., 9.

28 Catalano (1998) op cit, 147. I am grateful to Alessandra Catalano for suggestions of buildings to be considered in this section.

29 Lyall, J. 'Pulling Teeth and Filling Cavities', in Warren, Worthington & Taylor (1998) op. cit., 154–164.

30 (1996) *Casabella*, July-August.

31 (1997) *Architectural Review*, 1202, April, 78.

32 Binney, M., Machin, F. & Powell, K. (1990) *Bright Future: The Re-Use of Industrial Buildings*, SAVE, London, 94–7.

Saturday, February 6, 1965. An early start to Stoke with Molly in the official car. As I was driving through it I suddenly felt, 'here is this high, ghastly conurbation of five towns – what sense is there in talking about urban renewal here?' ..... I felt even more strongly that it was impossible to revive Britain without letting such places as Stoke-on-Trent decline. Indeed, I began to wonder whether it wasn't really better to let it be evacuated: renewal is an impossibility or alternatively a fantastic waste of money.

Richard Crossman, *The Crossman Diaries*[1]

From dereliction to sustainable urban regeneration:

the example of Stoke-on-Trent

Rick Ball ❙

Staffordshire University

Reproducing diary jottings, reminiscences reprised years after they were constructed, out of context and from a previous era of development, is not necessarily relevant or defensible. However, in this case, it seems rather appropriate, not least because of the enduring topicality of urban renewal in the late 1990s. As the quote implies, the image of old industrial areas has not always been positive. Indeed, cynics might argue that some elements of policy – at least as enacted at the central government level – have reflected the Crossman line ever since the 1960s.

There seems to have been a predilection for redevelopment of old industrial areas rather than refurbishment particularly in those areas under the jurisdiction of Urban Development Corporations.[2] The scarcity of research on industrial buildings means that the issues associated with their occupancy, vacancy or demise have not been widely explored. However, the perceived economics of refurbishment against redevelopment and reconstruction, coupled with the ever acuter sense of locational image, have combined to render the retention of older buildings a less than popular commercial option. Despite this, there is a strong argument that in many areas, assuming acceptable levels of demand, the costs of re-use are lower than new-build alternatives.

The debate over re-use or rebuild is a controversial matter and, along with 'sustainability' – in its various environmental, community and economic forms – it is ever more firmly on the planning agenda. Perhaps as a consequence, the industrial built environment has become an issue of great interest in the contemporary planning and economic development scene, even if it has not, until recently, been given prominence in media[3] or government publicity circles.

With its jumbled landscape of industrial buildings and housing, developed through infill and in piecemeal fashion over the years, and, in its heyday, with little formal planning,[4] Stoke-on-Trent presents both a challenge and an opportunity for regeneration through its industrial built environment. The area has long been burdened with an image of dereliction and decline.

Through an analysis of re-use potential, this chapter explores the broad policy arena and the effective use of industrial premises in old industrial areas.[5] The Stoke-on-Trent locality is the main focus of attention, with the analysis based around the results of major surveys of vacant industrial buildings completed in August 1994[6] and July 1997.[7] This includes aggregate local analysis and detailed case studies of reoccupation circumstances, constraints and end results, including a consideration of developer attitudes and experiences, a discussion about the Burslem-Cobridge Single Regeneration Budget (SRB) area of the city, and a comment on the less successful examples – persistent vacancies, including the ongoing saga of the Chatterley Whitfield colliery site.

Exploring the vacant industrial premises issue in Stoke-on-Trent

The lack of comprehensive reliable data, the apparent negativities of the basic market view, and the realization that there is much to be gained from investigating the urban built environment,[8] has led to a series of surveys in Stoke-on-Trent, where research on vacant industrial premises has been in progress since 1985.[9] This has produced a number of important and often unexpected findings.

The extent of vacancy amongst industrial buildings in Stoke-on-Trent is much greater than might be expected. Many of these vacant

buildings are of sound quality – mostly a variant of traditional red brick and tile/slate construction in work-a-day style, but with a variety of alternative roofing materials such as asbestos or metal profiled sheeting in some of the more modern buildings – and could be reoccupied with minimum effort and cost. The surveys have shown that there is a persistence of vacancy in some zones and in some (usually purpose-built) building types. In the case of re-occupation a degree of variability has been revealed. Some buildings are easily reoccupied, others are not, but the pattern has been difficult to read. This renders it hard to predict the fine detail of local development outcomes. However, it does suggest the importance of geographical considerations.

The most recent and extensive survey of vacant industrial premises (VIPs) in Stoke-on-Trent was completed in July 1997, as part of an Engineering and Physical Sciences Research Council (EPSRC) funded project in the Sustainable Cities Programme.[10] This charted change in the VIPs situation over the 1994 to 1997 period, focused on the reoccupation process and the investigation of developers and related organizations. The results revealed the scale of the VIPs problem in the area. As shown in Table 1a, there were 427 vacant properties with a cumulative floorspace of over five million square feet. The great majority of premises fell into the 1,000–5,000 square feet range. An average floorspace of just over 11,000 square feet reflects the existence of a small number of large vacant industrial buildings, all former pottery manufacturing plants of some kind. At the other end of the scale the survey recorded over 270 premises smaller than 5,000 square feet, representing 64 per cent of the total. Over 60 per cent of vacant buildings were constructed before 1945 although, typically in the manufacturing (ceramics and engineering) industry, these were often composites developed over many years with regular adaptation and piecemeal additions. For example, a recent survey at the former Dudsons factory, completed as part of the site investigation for a major redevelopment scheme, found that the existing complex formed a quadrangle around a surviving bottle kiln. The site had been completed in stages with the majority of the buildings dating from the mid-1880s and possibly some parts of the building having been converted from terraced houses.

(a) The basic structure of the vacant industrial building stock

Size of vacant buildings (sq.ft)	Number in survey
Less than 1,000	86
1,000–4,999	185
5,000–24,999	120
More than 25,000	38
Survey total	427

(b) Condition of premises and marketing status

Condition status	Marketed	Not marketed
Good	61	41
Structurally sound	75	165
Poor	8	61
Very poor/derelict	5	11
Total	*149*	*278*
%	*34.9*	*65.1*

Table 1
The vacant industrial premises problem in Stoke-on-Trent in July 1997.

(Source: Phase 1 Survey)

Table 2
Vacant industrial premises in Stoke-on-Trent: components of change, August 1994-July 1997.

(Source: Phase 1 Survey)

Situation	<- Buildings/Units ->		Floorspace (sq.ft)
Vacant industrial premises 1994	*464*		*5,026,111*
Sub-divided buildings	33		928,815
total number of sub-divided units		85	
Redeveloped (demolished) buildings	59		1,128,097
number of sub-divided and redeveloped units		5	59,977
Total redeveloped buildings and units		64	1,188,074
Reoccupied buildings	179		934,964
number of sub-divided and reoccupied buildings and units		53	316,279
Total reoccupied buildings and units		232	1,251,243
Persistently vacant buildings	193		2,034,235
number of sub-divided and still vacant units		27	552,559
Total persistently vacant buildings and units		220	2,586,794
Newly vacant buildings in 1997		207	2,126,089
Vacant industrial premises 1997		427	4,712,883

Important factors in re-use are marketability and physical condition. Indeed, market involvement reflects both the confidence of the property industry in saleability and the strategy of property owners. Less than 35 per cent of buildings were on the market at the time of the survey, although the great majority of all buildings were of good or at least structurally sound condition (*see Table 1b*). As such, it was interesting and initially surprising, that many of these were not on the market. This is a familiar and, to date, unexplained factor but it is partly a consequence of ownership patterns. Some buildings were unwanted but acquired as part of a wider portfolio; some were 'hoarded', or spaces that were simply not marketed because they were in difficult positions within complexes (on upper floors for example), or because they did not seem lettable at the time.

Aside from the documentation of the static picture, perhaps the most valuable survey-based insights derive from the extent and experience of re-use. From a base of 464 VIPs in August 1994, 179 were reoccupied by July 1997, and 33 were sub-divided producing 53 additional new occupiers (*see Table 2*). These were a mix of new small firms in manufacturing, some local services and distribution, expansions or branch establishment, relocations – mainly from within the North Staffordshire conurbation – or expansions, sometimes from adjacent premises. Several reoccupations involved niche pottery manufacturing or other specialist re-uses, but many were for relatively low grade uses, typically those such as budget furniture

3.1
Ephraim Court, Hanley.
Furniture making –
typical of the array of
small businesses that
seek out and re-occupy
low cost premises.

3.2
Carlton House,
Stoke-on-Trent.

making, which required low-cost operating space. Typically, the buildings were functional and structurally sound but modest in their visual attractiveness, often having been refurbished in a relatively piecemeal, low-budget fashion. Several buildings had been converted partly into student accommodation, sometimes to very high quality.

An example of this type of conversion is the former Carlton Ware pottery factory which closed in 1989. Of 15,000 square feet in a courtyard configuration, whilst retaining the broad character of the structure, it has been converted to mixed use, with small enterprise units on the ground floor and residential accommodation for 108 students on the two

upper floors. Vacant for six months prior to purchase, the site was acquired from the receiver by two local businessmen with the deliberate intention of developing student space as a business venture. Other buildings in the survey included a small number that were in leisure use as catering or related establishments. On the negative side, 220 were persistently vacant over the period, and 207 newly vacant premises were recorded, with a variety of more recently constructed buildings falling into (perhaps short-term) disuse.

Although there are many well-known disused buildings in a city such as Stoke-on-Trent, the survey revealed a level of vacancy that surprised even those with some expertise in the local property arena. Moreover, it generated a number of important policy implications, which related to the potential value of refurbishment funding to 'unlock' premises: the importance of generating a new attitude to the value of old and/or vacancy-prone buildings via a flexible approach to changing land and property uses; the idea that owners of non-marketed premises should be identified, located and contacted to encourage re-use via joint initiatives; and a clear need for the monitoring of VIPs to elicit localized trends and to improve local knowledge.

Picking up on the policy angles – challenges and questions

Given a commitment to intervene, which seems to pervade most urban authorities, the major local policy challenge is how to influence the incidence of vacancy in industrial buildings and, where they are of a suitable condition, how to encourage a process whereby such buildings are brought back into effective use. Of course there are constraints. In the global property arena, with competition between areas and so on, any notion of control in the local arena is likely to be constrained by feasibility of action. Are local policies really able to influence global businesses?

For local agencies, there are basically four options available in confronting the vacancy issue:

3.3
Roslyn Craft Studios,
Longton (former Roslyn
Works).

■ 'do little' – retaining the status quo and
relying on piecemeal activity by the private
sector

■ cosmetic improvement

■ large scale refurbishment

■ extensive redevelopment.[11]

Despite these options, for most areas the thrust
of policy towards industrial buildings tends
towards a reactive, opportunistic approach
within the constraints of financial resources,
although 'buildings at risk' surveys[12] or other
locally-based initiatives to record[13] or deal with
vacant buildings[14] are evident. By necessity,
there has been a concentration on a small
number of 'prestige' projects in an endeavour,
'phoenix from the ashes' style, to activate or
precipitate change. In Stoke-on-Trent, the
Gladstone Pottery Museum,[www] the Minton
Hollins site, and the divided and refurbished
ex-pottery factory that is now the Stoke-on-
Trent Enterprise Centre are prime examples.
Such a strategy is fine and, probably, expedient.
However, the main focus of vacancy in
industrial buildings is firmly on the smaller
categories and, more importantly, the
'piecemeal' approach implies incrementalism
and a lack of strategic direction.

The award-winning Gladstone Pottery
Museum has been running in some form since
1974. It is an example of a developing trend
towards the heritage tourism use of formerly
vacant industrial buildings. In combination with
the neighbouring Roslyn Works the site contains
seven of the forty-five pot-banks that remain in
the city, all of which are Grade II listed. Its
future performance will be a test of the strength
of association between heritage property and
tourism development, a matter that has rarely
been explored in research. The Stoke-on-Trent
Enterprise Centre, a former pottery complex of
33,000 square feet was acquired in 1986 and
subdivided in three phases into ninety-two
units by Stoke-on-Trent City Council in
partnership with Staffordshire County Council,
the Department of the Environment, and British
Coal Enterprise. Although tenant demand has
varied, it is a successful re-use, providing a
location for a wide array of new small
businesses in a range of activities.

Beyond that, the implication is that policy
has been severely constrained by the scarcity of
information about both the extent and the
context of vacant industrial buildings. As such,
a clear challenge for policy is for a better
informed decision base, and a fuller
understanding of business in the local industrial
property market. Ultimately, it should be
possible for authorities to engage in a much
fuller involvement with market players and
agents. This involves working to influence the
key players – owners and users, and the process
agents (commercial estate agents, local planners
etc.) – who have some power of influence over
the processes involved. Before that, there is a
need to know what local factors influence the

demand for industrial property. Factors of importance to establish are: who owns or controls the buildings; why they effectively 'hoard' their property investments; why are some buildings successfully re-used whilst others remain persistently vacant; and how do the attitudes and experiences of developers and related organizations relate to these situations. So far, policy has functioned in something of an information vacuum.

Exemplars and others: dispelling the Crossman view?

In order further to assess some of these policy challenges it is important to reflect on the information that is available and the implications or pointers that might be drawn from it. There are alternative routes. In the search for policy pointers there might be a focus on persistent vacancies, or on the viewpoints of local players, or report on some survey findings to monitor and reflect on policy successes and needs.

The idea of re-use potential needs to be investigated through a survey analysis that focuses on parameters of success, exploring reoccupation and re-use processes and problems. This can be done through aggregate analysis on a local scale, through a more detailed micro-scale focus on buildings/complexes or, through an investigation of developer attitudes and experiences. There is also benefit in investigating specific zones where particular circumstances might have sharpened the need for policy effort and/or generated supporting funds. In this section, using selected results from the 1997 surveys, some of these aspects are explored.

Focusing on re-use at the aggregate local level

Evidence from trends in VIPs dynamics should provide some pointers towards re-use conditions and hence to policy possibilities for the future. The evidence is particularly useful

because re-use, although widespread, appears focused on specific types of buildings, conditions, and locations. Indeed, as suggested above, at an aggregate level the incidence of successful re-use relates to local factors such as building condition and design, and the activities of 'process agents' – the initiators of re-use projects – and perhaps to less local factors such as the availability of funding through urban regeneration schemes.

These ideas are testable using findings from the 1997 surveys. Successful reoccupations between 1994 and 1997 were found to be focused particularly on premises that were, for example, in good or sound condition, accessible to a motorway interchange, with good local site access along with available parking facilities. The nature of the building design was of particular importance; for example, courtyard and island sites compared with street frontage sites recorded a very high reoccupancy level over the period. In general, reoccupations were focused on smaller buildings and units of less than 5,000 square feet.[15]

Within the context of these observed re-use conditions, there is a clearly variable rate of change in vacant industrial buildings, re-uses and redevelopments across the cityscape (*see Table 3 and Figure 3.4*). The reoccupancy rate (reoccupied floorspace as a percentage of total vacant industrial floorspace in 1994) is high in Fenton and Hanley, and relatively low in parts of Burslem, Shelton and Longton. The latter are the older industrial zones of the city where it has proved most difficult to effect substantial re-use. Both the occupancy and movement rates (reoccupied and redeveloped floorspace as a percentage of total vacant industrial floorspace in 1994) are relatively low in Shelton, Stoke and Hartshill. In the early to mid-1990s at least, these were the marginal spaces within the dynamic cityscape. The movement rate is high in Burslem, Fenton and Tunstall, which partly reflects the activities of local economic development that, via Single Regeneration Budget and European funding, has successfully focused the regeneration effort on areas such as Burslem.[16]

Local planning and economic development policy provides an important context for assessing local authority attitudes to the issue of vacant industrial buildings in Stoke-on-Trent. Although the city has tended to take a cautious

3.4
The distribution of vacant industrial premises; floorspace reoccupancy and movement rates in Stoke-on-Trent Wards, 1997.

Wards	VIPs 1997	Floorspace Reoccupancy Rate (%)	Floorspace Movement Rate (%)
Abbey	-	-	100.0
Berryhill	48	25.8	28.3
Blurton	10	59.5	59.5
Brookhouse	1	-	-
Burslem Central	22	37.5	45.6
Burslem Grange	54	12.0	82.2
Chell	1	-	-
East Valley	4	34.7	45.5
Fenton Green	49	50.9	77.9
Great Fenton	8	90.0	91.5
Hanley Green	18	55.0	55.6
Hartshill	30	11.9	26.7
Longton South	44	33.2	41.1
Meir Park	-	-	100.0
Norton and Bradeley	15	33.7	35.5
Shelton	53	18.7	25.0
Stoke West	17	23.9	23.9
Trentham Park	5	33.8	33.8
Tunstall North	45	21.7	61.9
Weston	3	31.5	31.5
City wide	*427*	*24.9*	*48.5*

Table 3
Indicators of vacant industrial premises (VIPs) dynamics in Stoke-on-Trent Wards, August 1994–July 1997.

(Source: Phase 1 Survey)

view over regeneration schemes involving some of the prominent vacant industrial buildings, generally it has been keen to resolve such problems. Detailed research[17] has been commissioned in an endeavour to attract European funding.[18] The successful bids have been partly deployed in building renovation and related areas, and have been actively sought to retain historic buildings in heritage tourism or other alternative uses.[19] The initiative has been driven by a desire to diversify the local economy, nurture businesses and jobs, and improve the image of the area.[20]

Re-use has been regulated by the 'listing' of some buildings[21] and that, to a degree, has restricted the array of new uses that are permitted. In most cases, however, the predominant factor is economic pragmatism combined with a determination to seek and secure funds for re-use. A case in point is funding secured through an early Single Regeneration Budget (SRB) bid.

Area-based analysis: selective investigation with a policy remit – re-surveying and reflecting on trends in the SRB focus area

In Stoke-on-Trent, the Burslem-Cobridge area has been targeted for specific support via SRB funding. In these terms, a major route for generating policy pointers is to focus on the vacant industrial buildings issue, reviewing the situation within this area after a three year period since the 1994 survey. This has two benefits. Firstly, it allows change to be charted and policy implications to be drawn out. Secondly, it allows initial judgements to be made on a refurbishment fund that was set up in 1995 to confront the vacant buildings problem.

From the 1997 re-survey work, it is useful to focus in particular on two aspects of the vacant industrial buildings problem in the SRB area – successful re-occupations and persistent vacancies (see Table 4).

Re-occupations provide real pointers for policy as it is possible to identify the buildings that were subject to successful re-occupations, who was responsible for the project, and what level of building improvement (refurbishment) was achieved. Future policy initiatives might try to create the conditions under which

(a) Status of re-surveyed premises

Status	Number in re-survey	
	before subdivision	after subdivision
Persistently vacant	21	23
Reoccupied	22	26
Redeveloped since 1994 survey	10	10
Subdivided	2	-
Total re-surveyed	*53*	*59*

(b) Persistently vacant premises – condition and market status

Condition status	Marketed	Not marketed
Good	1	3
Structurally sound	6	11
Poor	-	1
Very poor/derelict	-	1
Total	*7*	*16*

(c) Reoccupied premises

Nature of firms	Number in re-survey
New firm	6
Branch establishment	3
Expansion	5
Relocation within area	7
Status unknown	5
Total	*26*

(d) Reoccupied premises – condition and market status

Condition status	Marketed	Not marketed
Good	16	2
Structurally sound	3	3
Poor	1	1
Very poor/derelict	-	-
Total	*20*	*6*

Table 4

Selected 1997 re-survey results from the Burslem-Cobridge SRB area.

(Source: Phase 1 Survey)

successful re-occupation occurs or, alternatively, ignore the 'difficult to re-occupy' examples. The latter case relates to the situation of persistent vacancies – a condition that clearly represents a more intransigent problem.

The re-survey focused on the forty-nine vacant industrial buildings initially identified in August 1994, which were clearly located within the SRB area. This revealed that some twenty-one buildings were still vacant, twenty-two had been occupied, and ten had been redeveloped, usually involving total demolition of the original building. The floorspace re-occupancy rate was 15.4 per cent and the movement rate 84 per cent. Over 50 per cent of persistently vacant buildings were in good or sound condition. However, in many cases there was substantial evidence of deterioration in either the building and/or the surrounding land/site. Not only is there a potential, there is also an urgency for these buildings to be confronted by policy action.

An investigation of the re-occupations is equally interesting and relevant for the policy process. The re-survey addressed who was occupying the buildings, for what purpose and what level of refurbishment was completed. It was found that, of the twenty-six re-occupations, thirteen were either new firms or in-movers from within Stoke-on-Trent, whilst others included branch establishment and local expansions. This reveals that, over the limited time-period involved, Stoke-on-Trent vacancies were serving an essentially local need.

Most re-occupations involved good or sound premises that were being actively marketed (see Table 4), implying a potential for the successful re-use of buildings with appropriate promotional activity. There was evidence of refurbishment in many cases, albeit of a minor nature and, with the exceptions of local authority assisted re-occupations, involving modest expenditure.

In this sense another element of the SRB analysis concerns the tranche of refurbishment funds generated as a result of the August 1994 survey. Although early in the process, it is possible to make some initial judgements on this initiative. Certainly, the grant allocation was fully utilized without the need to market the existence of the fund; its potential was advertised via the property/business 'grapevine'. In its initial sixteen months, three refurbishment grants were awarded, using the full allocation of grant aid for the initial two years of the SRB project. These were for £134,000, £246,000 and £67,000. The first grant was made to a firm specializing in the production of children's party bags. 'Mr Luckybags' – a fast growing locally-based enterprise – needed larger premises and was thus persuaded to move into an SRB area vacant building. The refurbishment grant was viewed by the company as an important, if not necessarily crucial, component in the decision to locate in such premises. It was more a stimulus to create a higher quality, and potentially more sustainable, refurbishment. The other two recipients of a grant were manufacturing firms re-occupying vacant premises in or on the edge of the SRB area. Clearly, at least some of the SRB area premises are now functioning as important locations for indigenous economic activity.

From the array of evidence paraded so far, there is an implication that individual firms or organizations, and sometimes individual buildings, are catalysts for change. The existence of specialist re-use developers is important – these are the individuals with an interest in taking on older buildings rather than occupying characterless new structures, or those who recognize the cost advantages of re-use.

Investigating the re-use of individual buildings or complexes

Aside from aggregate data on the changing patterns of vacant, disused and re-used industrial buildings, the 1997 project included detailed investigation of a small number of single occupier re-uses and sub-divisions of former industrial buildings, as well as a detailed developer survey.

The survey revealed that the vast majority of re-used buildings had been returned to industrial or warehousing use, often with little or no substantive refurbishment. Only in a few cases had conversion into very different uses occurred or was likely to occur. The typical outcome for reoccupation involves small, vulnerable and uncertain businesses operating in cheap workspaces. Media attention on office or industrial conversions tends to be focused on the large, possibly contentious or exciting design. But, in reality, there have been relatively few stunning industrial conversions, and a great many modest re-uses. That said, there are 'success stories' and these may sometimes emerge as 'icons' of the 'new', and in some cases, as exemplars of sustainable re-use.

To give an example, a niche pottery manufacturer – employing around sixty staff – purchased, refurbished and occupied a plant (formerly owned by Wedgwood) of over 45,000 square feet in the Hanley area. The firm relocated from smaller premises elsewhere in North Staffordshire and selected an existing building because of the lower potential costs involved and the feeling that purpose-built space was unacceptable as it lacked character. Whilst the firm was virtually 'forced' to re-use a vacant building, occupancy brought some unexpected benefits. For example, the ground floor could be used for production, the first floor for warehousing, and there was plenty of space for car parking. More significantly, the building offered space with character, including a huge office which has been praised by staff. For a firm led by design, there has been a good deal of benefit from not operating out of a 'soulless shed'.

Other examples in the survey include a new firm that occupied a former pottery works for fibre glass moulding. The site was viewed as having a suitable form, size and configuration for their activities, and was attractive partly because of the solid building, but mainly for its low cost. Another example was an in-car entertainment retail and trade outlet which moved into a building of 23,000 square feet on the edge of Fenton, adjacent to a new link road access. The substantial refurbishment and re-use of the existing factory building followed from a need for wider accessibility to the site, good access to the town centre for passing trade, and the low purchase cost, although the building, vacant for over four years prior to acquisition, was only being partly used at the time of the survey.

In Stoke-on-Trent the acquisition, sub-division and re-use via letting is an important mechanism through which vacant industrial premises are returned to use. The survey found a number of specialist firms and public sector organizations engaged in such activity.[22] Local authority initiated sub-divisions, for example

the Roslyn Works (*see Figure 3.3*), were precipitated with the deliberate objective of creating managed workspaces in the city, often with local or European funding support. This former china pottery – a Grade II* listed building – has been refurbished by Stoke-on-Trent City Council under an Urban Pilot Project as managed workspaces for designers and makers in ceramics and related activities. Adjacent to the Gladstone Heritage Museum in Longton, the building of 9,000 square feet is on three storeys and has been subdivided into sixteen units. A key feature enhancing the flexibility of the building was the construction of internal staging via a gallery deck access within the inner courtyard walls to allow easy access to upper floors and thus to create flexible, small unit spaces.

Some sub-divisions of buildings are immensely successful as viable economic entities, with clear evidence from enquiries and actual lettings, subject to cyclical fluctuations, of generally high occupancy. Examples of such buildings are the Stoke-on-Trent Enterprise Centre, Carlton House, and the IMEX Business Park at Fenton. This former Ministry of Defence store, constructed in the early 1950s, has been converted into industrial units by IMEX, a subsidiary of Birkby plc. It is a single storey building of 68,000 square feet with brick external walls, internal steel frame and steel roof truss construction, clad with asbestos. The important feature of the complex is the internal routeway developed as part of the refurbishment to create access to the units.

3.5
IMEX Business Park, Fenton.

3.6
Lord Nelson Industrial
Estate, Hanley.

Other buildings have not sustained a high quality of working environment but still seem able successfully to let space. In most of these cases the buildings were structurally sound but in poor state of repair. At the Lord Nelson Industrial Estate in Hanley, a former pottery complex, the main buildings have been subdivided to create a variety of units. Although it is in poor condition and generally poor on sustainability criteria such as visual quality and energy efficiency, low rental values and flexible workspaces combine to generate a constant flow of low grade uses. These include retail catering, several small china manufacturers, kitchen furniture manufacturing, joinery, and metal polishing.

In Stoke-on-Trent the Hyde Park former steam locomotive and carriage works dating from 1842 has been subdivided and developed by Hyde Engineering, owners of the site. Adjacent to the A500 'D' road link to the M6, it has been a successful venture from the perspective of tenant demand.

3.7
Hyde Park,
Stoke-on-Trent.

Clearly, the response to repair and refurbishment needs is partly a function of access to resources and, where local authority or urban funding has been available, a better quality of refurbishment might be expected. However, the key distinction seems to be in the motive of the acquirers and, linked to that, their home base. Absentee owners, who have acquired a building cheaply as an investment with expected tenant income, do not appear to have sufficient commitment to maintain and develop their premises to a high standard. Where acquisition has been made by local business interests, particularly where it is part of a specialized, personal business venture – sometimes by those with a clear remit for sustainable development – then design, refurbishment and re-use qualities, and the quest for engineering innovations, are noticeably higher and keener.

There are plans to develop two neighbouring former pottery buildings extending to over 30,000 square feet and landfill sites adjacent to the Trent-Mersey canal in Tunstall to form the Middleport Environment Centre. This will be a visitor centre devoted to the theme of environmental sustainability, with a variety of community facilities around recycling, organic food production and teleworking enterprises. With the intention to refurbish the buildings to reasonably high and sustainable specification, these would be exemplars of sustainable re-use. Figure 3.8 shows one of the two buildings in the scheme, a Grade II listed former calcining mill, which has been altered in various ways since its construction in the late nineteenth century.

Focusing on the initiators: developers and related organizations and the re-use process

Whether a particular industrial building is occupied or not, and the extent to which buildings originally designed for another purpose are adapted for some economic activity, or industrial buildings adapted for non-industrial use, depends on a variety of influences – the policies of local authorities, the state of the local economy, and the willingness of developers and related organizations to initiate active change. As such, the 1997

3.8
Middleport
Environment Centre.

research project investigated who is active in the local industrial property market, through what process/processes they have developed their interest, the extent of their involvement and expertise in the use and re-use of industrial buildings, and the impact that they have.[23]

The respondents, mostly based locally, included: development companies directly involved with the acquisition, sub-division and re-opening of vacant industrial buildings, usually via self-managed letting; a large group of mixed property investment and development firms who acquired property as investments but were developing them as working buildings; a group who were involved via portfolio acquisition where one or more industrial buildings had been acquired for letting as an investment opportunity; a number of active manufacturing firms who had sub-divided and sub-let their premises as a parallel business venture; and several construction firms. It encompassed all of the large companies operating in the area, together with some smaller, more specialized organizations working with industrial buildings or developing design and build, mainly residential schemes.

For nearly 30 per cent of the organizations industrial refurbishment and re-use was more than 30 per cent of their core business; in some cases, the figure was almost 100 per cent. Around 40 per cent had some involvement, and another 30 per cent had no involvement. This shows a certain potential for enhanced activity, and provides a useful basis for assessing attitude variations across experience bands. The analysis focused on the relative costs and

related benefits and constraints of re-use versus new-build. In many cases, subject to appropriate after-use, it was felt that the costs of re-using vacant industrial buildings were lower than the equivalent costs of new-build. Of course, in some cases, deteriorating condition in structure and fabric after years of neglect pushed the costs way beyond any economic benefits, although there may still be sustainability gains to be made in environmental and community terms and these may be viable if funding support is forthcoming. For many structures however, where there are expected end-users of refurbished and/or reopened buildings, and hence some guaranteed demand, then the refurbishment/re-use route was seen as effective and profitable in economic terms. Re-use benefits were seen as not only lower costs, but also in the value of retaining style and character (heritage features) of buildings, in the solid build qualities, and in the appropriateness of their location.[24] Lack of demand for re-use was sometimes apparent, but, in general, there was no problem in filling refurbished and/or re-opened industrial space.

Icons of decline? – focusing on a key and contentious location: the Chatterley Whitfield site

As a final point, it is worth dwelling briefly on the less successful as well as the successful re-uses and re-users, and the Chatterley Whitfield site offers a salutary lesson. This is a high profile site in Stoke-on-Trent. It is a former colliery complex, latterly the site of a major mining museum, at one stage holding the now sold-off and partially dispersed British Coal collection of mining artefacts. The site contains a complex of some twenty-eight buildings, some of which are listed or Scheduled Ancient Monuments. Much of the complex operated as a mining museum following the winding down and eventual cessation of mining activity from the early 1980s. With a wide range of surface buildings intact, Chatterley Whitfield represents an excellent example of a colliery complex developed from the late nineteenth century onwards. Unfortunately, the escalating costs of refurbishment and re-use, the relative inaccessibility of the site, and local political pressures, have combined to weaken local commitment to its development. There were grandiose plans for the re-opening of a coal face to produce an authentic visitor experience but the need for subsidy in the face of a modest market led to its demise in the early 1990s.

Whilst there are continuing attempts to refurbish the site in order to develop it as a major heritage location, a recent consultant's report stresses the inhibitive costs involved in dealing with a wide array of structural and fabric defects and repair requirements.[25] Capital costs in bringing all buildings into effective repair amount to £13 million, leaving aside operating costs. Compounding this problem, the potential market for the refurbished heritage site is thought to be modest.

The case of Chatterley Whitfield provides clear pointers for policy on vacant industrial buildings of this type. Even with a strong heritage potential, accessibility and physical condition are important factors in re-use. Above all, there needs to be a guaranteed market of some size to precipitate interest in developing a suite of buildings. The alternative is to develop piecemeal, selecting buildings for concentrated attention, but even here there are negative legacies if premises in the vicinity are left untouched by improvement. Clearly, in a general sense, the re-use potential of a complex site such as this needs to be heavily marketed with private and public sector decision-makers.

3.9a & 3.9b
Chatterley Whitfield
colliery site.

From sustained to sustainable re-use

Having discussed the idea of precipitating a sustained use of formerly vacant industrial premises, the realms of sustainability require a wider evaluation. There is certainly a clear link between sustainability and urban regeneration. It is based on the view that key problems in the urban environment – dereliction, decaying infrastructure, or the various constrained locational qualities – are incompatible with sustainable development. This requires us to chart and understand relationships between problems of the relic industrial built environment and sustainable urban development; to explore the links between the physical and design challenges of old industrial buildings and the urban regeneration issues involved; and to pursue and establish an agenda and a set of good practice guidelines for refurbishment and conversion activity in the industrial buildings sector.[26]

Without exploring the detailed sustainability implications of their argument, the Department of the Environment in its 1987 report suggested that re-use of derelict buildings is important as: they have more character than contemporary structures; if left derelict, they inevitably blight the area; it is cheaper to refurbish an old building than to construct a new one; it offers a means of heritage conservation (especially with listed buildings); and it may generate economic developments in run-down areas.[27] The sustainability view might be developed here with the argument that, saving greenfield sites elsewhere, it is good practice to retain a building in flexible use, adapting it for resource-efficient operation and enabling it to contribute to the long-term development of the local economy and environment.[28]

Although there is a general view that economic costs drive decisions in the property arena, the 1997 surveys have shed some additional light on this area.[29] The survey of developers found a convoluted view of sustainability, framed within the narrow context of durability and longevity in new completed or refurbished buildings. Yet, these same respondents clearly recognized and accepted sustainability parameters such as the value of recycling materials, seeking energy efficient systems, relating to local communities, and so on. In essence, there are positive attitudes

towards re-use and frequently positive experiences of refurbishment and re-use by those who are initiating it.

Switching from attitude to actual activity, the research has revealed a wide array of technical and engineering solutions to re-use challenges.[30] These include: building refurbishment such as the use of overcladding techniques to improve appearance, lettability and insulation; the use of asphalt flooring to level rough concrete factory floors; the use of internal staging to add flexibility to building design; flexibility in the use of selective buildings – for example, as parking areas; or simple ideas that draw on the character of existing buildings (for example, making use of high buildings by using solar panelling). It is these kinds of activities that will generate sustainable rather than simply sustained re-use and that, from a policy perspective, might produce environmentally attractive outcomes. This may need to be combined with more effective and positive promotion of the potential for refurbishing and re-using vacant property in order to overcome the external constraints that often seem to work against local progress.

Reflections

Much previous research on vacant industrial premises has focused on the extent, character and useability of such buildings and on the potential planning solutions to their use and re-use. The research completed on the Stoke-on-Trent area probably represents one of the fullest and most complete investigations of this issue in Britain. In these terms, commencing from a solid base of experience and expertise in this area, a much fuller and more in-depth study of the process of use change and re-use has been made. This chapter has initiated, or at least opened up, a sustainability-tinged debate about the myriad roles of industrial buildings in old industrial areas. Is redevelopment the only answer – what are the consequences of vacancy-proneness – what opportunities exist for a more ambitious use of vacant industrial buildings – above all, what are the lessons to be learned from successful re-uses? The research agenda suggested here involves three key pursuits. These are: to further monitor and understand the activities of process agents, with both marketed and non-marketed vacant premises in mind; to assess the appeal or otherwise of vacant buildings via a flagging-up of both their existence and their potential; and to consider the sustainability implications of this part of the property arena. If these issues are further addressed, then our understanding of the local property market and its policy needs will be substantially and positively enhanced.

For Stoke-on-Trent in particular, there remains the irresistible chance here to comment on the irony of recent urban funding initiatives. The most recent outcome for this 'intervention backwater' has been a proliferation of urban and European funding, generating a claim that "we're in the money".[31] This 'winner' status claimed by the local authority reflects the shift in urban policy away from prespecified areas and towards 'competitive localism', and the bidding process. This is the irony of the issue. Just as stated by Crossman thirty years earlier, places like Stoke-on-Trent are potentially unpopular for business location and expensive for policy to deal with, but a recent 'cash deluge' appears to have transpired. In the late-1990s, sustainability is the name of the game and, so far at least, abandonment is not a feasible option; but then, politically, it never was!

Notes and references

1 Crossman, R.H. (1975) *The Crossman Diaries*, Hamish Hamilton/Cape, London.
2 Imrie, R. & Thomas, H. (eds) (1993) *British Urban Policy and the Urban Development Corporations*, Paul Chapman Publishing, London; although, for an exception, see *Planning for the Natural and Built Environment*, 1102, 20 January.
3 Hall, P. (1998) 'Vacant looks', *The Guardian*, 28 May.
4 See Phillips, A.D.M. (ed.) (1993) *The Potteries: Continuity and Change in a Staffordshire Conurbation*, Alan Sutton, Stroud, especially chapters by B.J. Turton, A.D.M. Phillips and A.L. Murray.
5 Ball, R.M. (1995) 'Charting the uncharted: vacant industrial premises and the local industrial property arena' in: R.M. Ball & A. Pratt (eds) *Industrial Property: Policy and Economic Development*, Routledge, London.
6 Ball, R.M. & Bord, D. (1994) *Vacant industrial premises in Stoke-on-Trent: a survey and analysis of the situation in August 1994*, Consultancy Report submitted to Stoke-on-Trent City Council and the Staffordshire Training and Enterprise Council, September.
7 See Ball, R.M. (1997) *The use and re-use of vacant industrial buildings: towards sustainability*, Fourth European Real Estate Society, Berlin, Germany; and Walljes, I. & Ball, R.M. (1997) 'Exploring the realities of the sustainable city through the use and re-use of vacant industrial buildings', *European Environment*, 7, 194–202.
8 Ball, R.M. (1997) 'The conversion of industrial buildings: stacks of potential for re-use', *Chartered Surveyors Monthly*, November/December, 36–37.
9 See Ball, 'Charting the uncharted: vacant industrial premises and the local industrial property arena' and Ball, R.M. & Bord, D. (op cit).
10 See Ball, *The use and re-use of vacant industrial buildings: towards sustainability* and Ball, R.M. (1998) *Vacant industrial premises in Stoke-on-Trent, 1994–1997: a review of the changing cityscape*, EPSRC Industrial Buildings Project, Working Paper, Staffordshire University.
11 See Ball, 'Charting the uncharted: vacant industrial premises and the local industrial property arena'.
12 Stoke-on-Trent City Council (1993) *Buildings at Risk: 1992 Survey of the Condition of Listed Buildings in Stoke-on-Trent*, Department of Planning and Architecture, Stoke-on-Trent, April.
13 Stoke-on-Trent City Council (1985) *City of Stoke-on-Trent Historic Buildings Survey, 1982–1985*, City Museum and Art Gallery, Hanley, Stoke-on-Trent.
14 Civic Trust (1987) *New Grist for Old Mills: Calderdale Feasibility Study*.
15 Ball, *Vacant industrial premises in Stoke-on-Trent, 1994–1997: a review of the changing cityscape*.
16 Ibid.
17 Ball, R.M. & Bord, D. (op cit).
18 As with the Gladstone/St James Ceramic Design Quarter concept which, part-funded by the European Commission as an Urban Pilot Project, has successfully initiated and sustained a focus on regeneration in part of the Longton area of the city.
19 For example, see Stoke-on-Trent City Council *City of Stoke-on-Trent Historic Buildings Survey, 1982–1985*.
20 See Stoke-on-Trent City Council (1991) *Economic Development Strategy, 1991–2001*, Stoke-on-Trent.
21 Stoke-on-Trent City Council (1998) *Listed Buildings*, Department of Planning, Development and Environment, Stoke-on-Trent.

22 Ball, R.M. (1998) *Developers and the re-use of vacant industrial premises in Stoke-on-Trent*, EPSRC Industrial Buildings Project, Working Paper, Staffordshire University.

23 Ibid.

24 Ibid.

25 Building Design Partnership (1995) *Chatterley Whitfield Colliery: a Strategic Assessment*, May.

26 Ball, *The use and re-use of vacant industrial buildings: towards sustainability*.

27 Department of the Environment (1987) *Re-using Redundant Buildings: Good Practice in Urban Regeneration, Inner Cities Directorate*, London.

28 See Ball, *The use and re-use of vacant industrial buildings: towards sustainability* and Walljes & Ball, 'Exploring the realities of the sustainable city through the use and re-use of vacant industrial buildings', 194–202.

29 Ball, *Developers and the re-use of vacant industrial premises in Stoke-on-Trent*.

30 Ball, R.M. (1998) *The use and re-use of vacant industrial buildings*, Final Report on Project GR/K93464 submitted to the Engineering and Physical Sciences Research Council, June.

31 Howle, N. (1996) 'At last – we're in the money! How £75m cash deluge will change face of city', *The Sentinel*, Stoke-on-Trent, 12 April.

Tornqvist, A. (1995) *Buildings for Small Firms: Managing the Culture of Entrepreneurship*, Working Paper IACTH, Göteborg.

Acknowledgements

The basic survey work was skilfully completed by my Research Assistants – Hannah Lorenzelli, Richard Chadwick, Paul Armstrong, Sarah Crompton and Alice Evans, and in conjunction with Ms. Ilka Walljes, Research Associate on the project. We must thank all those process agents who offered information during the 1994 and 1997 survey phases. In addition, Adrian Bond and Kevin Birks at Stoke-on-Trent City Council, Richard Day of Daniel and Hulme, Roberta Cameron at Seddons, and Phil Gratton of Hulme Upright provided valuable advice and support for the research activity, and Andy Roberts of InStaffs (UK) Limited provided invaluable technical computing facilities and support.

Further reading

Ball, R.M. (1995) *Local Authorities and Regional Policy in the UK: Attitudes, Representations and the Local Economy*, Paul Chapman Publishing, London.

Carley, M. (1995) 'The bigger picture: organising for sustainable urban regeneration', *Town & Country Planning*, 64, 9, 236–239.

Engineering and Physical Sciences Research Council (EPSRC) (1996) *The EPSRC Sustainable Cities Programme*, August.

Handley, J.R. (1987) 'Industrial Improvement Areas – success or failure?', *Land Development Studies*, 4, 35–53

Hirst, C. (1996) 'New solutions to urban issues', *Planning Week*, 5, 33, 12–13.

Punter, J.V. (1992) Design control and the regeneration of docklands: the example of Bristol, *Journal of Property Research*, 9, 49–78.

Thrift, N. (1994) 'Taking aim at the heart of the region', in Gregory, D., Martin, R., & Smith, G. (eds) *Human Geography: Society, Space and Social Science*, Macmillan, London.

Part **2**

New Communities
and Markets

4.1
Sowerby Bridge
canal basin.

Chapter four

Regeneration

Through Heritage:

combining

commercial skills and

community interests

Fred Taggart

Director, Regeneration Through Heritage

In the past, Britain's towns and cities were shaped by the needs of industry; the need for water, transport, energy or raw materials determined where the large manufacturing enterprises would locate and this in turn determined where people would live. Given the fundamental shifts consequent upon the collapse of Britain's traditional manufacturing economy, and the inheritance of vacant factories and industrial buildings, local communities with strong connections to these areas are now at a decisive point in their development. People are increasingly resistant to the proposition that they should move away from their communities to find a future in other parts of the country or indeed the world. Rather, local communities are pressing the government and agencies responsible for regeneration to explore the process of reinventing economies in these locations and – in consequence – to reinvent the communities where people already live. This inevitably means that there is a need to recognize the value of the investment that already exists both in the people and the built environment. Regeneration strategies in future will have to include an explicit recognition that much of the built environment, and especially heritage industrial buildings, represents a sustainable resource from past generations which is capable of being recycled for new uses and forms part of the current agenda of 'sustainability'.

The private sector has successfully adapted a number of such buildings for new uses. Dean Clough in Halifax[www] was perhaps the first major project to achieve national attention. Sir Ernest Hall converted this massive former

4.2
Dean Clough Mills,
Halifax, West Yorkshire.

(Photo: Dean Clough Ltd)

4.3 & 4.4
The *1853 Gallery* at Salts
Mill (*see Plates 3 & 4*)
created by Jonathan
Silver for works by
David Hockney.

*(Photos:
Christopher Cormack)*

carpet mill for a multiplicity of new uses
including offices, workshops, theatre, art
gallery, restaurant and gymnasium. At
Saltaire^{www} near Bradford another great
Yorkshire entrepreneur, the late Jonathan Silver,
transformed Titus Salt's monumental mill to
create a new art gallery for works by Bradford-
born artist David Hockney, a restaurant, quality
retail shops and space for high value
manufacturing. Throughout the country there
are many other examples where developers,
entrepreneurs and local authorities have
successfully tackled smaller and less daunting
heritage industrial buildings and brought them
back into contemporary use (*see Chapter 11*).

Increasingly, public policy makers and local
communities are recognizing that, with ideas
and skills, the private sector can adapt even the
most unlikely heritage industrial buildings for
contemporary purposes. At the same time there
is also a much wider recognition of the
importance that these buildings retain in the
eyes of the communities where they are
situated. People who worked in them see them
as part of their lives, are proud of what was
achieved there and appreciate the buildings as
icons for their local community.

Notwithstanding the efforts of the private
sector, there are still many buildings where the
level of investment needed, or local conditions,
are such that regeneration is not being
achieved. Instead, building preservation trusts,
local authorities, regeneration agencies and,
increasingly, local community and voluntary
organizations brought into being for this
purpose, are seeking new ways to bring these
assets back into sustainable contemporary
economic use. However, regeneration is
operating in a new economic order where the
prospects of attracting mobile investment in
manufacturing from other parts of the country
or abroad are diminishing. An economy is
emerging based on knowledge and information
technology rather than manufacturing, where
location is not the economic determinant it once
was. Communities with an inheritance of
heritage industrial buildings can now with
greater confidence identify activities within this
new economy appropriate for these buildings.

Until recently there was no national network
to exchange information and experience or
provide advice and support to communities
that have large vacant industrial buildings they
wish to see brought back into use. Regeneration
Through Heritage, which was established in
1996, seeks to fill this need.[1] The initiative is
part of Business in the Community, the
organization supported by Britain's largest
companies to promote private sector
involvement in social and economic
regeneration. Regeneration Through Heritage
has been working with a number of projects
throughout the United Kingdom seeking to
help community groups and not-for-profit local
partnerships to develop realistic and
economically sustainable proposals for the re-
use of heritage industrial buildings and secure
the necessary funding. These projects include
buildings of a range of size and former usage,
and many different types of voluntary
organizations and partnerships. While the
projects are at different stages of development,
all are sufficiently advanced for certain key
lessons to have emerged, which include the
need to: establish a steering group; understand
the building; consider the key characteristics of
the building; develop a vision; carry out a
feasibility study; appoint consultants with care;
and not to get over-fazed by the intricacies of
funding. This chapter looks at those lessons in

more detail in an attempt to give a starting point for community groups and others who might be considering embarking on such a project. Finally it gives a flavour of what might be achieved through two Regeneration Through Heritage projects.

Establishing a steering group

For a project to be successful it should be supported by a very real sense of ownership and identification on the part of the local community. Communities need to understand the proposal, see how they will benefit from it, and in turn support the group developing the project. Accordingly, groups should seek to be broadly-based with wide ranging skills and interests. However, there is no need in the early stages to have a strictly formal organization in place, although formal arrangements will be needed later on. Rather, the most effective way forward is to establish a steering group for the project which is representative of all the key local interests, and to have genuine participation by the community. The group should include a range of people with different skills, which in some communities can be scarce and may require the group to draw on expertise from a wider area. In addition to people with a general interest in or commitment to the local community, the building, or a particular need to be met by a proposed use for the building, the group should seek to include people with some of the following:

▌ financial skills, e.g. accountant, bank manager

▌ legal skills, e.g. solicitor

▌ general business skills, e.g. business owner or manager

▌ conservation and building skills, e.g. architect, planner, conservation officer, or with experience in a civic society or building preservation trust.

In Britain the role and goodwill of the local authority is of fundamental importance and every effort should be made to secure cross-party councillor and officer support, particularly that of the local authority conservation officer (if there is one) who can be an invaluable source of information and advice. In addition, well known local public figures could also be invited to act as patrons for the project as their influence and support can be crucial in its later stages.

Understanding the building

Projects start because local people see vacant buildings for what they are – as opportunities. So groups should research and understand the building's history and role in the community, and understand why it is important. It is necessary to research its architecture, check its condition and listing status, clarify any local or central government policies that might affect it and determine whether or not the local authority has taken, or is contemplating, statutory action on any outstanding repair issues, and how it might exercise any statutory powers, particularly if the building is listed.

The attitude of the owner is critical. Often such buildings have little value because of the extent of repair work required, but as soon as a community group expresses an interest, particularly if it can attract money not available to the private sector, owners can see an enhancement in its value. However, groups can usually assume that if the owners could have done something with the building then they would already have taken the opportunity. A building will probably have been vacant or underused because it has not been economic for the owner to sell or rent it, or even do any necessary repair works. In these circumstances local groups can be in a strong bargaining position and, when it comes to acquisition, early discussions with the owner are essential. Very often the local authority can spell out the financial liabilities attached to listed buildings which are in poor condition and so help limit speculation.

Before any proposals for new uses are made, groups should undertake a conservation study of the building. This will help them to understand their building, see its strengths and limitations, and the extent to which its structure, character and history will influence what can or cannot be done with it. The conservation study will identify key elements of the building and help groups to ensure that any conversion work is sympathetic and in keeping with its character. It will also help the group to develop a strategy for the maintenance of the building, which is a major future revenue cost, and guide it towards a specific philosophy of how best to 'live' in and operate within the limitations of its design. For this work the advice and assistance of qualified professionals will be required. In particular, an architect with conservation expertise, preferably one with a particular knowledge of and interest in industrial buildings, should be called upon for advice. If a building is listed, Listed Building Consent will be required for any changes, so a dialogue with the planning authority is essential. More than one keen group of local people has ripped out the key architectural features of the building they were seeking to conserve because they didn't understand its architecture or structure, didn't take professional advice or appreciate that changes to listed buildings require specific listed building planning consent – a classic case of throwing out the baby with the bathwater!

The conservation study will define the limits of change and the means by which the character and architecture of the building's shape can contribute towards the changes that are necessary to make it suitable for new uses. In any event a number of potential key funders, such as the Heritage Lottery Fund and English Heritage (and their equivalents in the other United Kingdom countries) will require a Conservation Plan.[2] This sets out the proposals for refurbishing the building, including any structural changes, together with proposals for its upkeep and maintenance. The conservation study is essential background for this work.

Building considerations

In order for a group to understand a building, it can be helpful if they spend time together examining its characteristics. An examination

can begin to secure collective agreement about any key features that must be preserved or enhanced, including stonework, brickwork, decorative features and fenestration. An understanding of the external appearance of the building helps shape thinking about what changes might be possible or constrained internally. For example blocking up windows may make perfect sense for the uses on the inside but can destroy the external appearance of a building.

An examination of access can be quite revealing. The Victorians didn't always pay much attention to the rights of their workforce and there were no such things as health and safety requirements as we now know them. Accordingly, historic buildings often have poor access which will not meet contemporary requirements. New access provision may be needed which would require structural alterations to floors or the construction of external lift shafts. Decisions on these matters will affect later decisions on the usage of the remainder of the building.

The internal size of rooms and apartments fundamentally shapes thinking about what can be done within the building. Furthermore, decisions on internal alterations must be informed by an expert analysis of load-bearing capacity of the structure. Demolition of internal walls requires careful consideration. Ceiling height can also be important. Low ceiling heights, as found in building types such as maltings, may mean that an internal floor level has to be removed to give sufficient headroom to meet the building regulations, whereas high ceilings in many cotton and woollen mills are sufficient to enable artificial floors or ceilings to be inserted to conceal new servicing ducts and cabling.

Allowance should also be made for the extent to which usable space accommodation will be reduced by the inclusion of new services, particularly air-conditioning, which require a considerable amount of space. Many mill buildings have very large windows, which were necessary to provide light for textile manufacture, but these can present real problems of daytime solar gain which can limit the range of new uses. The size of windows also needs to be taken into account when calculations are made about reglazing, installation of tinted glass and central heating

4.5
Salts Diner at Salts Mill;
the former cotton mill
has well proportioned
ceiling heights and large
windows which add to
the attraction of this
highly successful
restaurant.

(Photo:
Christopher Cormack)

requirements. In addition, windows may sometimes be inadequate for modern standards of daylighting towards the centre of the building and this space may have to be used for storage or short-term activities such as meeting rooms or kitchens. This will affect the amount of lettable workspace.

A detailed analysis of all these considerations by the group as a whole helps create an awareness of the constraints and opportunities offered by the structure of the building, and moves it towards a consensus about what can be achieved. People stop thinking about how to cram as many uses as possible into the building and start to think about how they can work with the 'grain' of its structure and architecture. In short, they begin to understand and perhaps even to like the building.

In evaluating the potential of the building, groups may find it helpful to agree a checklist of basic alterations which they wish to consider. These might include: new electricity and water supplies; a new central heating system; an air-conditioning system; new sanitation arrangements; new access and egress arrangements; the location of any major insertions such as lift shafts, either internally or externally; and the construction of any new extensions. Not all groups will wish or need to undertake all of this work but options should be considered at this stage.

Recognizing that these buildings represent an inherited investment in time, material and skill, some steering groups are considering concepts such as environmental sustainability and local Agenda 21.[3] This is still relatively uncharted territory for heritage industrial buildings, but an explicit commitment to these concepts can have a positive environmental impact and, in the long-term, help groups to reduce running costs. If substantial work is required to a building then the opportunity exists to build-in environmentally friendly concepts with respect to heating, use of materials, maintenance, lighting and insulation.

4.6
At India Mill, Darwen,
Lancashire, lifts have
been installed and a
partition system is
available to divide large
floors of this former
cotton spinning mill into
bespoke office spaces (*see*
Plate 24).

(Photo: John M. Fryer)

All of these factors need to be talked through and the local authority planning and building regulation officers, and the fire officer will always be willing to give an initial opinion. Since the approval of these officers will be required for any final proposals, it is a good idea to involve them from the beginning.

Developing a vision

Most people will have become involved with the project either because they appreciate the building and want to see it saved, or recognize its potential to accommodate new economic, social and cultural uses for the local community. Many will have a mixture of both considerations. Having examined in detail the characteristics of the building, the steering group will have acquired a better understanding of what can be achieved and, hopefully, recognize that, whatever new uses are proposed, the building must retain its 'architectural wholeness.'

Voluntary organizations invariably will attract a wide range of people each with differing aspirations and their own 'lists' of proposed new uses, many of which might not be compatible. It is a good idea for groups to visit completed projects which include some of the uses they have in mind, to find out what went well and what didn't work or presented unforeseen difficulties. It is important to talk to people who have been through this process before, as this can save time and frustration, and open up new possibilities. These can include private sector entrepreneurs and developers, or community groups. Fortunately, most people with successful projects are usually only too happy to talk about their successes, so steering groups can get new ideas, see good and bad designs elsewhere, and raise their own aspirations. They will also come to recognize the need to achieve a 'balance' in their buildings – that is the balance and harmony between the uses they want to see and a synergy with the building itself.

One of the first priorities should be to seek to identify a 'vision' or 'theme' for the building. This will determine the broad 'function' of the building, and make it easier to market or promote it. Although groups may lose some of their support at this stage, experience suggests that saying 'no' to non-compatible uses is essential. The non-compatible uses usually drive out the better ones, and uses that might appear to bring in secure money can often undermine the long-term credibility of the project. In general the most popular uses include:

▌ Housing

▌ Offices

▌ Workshops

▌ Manufacturing space

▌ Storage space

▌ Art galleries

▌ Restaurants

▌ Bars

▌ Performance space

▌ Shopping facilities

▌ Community facilities

▌ Leisure facilities.

A 'twenty-four hour' building is probably not desirable but more and more projects are finding that they can do better than assemble a group of activities which are active only during the working day. Activities that attract people in the evenings and weekends, even if they require part of the building to be closed off, create an occupied and busy building which is both an attraction to the local community and can often offer greater security to tenants. This is also in many cases the only way to reach economic viability.

Most projects require a mixture of uses, some of which will make money and others that will not. However it can often be a mistake to allow one key tenant who is absolutely required as a reliable source of income to have first choice of space – usually the most accessible prime space – leaving the steering group with the less attractive or inaccessible parts of the building somewhere else. It is important to bear in mind that public access space needs to be near the main entrance, not in the roof space, and that is usually where the key tenant would like to be. The steering group will therefore need to have an overall 'plan' for uses before any space is actually let.

Members of the steering group will have their own ideas and proposals for the building but the views of local people are crucial. There is a need to consult on the options with the local community and, accordingly, groups are increasingly undertaking detailed surveys with local people about what they feel is required. This can very often duplicate the thinking of the group, but more often than not will add fresh ideas and perspectives. It is essential that local people see the refurbished building as being relevant to their needs and promoting local interests. Nothing can be worse than a building, refurbished at considerable public expense, which local people feel is a waste of money and is not meeting their needs. Regeneration Through Heritage has always placed great emphasis on 'planning for real' events at which as many local people as possible with an interest in the project are invited to spend a day or two looking at the building, its environment and considering local needs and opportunities.

4.7
Public participation at the Wakefield Planning Day.

Some groups have found it is helpful to have an 'open day' when local people can see the inside of the building, which may well have been shut up for many years, and perhaps an exhibition of the proposed new uses. (This of course will be subject to necessary public liability insurance etc.). The open day will afford an opportunity for people to talk to members of the steering group and any advisers, and input their own ideas. If the public don't like what the

steering group is proposing then it is wise to return to first principles and re-examine objectives. These events generate a range of ideas and give a very good indication of local hopes, aspirations and fears about the building, which can then be taken away and evaluated by the steering group at their own planning day.

Experience shows that there should be a clear emphasis on quality. A quality product is easier to sell, not just to potential funders, but to local users and the people or groups needed as tenants. In addition, by agreeing a 'vision' or 'theme' it is possible to add value through the propinquity of comparable activities or businesses; that is the additional value achieved by kindred activities locating together when the total is greater than the sum of the parts. There is a great deal of evidence to show how people or small companies working in the same fields and located together can work together to generate employment and contracts for each other, and provide a mutually supportive ethos and atmosphere which in turn generates more growth.

In a world where, increasingly, the only new business in some communities is likely to be that developed locally, there is a very high dependence on people generating businesses themselves. Sympathetic low-cost or managed workspace is an effective way of getting new businesses started. Very often there will be people working on their own, often in inappropriate accommodation, who are ready to move into a structured business environment. Of course there will be a failure rate but there will also be successes. Groups need to think about how they can help 'grow their own' new businesses in their building. They also need to realize that new businesses, especially in the 'cultural industries' sectors, or the IT and knowledge sectors, are as 'real' and income-generating as traditional employment. Indeed, cultural activities can bring local people and visitors into the site who would otherwise have no reason to come, and this in turn helps the project become known, gain credibility and so helps create more jobs.

Before any final decisions are taken there should be an opportunity for market testing of ideas in the local economy. Proposals will invariably include some uses that exist elsewhere in the local community – workshops, offices, industrial space – and it is important to seek expert advice on what local market conditions can stand before planning further provision. It is necessary to determine realistic potential rent levels and the extent to which provision of new space can meet a need in an existing local market. This is also very helpful in determining realistic expectations about what local market conditions can pay. A business plan can be fatally undermined by the inclusion of unrealistically high rental income levels.[4]

Some groups have found it feasible to 'head hunt' tenants by circulating good quality publicity and making direct approaches before construction work has actually commenced on the building. Apart from other considerations this enables the steering group to get a realistic feel for what is achievable and not get caught up with aspirations that the market cannot stand. If they are able to demonstrate that they can secure anchor tenants then it is more likely they will feel able to take a risk with some other more marginal commercial users.

New young business needs a break, but they can in turn grow and become reliable tenants. It therefore makes sense to adapt part of the building for these sorts of uses. It is also not necessary to fill the entire building before the project begins. Circumstances change very quickly and once work begins on the building local interest will increase. However it would be unwise to proceed unless the steering group can be fairly sure that it can fill at least 70 per cent of the building at the outset – and the rest will fill up as the project becomes established. Market research will also inform decisions about the level of quality the steering group should seek to achieve in its conversion work. There is no point developing workspace which the local market does not require to be fitted out to the best quality. Basic provision may be all local businesses and entrepreneurs want. So there is something to be said for fitting out to a basic level and allowing tenants to complete the work. The same may also be true for housing provision as there is a market among people in some parts of the country who want only a basic shell and the freedom to fit out the unit as time and their resources permit. This more basic level of construction will also reduce the steering group's capital costs for conversion.

Steering groups should also talk to the owners of all neighbouring properties. Other landowners and property owners will have a view about the building and usually it is not negative. If a building has been empty for a long-time and proposals are in hand to regenerate it then adjoining landowners will recognize that this can not only help, but enhance the value of their own property. In addition, it is also helpful to seek advice from specialist organizations such as English Heritage, CADW in Wales, Historic Scotland, the Georgian Society, the Victorian Society, the local authority conservation officer, or any local or county-wide organizations concerned with conservation and the environment. These organizations and individuals are usually very glad to help and often can be very encouraging.

In the light of these discussions and consultations, the steering group will then be in a position to shortlist potential new uses and 'pencil in' appropriate locations within the building. By this stage the steering group will have a good idea of the kind of changes they wish to make to the building and the uses they would like to see in it. However, the initial vision and concept will need to be supported by a professionally prepared feasibility study.[5]

Appointing consultants for the feasibility study

Surprisingly, there are few private sector consultants with the full range of architectural, conservation, technical, structural and business planning skills to undertake all the necessary work. Accordingly, groups are likely to receive tenders from a 'lead' consultant who will be accompanied by separate professional consultants retained to do particular work. For example a consultant may want to prepare the business plan and funding applications but to sub-contract the architectural design work to a separate company. This is normal practice. It is therefore important that the brief for the feasibility study is carefully written and understood by the steering group as a whole, as it is likely that different elements will be undertaken by people from different consultancies and each element of the work to be undertaken will need to be carefully specified.

There is no national list of professionals who are qualified to undertake this work and therefore discreet investigation on the part of the steering group will be necessary. If the group has visited other completed projects and is impressed by the quality of design and other work then it is worth finding out the names of the consultants responsible for advising. Advice can also be taken from national organizations, the local authority's conservation officers, English Heritage, the Architectural Heritage Fund and the Regeneration Through Heritage website (www.bitc.org.uk/rth).

A brief for the work should be prepared which reflects the desired outcomes in the feasibility study. The secret is not to try and be too clever. The consultants should be clearly advised of the steering group's expectations with respect to alterations to the building, any views they may have on the quality of major alterations or extensions, the views of the local community, and a very focused statement on the uses that the steering group wishes to see located in the refurbished building. There are cases where groups have failed to sufficiently brief consultants who have then investigated a range of potential uses that the steering group does not want or are unsuitable for the building. This is a costly and time-consuming business. It is therefore essential that groups specify what they want to do in and with the building and it is then the consultant's job to advise if this can be achieved within the constraints of the building and the likely capital and revenue resources.

In preparing a brief, steering groups should look at those prepared by similar organizations for ideas on length, structure, presentation and key points on content. The brief can be sent to those invited to tender with a deadline for response. Groups should remember that it costs money to submit a tender, and only those who are suitable and have a realistic prospect of being appointed should be approached. If steering groups are unsure of the process they should ask their local authority, or a friendly building preservation trust, to provide an experienced or professional adviser. Shortlisting of tenders received should be against an agreed list of criteria and then no more than three or four tenderers invited to interview. The group may wish to delegate this task to a small sub-committee plus some external advisers.

Steering groups need to be sure that the people who are doing the presentation will be the people actually doing the work. It has been known for firms to send their senior staff to present the tender and then have their junior and less experienced staff do the work. The most senior person undertaking the work should be in attendance. Once an appointment has been made it is worth having some further professional advice before everything is signed, and it is always a good idea to look at other people's contracts. The steering group also needs to set in place a formal procedure for consultation with the consultants while they do the work in order to make sure they are working to the steering group's ideas and not their own.

Funding for this work will be required, so approaches should be made to as many different sources as possible, even if only for small amounts. The more people who are financially supporting the project, the better the chances of success and the easier it will be to demonstrate to the major funders that the project has local support. Accordingly, local authorities, parish councils, local businesses, endowment trusts and charities as well as larger organizations such as the Regional Development Agencies and the Training Enterprise Councils should be approached for contributions. The Architectural Heritage Fund can make grants for this work if the applicant is a Building Preservation Trust. English Heritage may offer some support and it may be possible to acquire funding from the landfill tax credit scheme provided the organization registers with ENTRUST – the body which administers this scheme – and can identify a sympathetic landfill operator who will support the project.[6]

The feasibility study

The feasibility study should address the following points:

▎ Appraise the building

This should cross reference to the conservation study undertaken earlier, and set out the objectives of the steering group with respect to those elements of the building they wish to conserve and enhance and those which may need to be changed, or where new building extensions are contemplated.

I Examine the opportunities

This will involve setting out the needs and requirements of the steering group, the local community and economy, and the extent to which the building can provide a framework for these new uses. This will cross reference to the consultation work on local opinion and any market research that has been done on the needs of local businesses.

I Evaluate the development options

This will examine the range of development options proposed by the steering group, take account of any feedback or proposals from the community, set out the extent to which the building can accommodate these options and the case for each, including the option of doing nothing.

I Test preferred option

This will set out the case for the preferred use or package of uses the steering group wishes to see, or any alterations to the package of uses which the consultants would recommend in light of their appraisal of the building and the achievability of the options considered. It is possible that the consultants will have developed some other proposals or configurations which have not previously occurred to the steering group but will have been discussed with the steering group during the course of work if the supervision mechanism is working properly.

I Assess financial requirements

This is the part of the process which most frequently goes wrong and where hope often triumphs over experience. It is essential that the preferred option is realistically costed and if necessary cross-referenced back to some of the earlier options which have been considered but discarded in case some

rethinking is required. This part of the process must involve a realistic assessment of the capital works required to refurbish the building and to construct any new extensions or alterations to the building.

I Determine the final proposal

This will then be the consultant's recommended final package of uses together with the financial implications which will set out the parameters within which a business plan must now be developed.

I Develop programme of implementation

This will be the consultant's best estimate of how the project can be undertaken, setting out a construction programme and projected spend. It is important that appropriate provision is made for capital grant draw down and likely cash flow considerations. Groups must allow for paying contractors for work completed before they receive grants from their funders.

The feasibility study will need to set out, either as part of the study or in a separate volume, the consultant's recommendations with respect to the physical alterations of the building and the design considerations which will define any new construction. Since all buildings are different there can be no rules for new internal design work or for new extensions. Buildings need to change and grow but getting the design element correct is important. The consultants should therefore seek to provide the steering group with a clear set of parameters within which subsequent detailed design work can be commissioned. Broadly, they should identify the features in the building that must be respected and protected at all costs. They should also define the context within which the building is located and set out some guidelines as to how the refurbished building should relate to its environment. If the building is in a particularly poor state there may well be a tendency to 'over restore', to create almost a pastiche of what was there before. Over-restoration can be enormously damaging to buildings and the most sensitive of architectural advice is essential. In addition, the consultants should generate guidelines with respect to the quality of design of any new additions. Modernity and new materials are both appropriate and possible but must work with the grain of the building. Bright new materials, including glass and steel, can set off and enhance a stone or brick building and the feasibility study should put forward recommendations on the quality of work possible, together with indicative drawings.

Funding for capital works

At the early stages in many projects there is a central preoccupation with the amount of public subsidy that will be required. Through time this can change to an understanding that steering groups are creating an organic, adaptive place for activities which can be funded in many different ways.[7] Money can then cease to be the central driver of the initiative when people realize that quite small sums can be used to achieve a great deal. Similarly it is not essential to obtain outright ownership. A multiplicity of tenures – leasing, tenancies, part ownership, and trusts – is possible to reflect the various interests. Indeed a single ownership can be as much a problem as a solution.

Many funding agencies will only make capital grants or loans of any size to organizations that are legally established as trusts or registered charities. However, a number of enthusiastic, ad hoc groups who have come together to consider the regeneration of a heritage industrial building have become bogged down in the mechanics of how they should organize themselves – should they become a building preservation trust, a charity, a company limited by guarantee, or a development trust? While these are important issues, which need to be resolved before the steering group can actually take charge of any significant money and engage in legal contracts, there is no need to take immediate decisions about this. A better way forward in the early stages can be to establish a semi-formal organization with proper membership objectives, officers and arrangements for meetings. This will be sufficient to enable

projects to get off the ground, engage in formal negotiations and prevent them being dominated or hi-jacked by local factions. A strong independent chair and secretary are absolutely invaluable. Applications for funding can be submitted by this sort of group as long as they appreciate that a formal structure must be in place by the time any grant becomes payable.

Even at the early stages of the project, a semi-formal organization will be required to handle money, probably up to and including the stage of commissioning the feasibility study. If the organization has no formal status at this time, it is worth considering approaching a friendly existing neighbouring trust, or the local authority if they are participants, to see if they would be willing to handle this money on behalf of the group. Donors are also much happier making money available to a formally established organization with a proven track record in accounting for expenditure.

A sub-group of the steering group should be charged with investigating the most appropriate options to put the organization on a long-term formal basis. The Architectural Heritage Fund[8] and the Development Trusts Association have model constitutions which are acceptable to the Charity Commissioners and Inland Revenue. These are usually adequate for the purposes of most local community-based organizations and a good initial first step is to look at these models and talk to the two organizations. If the steering group wishes to develop a custom-made constitution for its own objectives, this can be expensive and will require specialist legal advice. It therefore makes more sense if possible to adapt a constitution which has already been recognized by the Charity Commissioners. Arrangements in Scotland and Northern Ireland are slightly different from those in England and Wales but the Architectural Heritage Fund has produced separate guidance notes for each to assist organizations to make the necessary adaptations.

Steering groups are finding increasingly that they need more than one formal mechanism to implement their project. Ideally a 'not-for-profit' umbrella trust to be responsible for the conversion and maintenance of the building can be established with the small number of trustees who have the appropriate experience and skills. It is not necessary for all members of the steering group to be trustees but, as this role entails legal and financial responsibilities, a core group should be identified which is willing to serve for a long-term period.

When the trustees are in place, tenancies can then be granted to the users of the buildings. These can be commercial tenancies to private sector companies or to activities approved of by the steering group (and therefore the trustees). These might include separate trading activities established as legally separate commercial arms of the project whose profits will then be recycled back to the trustees and hence used to subsidize non-moneymaking activities elsewhere in the building. It is usually the non-commercial activities that make projects attractive to people living in the area. It is also worth bearing in mind that the trustees can have standard leases for commercial tenants that govern the use of the building and, for example, require them to use services such as catering and office support, provided by the trust for the building as a whole.

Proposals for funders

When the consultants have completed their work the steering group should set aside sufficient time to consider the draft report, give feedback, question the consultants on the logic, reasoning and nature of their proposals and give instructions regarding any amendments they require.

Once the final consultant's report has been accepted, a separate document can be prepared for submission to potential funders.[9] Funders have very real requirements about the information they need from community-based projects without which they will not proceed, but by this stage most of the information will be available. Broadly, the documentation should include the following:

I description of the building

I condition and characteristics

I locational factors and setting

I conservation plan

I proposed uses

I market study

I financial plan

I architect's drawings

I specifications.

The realization of the project

It may take time to acquire the necessary funding. For example, the Heritage Lottery Fund and other major funding bodies can take six months or more to consider any application. However, once the funding mechanisms are in place, the real work on the building can begin and the project will gradually start to take shape.

In considering all the advice that has been laid out in this chapter, perhaps the most important asset that any group can possess is patience. It takes time for people coming together for the first time in 'partnerships' or 'steering groups' to recognize that all involved in these projects – residents, businesses, local authorities, owners, pressure groups – have different interests and objectives. Each will have different 'ownerships' and perspectives on the building and it takes time to unravel these in order to create a shared agenda. The process of putting together a set of proposals places everyone on the same 'learning curve.' If handled sensitively this process can unlock potential in individuals, steering groups and even communities and since nothing succeeds like success, people of all kinds are encouraged to get behind the project and help it to fruition.

Regeneration Through Heritage has shown that an external agency, with no direct interest in the project, can be the essential element which brings together the various strands of opinion, brokers the compromises, raises aspirations, helps maintain morale, and sets the pace. However, essentially it is the process of understanding the project which binds the group together and creates the sense of ownership and empowerment which are the factors needed to ensure success.

Regeneration Through Heritage pilot projects

To show what can be achieved through applying the above approaches, two of RTHs pilot projects now follow as case studies. They demonstrate that, for projects to be successful, the needs of both the community and the building must be fully understood and strong partnerships must be forged. Above all, a great deal of patience is required by all involved. Both of the projects described have been slow to evolve. However, the time and care taken to develop a strategy will help to ensure success for the projects and breathe new life into communities that have been long neglected.

Navigation Warehouse, Wakefield[www]

The Grade II* listed Navigation Warehouse (*see Plate 6*), built in 1790, which fronts the River Calder at its junction with the Calder Hebble Navigation canal in the city's industrial core, is being used as a catalyst for the regeneration of the entire waterfront area. The Trustees of Barbara Hepworth, the Wakefield-born sculptor, propose to gift many of her works and workshop tools to a new trust, which is seeking to refurbish the warehouse as the centrepiece of a new Hepworth Gallery. The City Council is also to donate its own collection, which includes works by Hepworth and Henry Moore, who was born in nearby Castleford. This will form a new gallery of national significance.

4.8
Navigation Warehouse overlooking the River Calder at Wakefield.

(Photo: Wakefield Waterfront Partnership)

4.9
Victorian mills
in the waterfront
conservation area.

*(Photo: Wakefield
Waterfront Partnership)*

The Regeneration Through Heritage-inspired Waterfront Partnership, which has brought together the key players, has agreed a strategy to use the gallery as the engine to regenerate the wider area and create a new Wakefield Waterfront Quarter. English Heritage has listed the adjoining Victorian mills, and the City Council has established the Waterfront as a conservation area.

A strategy is now in place for new canal-based recreation facilities, a quality hotel, new retail, office, craft, and entertainment facilities, as well as new studios for Wakefield's existing vibrant artistic community. By finding an appropriate re-use for a redundant heritage industrial building, putting together a partnership and defining a strategy, the project has enabled Wakefield to save an old industrial area from continued gentle decline and to create a new quarter which is a heartbeat for the city.

Sowerby Bridge,^{www} West Yorkshire

The project at Sowerby Bridge has its roots in the community around the canal basin (*see Figure 4.1, page 73, and Plate 2*). Two largely vacant Grade II listed eighteenth-century warehouses sit in the centre of this unique remnant of the canal age. A local partnership was created to develop a regeneration strategy for the whole basin which, rather than displacing existing activities, seeks to build on them to create a hub of new activities reflecting its potential for canal-based recreation, architectural heritage, and intrinsic attractiveness as a location for businesses.

Sensitive proposals were developed for the refurbishment of the two buildings to implement these objectives. The necessary business plan has been prepared to support applications to the funding bodies and the

4.10
The Salt Warehouse
at Sowerby Bridge.

(Photo: Michael Stratton)

partnership has identified a number of potential tenants from the high-tech and cultural industry sectors who are looking for quality production and office space. Already the market is expressing interest in the development potential of all the other under-used or vacant canal buildings that surround the basin. The catalytic effect of the warehouses to be refurbished is already evident with the construction of a new access road, new street lighting and the improvement of adjoining heritage buildings.

Notes and references

1   For further information and contact details see the Regeneration Through Heritage website www.bitc.org.uk/rth

2   See: Heritage Lottery Fund (1998) *Conservation Plans for Historic Places*, London.

3   Agenda 21 stems from the 1992 'Earth Summit' in Rio which drew up a framework for future action on sustainable development across the globe. Since Rio, UK local authorities have helped lead the way internationally in promoting Local Agenda 21, a comprehensive action plan at local level for the 21st century. Further information: www.environment.detr.gov.uk

4   For advice on preparing a business plan see 'Preparing your business plan for a capital project' published by the Heritage Lottery Fund.

5   Architectural Heritage Fund (1998) *Feasibility Studies: A Guide for Buildings Preservation Trusts*, London.

6   The Landfill Tax Credit Scheme channels portions of funds from landfill tax towards bodies with environmental objectives including reclamation of contaminated land, provision of public parks and amenities, restoration of buildings, etc. ENTRUST is the regulatory body that decides which schemes qualify to receive money. Further information: www.environment.detr.gov.uk

7   Architectural Heritage Fund (1998) *Funds for Historic Buildings in England and Wales*, London – a comprehensive directory of sources of funding; it includes invaluable references to other documents that will help with funding applications. Available from The Architectural Heritage Fund, Clareville House, 26–27 Oxendon Street, London SW1Y 4EL. E-mail: ahf@ahfund.org.uk www.ahfund.org.uk

8   Ibid.

9   Heritage Lottery Fund (1997) *Application Pack*, London – a good example of the kind of information that all funding bodies will expect from applicants. Available from Heritage Lottery Fund, 7 Holbein Place, London SW1W 8NR. Tel: 0171 591 6041.

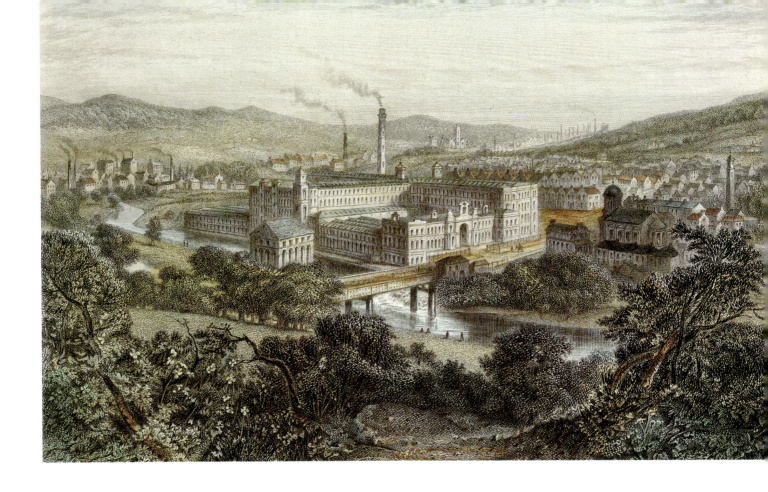

Lingotto Factory, Turin.

8 (top)
The 'Bubble – VIP meeting room' on the roof of the building which was formerly used as a test circuit for vehicles. Architect: Renzo Piano.

(Photo: Shunji Ishida)

9 (bottom)
Interior of the 'Bubble – VIP meeting room'. Architect: Renzo Piano.

(Photo: M. Denance)

10 *(top)*
Concept photograph of
how the Bankside Power
Station will look when it
opens as the Tate Gallery
of Modern Art.

(Photo: The Tate Gallery)

11 *(bottom)*
Stanley Mills, Perth.

(Photo: Louis Flood)

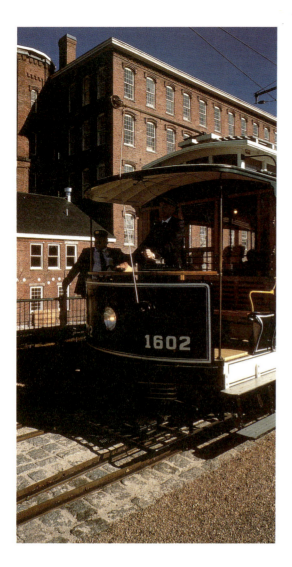

Lowell National Historical Park, USA.

12 *(top left)*
Replica nineteenth-century trolley buses shuttle visitors.

13 *(top right)*
Weaving Room exhibit at the Boott Cotton Mills Museum.

14 *(bottom)*
Market Mills.

(Photos: James Higgins courtesy of Lowell National Historical Park)

Chapter five

At the end of a century, let alone a millennium, there is an interest in new ideas, and an opportunity to rethink the way that we treat our heritage of old industrial buildings. Although ideas of adaptive re-use have been taken from the USA, applied in many cities in Britain and exported to the rest of Europe, there is still a huge rift between the guardians of our heritage and the entrepreneurs and professionals who bring old buildings back to use. Having spent over twenty years as a consultant, during which time URBED has been involved in many pioneering projects and research reports, it seems appropriate to look forward to the next twenty years, and to set out some lessons from our experience that may guide the next generation of re-use projects. In this chapter I have sought therefore to tackle three issues:

▌ How are the challenges changing in terms of supply and demand of buildings, and what are the the factors influencing re-use?

▌ What lessons for good practice can be drawn from a range of projects with which URBED is associated, including some failures as well as successes?

▌ What can be done to ensure that the resources needed for sustainable regeneration are available on the scale required?

Challenges for the twenty-first century

It is so common to focus on problems and buildings at risk that one easily forgets how much has been achieved in terms of saving and reusing industrial buildings over the last twenty years. People now generally see the value of old buildings that they once wanted demolished, and recognize the potential for new uses and for reusing upper as well as ground floors. Much of the original inspiration came from examples of adaptive re-use documented by Sherban Cantacuzino in his two books, *New uses for old buildings*[1] and *Re-architecture: old buildings/new uses*,[2] which illustrated examples in the USA such as Quincy Market in Boston. However, to show the way forward, it needed the work of

New uses for old industrial buildings

Nicholas Falk ▌

Founder Director, URBED ▌

pioneering developers like David Rock with *5 Dryden Street*, a 'working community' in Covent Garden. The potential of this project was demonstrated and publicized through magazines like the *The Architects' Journal* and its series on reusing buildings for small enterprise.[3] Research by URBED, *Reusing Redundant Buildings*,[4] provided lessons on good practice. This has been used by a host of developers and local authorities up and down the country.

Hence, there is no need to reinvent the wheel, though it sometimes may be necessary to encourage people to think creatively before reaching conclusions on what to do with a problem building. Perhaps the greatest evidence of a general change of heart is the publication of a popular guide to re-use by John Timpson, *Timpson's Adaptables: Travels through England's Hidden Heritage*, which suggests that we are all conservationists now.[5] However, just when it looks as though many of the most important groups of buildings are being saved, new challenges are arising, which call for different approaches.

The first challenge is that problems associated with inner city decay, once found only in large cities, now are experienced in many smaller towns. Not only do these areas lack the organizational capacity to take on complex development projects, they also lack access to the sources of grants that made marginal projects viable in the past. The second challenge is the growth in car dependence and the related trend towards population dispersal, which is leading to black holes in the hearts of town centres. As soon as vacancy rises above a certain level, it scares off potential new users and developers and makes regeneration more difficult. Many of the key buildings at risk now are in the secondary areas of town centres.

A third challenge is the aversion of institutional investors, including the banks, to over exposure to the property market; the continuing low level of inflation and growth in the stock market makes it hard for property to compete as a source of investment. As a consequence, projects will more and more have to be driven by 'social entrepreneurs', applying the key factors that lead to successful re-use. According to URBED's action research, which has included the promotion of a number of innovative schemes, the recipe for a successful project boils down to five elements:

▌ Shared vision that unites both the owner of the property and the local authority and other regulatory bodies, so that there is the minimum of time wasted in conflict.

▌ Impetus for collaboration, which may come from the promise of grants, or of the need to catch a wave of demand, or even sheer desperation at seeing a prominent building decay.

▌ Balance of uses, and also a balance between pilot projects, that can be implemented fairly quickly to build confidence, and flagship projects that help turn an area around.

▌ Driving force with the guts to take an innovative approach to development, to control and avoid all unnecessary costs, and to generate activity and interest.

▌ Financial package or process that generates the necessary yield to satisfy both private investors and also sources of grants.

These basic principles, from URBED's 'Vision to Results' model,[6] have been applied to a number of successful projects, some of which are summarized below. They illustrate the range of possible new uses and different approaches to the regeneration of industrial buildings.

Lessons from good practice

Initial experience in Rotherhithe

URBED's first experience was drawn from its involvement in a number of pioneering projects in the St Mary's conservation area at Rotherhithe, London.[7] The projects involved setting up a trust, the Brunel Exhibition Project, to renovate the derelict engine house used in building the Thames Tunnel, and turning it into an interpretation centre linked by landscaping to the underground station and the river. Some twenty-five years on, the engine house is still run by volunteers and is open to the public at weekends. The project shows that it is possible to tap voluntary enthusiasm where there is a specific cause, and where a partnership can be set up between the local authority (who still hold the lease) and a group of enthusiasts, who basically see the project as a 'labour of love'.

The second project, undertaken through a separate trust called the Industrial Buildings Preservation Trust, was to refurbish a group of early nineteenth-century warehouses as craft workshops, including a community workshop and a community arts centre. While the community spin-offs from both projects were high, the local authority who took over the buildings eventually sold them to a developer for luxury housing. What was once a community of creative people and potential visitor attraction is becoming an exclusive residential enclave in what remains a relatively poor area. This shows the difficulty of relying on a local authority to pursue complex objectives. It calls for formal agreements to specify long-term obligations, rather than depending on goodwill.

Kirkaldy's Testing and Experimenting Works

Subsequent experience was gained through a number of consultancy assignments, including refurbishing Kirkaldy's Testing and Experimenting Works as a museum with workspace above. This project enabled the Industrial Buildings Preservation Trust to build up a significant nest-egg, which it reinvested in other projects. It also left behind a well-provided specialist museum, as well as injecting a boost into what had been a very run-down part of Southwark, London. The project was a breakthrough in that a deal was set up with the building's original owner, The Crown Estate, which in return for the building received the existing use value, plus the promise of a share in the proceeds if the building were resold. National Westminster Bank was persuaded to provide a loan secured against the increasing value of the building, to enable the promise of a 'soft loan' from The Architectural Heritage Fund to be repaid. The project showed how small enterprises can often be the urban regeneration 'shock troops'. Small businesses and artists will move in before others are willing to occupy an area. Hence, they help to show the way towards long-term regeneration before the environment or accessibility is good enough to attract larger occupiers. This in turn confirms the importance of interim uses, with

licences rather than leases, although it does seem unfair that the pioneers, who are often creative individuals, tend to be kicked out of the property once the market improves.

Sheffield cultural industries quarter

The cultural industries quarter in Sheffield provides a good example of the benefits gained from clustering similar activities in the same area where they can achieve a critical mass. It also illustrates the value of adopting a balanced incremental development strategy, by reusing redundant buildings gradually as resources allow. The development of the quarter began in 1986 with the opening of the Red Tape rehearsal and recording studios followed by an audio-visual enterprise centre, both in former car showrooms, both of which responded to local demand, using public funding.

The second stage of the project was the conversion of the former Kenning's Garage into the Workstation cultural business centre, following a feasibility study by URBED which

5.1
Entrance to the Workstation, Sheffield, formerly Kenning's Garage.

(Photo: Allen Tod Architects)

showed how the scheme could be developed in phases. This was completed in 1997–8, some ten years after the original study, with the final phases of the Showroom cinema and café bar. This development, which is a scheme of regional significance, has created some 70,000 square feet of workspace. It has been developed and managed by a group of not-for-profit companies set up by the local Council. Tenants include the Independent Television Commission and the Northern Media School. Alongside are a range of conference and exhibition spaces as well as back-up services.

Stage three involved setting up the National Centre for Popular Music in 1998 and will lead on to the project securing an international profile through the Metropolis Live and Performing Arts Centre in the former Leadmill bus garage. Both of these projects are being developed through independent trusts. In addition, a number of other projects in the area, such as the Leadmill night club and students' residences in a former factory, have tapped private finance to diversify the area's attractions. The development has transformed an important gateway to the city from the railway station and, along with the adjoining science park and nearby Sheffield Hallam University, it has helped to diversify a city centre which had lost much of its traditional base.

An audit carried out in 1995 showed that the scheme had attracted £35 million of private capital in response to £6.1 million of public funding. 250,000 square feet of space had been developed, largely in refurbished buildings, which accommodate some 150 new or relocated cultural businesses including film, music, design and photography, employing over 1,000 people, with an annual turnover of £20 million. They provide also 1,500 media training places a year.

The next stage is expected to total £120 million and should establish the area as a visitor destination, with a forecast of 400,000 visitors for the National Centre for Popular Music in its first year, three times the current level.

To ensure the momentum is maintained, the City Council's Department of Planning and Economic Development, which master-minded the process, has produced an action plan for consultation. It has commissioned consultants to prepare a vision and development study, which will be implemented through a cultural industries development trust. The Cultural Business Network comprises ten charitable companies and their trading subsidiaries. The partnership is also made up of the City Council, the Chamber of Commerce, Sheffield Hallam University, the Science and Technology Park and the Yorkshire and Humberside Arts Board. The lesson to be learned is that a policy of promoting networks of activity can enable old cities to find new economic roles.

Merton Abbey Mills, South London

Most of the initiatives described so far have been in declining areas and depended heavily on local authority support. An alternative model is Merton Abbey Mills in South London, which provides high quality studio and office space over shops and showrooms, a number of which specialize in crafts. The area becomes animated by a weekend craft and specialist market with over 200 stalls. Other attractions have been developed, including a working water-wheel and a children's theatre. The development was undertaken in partnership with the land-owner, and community uses are managed by a trust, which is concerned with conserving and promoting the heritage of the River Wandle.

5.2
Merton Abbey Mills, brought back to life through partnership with the developer of an adjacent shopping centre.

5.3
Exeter Quayside.

(Photo: Michael Stratton)

One of the reasons for the success of Merton Abbey Mills is that the owners of the land (Sainsbury's) were persuaded to organize a partnership to develop and manage the site. A company was set up by URBED with Urban Space Management (who run Camden Lock and other market places). This company converted the buildings relatively economically, and then found occupants who would not have normally been accepted as tenants, for example three second-hand bookshops. Though the scheme is management intensive, it has been profitable for all concerned and has enabled a large number of new enterprises to get started.

For private sector initiatives to succeed, there not only needs to be an attractive environment to begin with, such as water or historic buildings, but there also has to be a successful entrepreneur with artistic interests to steer the project. Alternatively, some form of development trust may be used that packages funds from different sources. A scheme like this can be greatly helped if the landowner invests in the partnership that develops and runs the site.

Exeter Quayside

Exeter Quayside[www] development comprises an area stretching over some sixteen acres where the river meets the head of the sixteenth-century canal. There were groups of warehouses on either side of the river, together with what had become wasteland. The land was largely in local authority ownership and for years arguments had raged over what should be done to make the area attractive. Through a competition in 1986, URBED with Niall Phillips Architects were appointed to draw up a master plan and advise on how the area should be regenerated.

The plan divided the area into five distinctive quarters, each with a different role. The historic quayside was cleared of traffic by creating a new car park accessed by a pedestrian bridge. This in turn was financed by selling off sites for housing; the developers were chosen through a limited architectural competition. At the same time the Maritime Museum, which had spread throughout the area, was concentrated around the canal basin and revamped as the *World of Boats*. The empty warehouses were then turned into offices above shops and a pub. This development, along with a number of other projects, was carried out through the Exeter Quay and Canal Trust, a pioneering development trust set up by the city to take over historic buildings and to find new uses and financial packages.

The resulting scheme has put the area on the map for thousands of visitors as well as creating homes and employment opportunities. The quayside won a Europa Nostra award and the whole regeneration process has been undertaken at relative little cost to the local authority but with the Council very much in control. The development shows how quality and relatively high density housing can be used to create places that are a pleasure to walk around.

Chubb Media Centre

Wolverhampton is the proud possessor of a £2.4 million media centre that was formerly the old Chubb & Sons Lock and Safe Company factory and headquarters. Built in 1898, the factory had been empty since the mid 1970s. There was pressure to bring this listed building, in a prominent location in the city centre, back to life. A mix of funding has helped the transformation of the old building, of which £1 million was contributed by the Urban Programme. This was one of the largest Urban Programme grants ever awarded. The rest of the funding came from Wolverhampton City Council, the Midlands Industrial Association and the British Film Institute.

The inspiration for the project was to create a 'beacon of hope' at the gateway to the city through an unusual mixture of public space and themed workspace, by reusing a prominent old building that had become a white elephant. The City Council had already designated the area as the 'entertainment quarter' of Wolverhampton and was looking for a flagship scheme and a use for the building. It reacted enthusiastically to the Midlands Industrial Association's proposals.

The design exposed the original brickwork and timber floors and some of the timber ceiling joists. The Victorian panelled windows have been retained. In contrast, the interior is high-tech with an atrium linking the old and the new buildings, and providing space for two restaurants. Within one month of completion

and without intensive marketing, ten firms were close to taking space, including a video producer, publisher, public relations company, telecommunications firm, accountant and a graphic designer. Most of the firms relocated from unsuitable premises in other parts of the city. Wolverhampton's Light House Media Centre has been involved in the project since the early days and is the key anchor tenant, in the new part of the building. It provides a book and video shop, the regional media reference library, the Arts Council's video access library and two cinemas available for hire. The building has become a popular venue for meetings.

The Chubb building shows the value of mixing new with old, and the way in which development trusts can package funds and promote mixed uses through partnership with the local authority. It also demonstrates the importance of having a vision, and developing the edge of the town centre within a creative theme.

Stroud Valley, Gloucestershire

My final examples are taken from two very different areas. In the case of the Stroud Valley, our survey revealed that there were still over one hundred surviving woollen mills, most of which were in some kind of use, if not always ideal. However, the largest and most prominent buildings at the time, Dunkirk Mills in Nailsworth and Ebley Mill,ᵂᵂᵂ were vacant, and there was no mechanism for encouraging investment in the area's heritage. The strategy we produced formed the basis for designating a series of conservation areas, which then won significant financial support from English Heritage. The Stroud Valley project was set up to act as a champion for projects to improve the environment and, to lead the way, Stroud District Council decided to consolidate its offices in Ebley Mill, rather than moving into a new building, as originally proposed. The late eighteenth-century Dunkirk Mills was taken over by a developer for luxury housing, but the scheme was over-ambitious, and he and a successor went bankrupt, in part because too high a price had been paid for the site. Ten years later, the smaller mills are gradually being renovated and adapted to new uses, and conventional planning policies probably can cope on their own without further incentives, as the idea of adaptive re-use is more widely understood. Significant investment by English Heritage provided the Council with a welcome boost, and helped to turn the tide.

roots, and while the resulting renovation was done to very high standards, Elsecar Heritage has not yet attracted all the visitors it needs. The examples of Stroud Valley and Elsecar show the importance of matching the response to the economic situation, and the need for area-based approaches that can promote and sustain new roles, taking a long-term perspective.

URBED has played a key role in many other regeneration projects, in particular at the riverside in Sowerby Bridge,[www] which was its first major consultancy assignment to produce an area development strategy. At Bradford's Little Germany,[www] a large area of woollen textile warehouses, and in the Birmingham Jewellery Quarter,[www] it was asked to devise a strategy for reusing the empty spaces; both schemes won the BURA Regeneration Award.[8]

Resourcing regeneration through heritage

Elsecar Heritage Centre

A very different situation applies in an area such as Elsecar in Barnsley[www] where there is much less demand for new uses and therefore a greater need for public investment. An opportunity arose to promote new uses for a complex of buildings that had been colliery workshops, and which included the oldest Newcomen pumping engine still in situ. While the site's location close to the M1 motorway was appropriate as a visitor attraction aimed at rebuilding local pride, we put forward a strategy that envisaged a heritage park but with the bulk of the space given over to appropriate small enterprises that could generate activity and revenue when visitors were not around. The scheme attracted the local authority to take over the site and, with limited funding initially, efforts focused on creating an attractive entrance to the site. The project then attracted over £3 million in public investment through the City Challenge process, and some quite ambitious exhibits were installed. In the process, however, the project lost its community

While the above examples show that re-use can be made to work, they raise the complex issue of how best to 'prime the pump'. The pioneering projects to re-use redundant industrial buildings over the last twenty years have been a response to a fundamental restructuring of British industry, and to technological changes that have eroded the economic base of large areas in many parts of the country. Research undertaken as part of URBED's re-use of industrial buildings service, uncovered over 600 examples, involving every imaginable kind of building and use, suggesting that the physical problems are capable of resolution in most contexts.[9] However, local authorities generally have less capacity to devise and implement projects than they used to, and this is particularly true of the many smaller district councils who find it hard to focus much in the way of time and resources on any one area. With a change of government, but no increase in public expenditure, it becomes essential to adopt an approach to regeneration that balances the strengths of both the public and private sectors, and avoids their weaknesses. This 'third way' is at the heart of the idea of 'regeneration through heritage'. Just as those involved in regeneration have learned that it is not enough to throw money at a problem, or to rely on property development by itself to regenerate an area, we need to embody a more holistic and entrepreneurial approach to physical development within a framework that involves and engages the local community and promotes viable new roles for old industrial areas.

We have called this approach 'balanced incremental development', as it contrasts fundamentally with the 'big bang' approach to urban renewal that characterized much post-war development. The principles of going from 'Vision to Results' through a number of steps has been set out in a range of publications, including *Vital and Viable Town Centres: Meeting the Challenge*,[10] and *Town Centre Partnerships: Organisation and Resourcing*,[11] as well as in a new book, *Building the 21st Century Home*,[12] which brings to a climax work on what it takes to develop the sustainable urban neighbourhood. This focuses on how the process of managing urban change can be resourced and the underlying objectives satisfied, using ongoing projects to regenerate Newark Riverside[www] and a set of maltings in Mistley, Essex as case studies.

Responding to demand: Newark

The limited powers and resources of the public sector make it essential to devise strategies that respond to demand, and that package finance from all the available sources. This can be particularly difficult in smaller towns not experienced in promoting development projects. The example of Newark riverside could apply to many other places that are not sure what to do with a collection of redundant buildings. Newark is a town of around 20,000 inhabitants located on the main east coast railway line in south Nottinghamshire. The town for many years was dominated by brewing and malting, which left behind a collection of large buildings, many of which were attacked by fire, and became derelict.

One of the maltings[www] was owned by British Waterways, who commissioned a feasibility study from Allen Tod Architects, and URBED undertook a demand study. The building was

5.5
The concrete façade of the maltings, Newark, before construction of a new office block within the shell.

(Photo: Michael Stratton)

listed Grade II* because it was one of the first concrete buildings; but it had been ravaged by fire. However, this enabled a scheme to be devised for constructing a new office building within the shell of the old structure, thus filling a gap in the market, and helping to create new employment opportunities in an area of high unemployment. The demand study showed a lack of office available for letting, despite Newark's relative accessibility. Implementation was made possible through a package of grants, including significant help from English Partnerships and, even before the building work was finished, strong demand was expressed from telecommunication companies. Undoubtedly, the scheme benefited from the development alongside of new housing and a Waitrose foodstore.

The local authority commissioned a development strategy for the opposite side of the river, which included an old brewery, and a collection of smaller buildings, plus a scrap yard. The resulting proposals encouraged the government regional office to provide a package of Single Regeneration Budget and Capital Challenge funds to enable work to start on upgrading the riverside for a mix of uses. An action planning event was used to help develop a shared vision and involve representatives from the local businesses and other members of the community in the process. Our strategy is to locate new housing close to the town centre, to use the brewery to provide some missing arts and leisure facilities, and to encourage adjoining owners to develop their land nearest the station as a business park, linked by a new footbridge to the earlier developments on the other bank.

Planning holistically: Mistley

Mistley,[www] like Newark, also contains maltings but is in a very different location. The town is special in being a small industrial port on the River Stour in a part of Essex that has become a backwater, with a history as a failed spa. Although it is still a major centre for malting grain for brewing, the area needs to find new roles. Hence it exemplifies all the challenges that regeneration projects need to tackle in the twenty-first century and that a holistic development strategy should cover.

The physical challenges include not only a heritage of substantial but under-utilized industrial buildings that have lost their purpose, but also streets that are at times congested with heavy lorries and cars en route to the port of Harwich. Although there is a railway station opposite the site, public transport is rarely used, while the river carries occasional coasters but little else. The process of dispersal and urban sprawl is not being contained by conventional planning policies,

despite a host of conservation areas, Sites of Special Scientific Interest, and initiatives like the *Essex Design Guide* and Agenda 21. Yet the stock of empty buildings could be used to promote a regeneration initiative that will not only conserve buildings of national interest, but also restore the heart of the town and bring it back to life. It is therefore essential to find uses that are not only appropriate for the buildings but that will generate sufficient income to keep them properly maintained and managed for the benefit of future generations. It is important not to be too purist.

The economic challenges include not only levels of unemployment that are much higher than the national average, but also pockets of real poverty resulting from concentrations of public housing and housing allocation policies that result in people with the least capacity to cope being placed in peripheral areas. Good jobs are hard to find locally, and children are confused about what skills they need to survive in a changing world. Yet regeneration of the heritage could broaden the range of local jobs, and provide training opportunities and work experience. It could help to attract new forms of work that are knowledge-based. Many creative people prefer working in flexible spaces that offer a higher quality environment than a

5.6
Mistley, Essex.

(Photo: Michael Stratton)

conventional industrial estate or office block. The president of the vast computer firm Digital, which grew up in an old mill north of Boston, USA, commented that it simply made economic sense to use cheap space when your business is changing fast.

The social challenges include not only a divided community, with major differences between old established residents and newcomers, but also feelings of isolation and lack of self-esteem that cause people to object to new housing being built without compensating action to improve facilities for the existing community. Yet the heritage can provide a practical means for rebuilding a sense of pride. The results of local consultations (which involved as many as a third of the community) showed that far from being apathetic, local people wanted to be involved in a regeneration initiative and to ensure that it was not exclusive, but made some contribution to improving opportunities for everyone. As the English Heritage research report, *The Value of Conservation*[13] points out 'conservation is an important means by which people maintain their socio-cultural identity, and has the potential to improve perception of the area'.

Assessing the feasibility

One of the principal ways in which the re-use of a redundant building can be encouraged is through feasibility studies, therefore a few guidelines on what leads to an effective study are called for. The first point is that successful schemes are based on the conviction of the developer that re-use is viable and profitable. Unless he or she believes this, no amount of calculations will make any difference. That is why precedents are so important, and why URBED puts a great emphasis on its database of examples and slide collection of successful schemes. However, while some of the most successful schemes have gone ahead without much more than a back of the envelope calculation, progress can be made much more simple if the building's owner, the planning authority, and any grant giving sources are in agreement over the likely costs and values of undertaking whatever schemes are appropriate.

When URBED first became involved in regeneration, a great deal of effort was put into developing typologies of buildings. The results were published as a series in *The Architects' Journal*, and subsequently as a book.[14] While there is a great deal to be gained from analysing the structure, it is even more important to understand the context, and how it is changing. It is potential demand, not finance, that needs to drive a successful scheme. Consequently, today our feasibility studies focus on identifying what kinds of uses would be viable in the short, medium and longer terms, and on understanding where it will be easiest to make a start. Rather than starting with the fundamentals such as replacing the roof, it often makes more sense to start with seemingly superficial elements like creating a prominent new entrance, to help draw attention to the project and build confidence in the potential.

The most difficult problems occur where either the building is isolated, as in Mistley Maltings, or where there is such an excess of empty space, as in Little Germany,[www] Bradford. In both cases it is very hard to demonstrate that a market exists. Public agencies have an important role to play here, both in pump priming the first demonstration projects and in improving the overall environment. Little Germany Action also showed the value of a locally based team to animate the area. This is better done by some form of development trust or not-for-profit agency than leaving it to a developer, who inevitably is concerned about short-term profit rather than long-term value. In some cases, it may be possible to set a brief that safeguards the public interest. Too often new buildings go up and the historic buildings decay to the point where re-use is fruitless. As it only takes a couple of years of neglect for water to start penetrating and rot to set in, feasibility studies need to specify early action programmes to 'mothball' what is valuable, and to 'facelift' what will encourage new activity.

In undertaking a successful feasibility study, it is vital to pick the right team. In URBED's experience, adaptive re-use is a very specialized form of development; not all architects are able to adopt a developer's perspective, and focus on how to add value rather than just costs. It helps to use a firm of cost consultants or building economists that understands the entrepreneurial approach to refurbishment, and who is used to schemes that are undertaken incrementally as grants allow. Where parts of a building need to be demolished, or where there are structural issues, consulting the right engineers can also make a major difference. In contrast, it is noticeable how some of the most famous architects have been involved in a series of expensive studies that failed to produce successful schemes, perhaps because they were more interested in stamping their own personality on the buildings, or employing a large practice, than on solving the local problems efficiently. Hence, it often helps if a re-use project is managed by a firm of consultants who understand the management and marketing issues, and who can employ the right professional team. There needs to be an adequate budget for the initial feasibility study, which will be more than repaid if it unlocks the building's potential or attracts further grants. However, of equal importance is providing the right brief, and forming a steering group to represent the main interests. The brief should include a description of the context and main issues that have been identified for resolution. There also needs to be a sensible time frame (three to six months if consultation and a high quality report are important), and a limited number of competitors. Better proposals will be submitted when only four or five firms are invited to tender, and if the briefing has been done properly it should not be necessary to interview more than two or three firms, to save wasting everyone's time.

Restoring the balance

So, if regeneration through heritage is generally such a good thing, why does it still prove so difficult? The answers lie in the relationship between risk and reward, which governs investment. When the returns from refurbishing an old building are less than building anew, and when it is far harder to control the costs and to raise finance for the project, it is understandable that developers will focus on new-build, usually on greenfield sites. Unfortunately, the public finance system actually compounds the problems rather than redressing them, in four main ways:

I   Reliance is placed on negative planning policies, which add to the cost of refurbishment. It is hard to get owners or

developers to invest the necessary time in putting forward proposals in areas of decline.

I   The costs of refurbishment are higher than new-build, partly because VAT is not levied on new construction, while new roads, built at public expense, open up peripheral areas, while conservation projects have to cope with ageing infrastructure, and possibly parking charges too.

I   Property taxes in the form of the business rate are waived on empty buildings, but imposed the moment a building is ready for occupation.

I   The system of grants, which is used to close the gap, is cumbersome and unpredictable, and hence does not appeal to the kinds of developers who are most likely to make a success of regeneration projects. Furthermore the amounts available through bodies like English Heritage are trivial in relation to the costs of refurbishing large buildings, while the cost of preparing bids to the National Heritage Lottery is beyond the range of most projects, and professional skills are dissipated in chasing rainbows.

Britain has not yet learned from the experience of regeneration in the USA and a number of European countries like the Republic of Ireland, that tax incentives are a far more cost-effective mechanism than grants, particularly if they are confined to areas and projects from which regeneration benefits will flow. However, the need to reform the Business Rate, to harmonize our fiscal policies with other European countries, and to make development more sustainable could provide the opportunity to introduce an 'intelligent tax system' that rewards caring for old buildings rather than pillaging them.

The move towards regional development agencies, and the principles already set by the process of 'challenge funding' suggests that while local authorities will never have the resources to implement complex regeneration projects on their own, they can still play a vital role in championing regeneration projects, establishing local partnerships, and commissioning the advice and studies needed to satisfy investors. By identifying areas as well as buildings that are at risk, and then setting up task forces that bring together the main interests, they can overcome the limitations of conventional physical planning and bureaucracy.

As public policy tends to follow precedent, we need to create model demonstration projects, which apply good practice at the three stages of planning, development, and management to make the process more sustainable. Below are the principles that we are testing out in Mistley, which come out of URBED's earlier research and experience.

Sustainable planning means using publicly funded feasibility studies to reduce the risks, including:

▮ Involving the main stakeholders, which include the owners of the property, the local authority, and those concerned with conservation at a national level in finding solutions to difficult buildings in areas where demand is weak.

▮ Identifying options based on experience elsewhere and through brain-storming exercises to test out and refine ideas.

▮ Consulting communities about their preferences.

▮ Assessing the condition and capacity of the buildings as well as their context in order to come up with a strategy for bringing the space back into use incrementally as resources allow.

▮ Devising a vision that satisfies the main concerns of all the interests, and that can be used to attract funding.

▮ Securing agreement on planning briefs that cover uses, densities, access and car parking.

Sustainable development means using partnerships to combine resources from both the public and private sectors, including:

▮ Encouraging owners to see the potential in reusing historic buildings, by providing advice, and using the business rate as an incentive for occupation (as in Enterprise Zones, but focused on areas of existing buildings in locations that are highly accessible).

▮ Using Compulsory Purchase Orders where buildings have been empty for several years and are at risk of becoming derelict, with correspondingly higher costs for refurbishment.

▮ Setting up joint ventures with appropriate developers for specific uses, including working with small specialist builders to build housing for sale, and with housing associations to develop and manage for niche markets such as sheltered housing for the elderly or foyers for the young, both of which can make good use of historic buildings.

▮ Economizing on the building costs by deferring work until necessary, and by setting up training projects to undertake basic renovation work.

▮ Incorporating a mix of uses that generate some early returns, for example by selling off parts of the site, so that funds can be reinvested in the remainder.

▮ Transferring difficult elements that can only be viable through voluntary effort and grants to a development trust that brings together the public agencies and committed local people.

▮ Safeguarding the rights of those who put in 'sweat equity' through their involvement in the development trust, which might for example play a longer term training and educational role for which charitable status and grants can be secured, for example from the European Union.

▮ Establishing a project manager who can call on professional and other services as required, and who is committed to maximizing the value of the occupied space, and controlling the development costs.

▮ Avoiding materials or processes that are known to be environmentally harmful.

Sustainable management is a more elusive concept, but might include:

▮ Organizing occasional open days and participating in events where the renovated buildings act as a focus for community involvement and animation.

- Providing a range of space on flexible terms, for example including space on 'easy in easy out' licences, and enabling occupiers to take on shells which they improve and fit out to meet their own needs.

- Installing high levels of insulation and other measures to minimize the consumption of energy.

- Encouraging the use of public transport and car-pooling.

- Enabling spare space to be used for community and other appropriate non profit activities.

One of the hardest and most important tasks is coming up with the right uses for an empty building. It can be very hard for those who know the area best to literally 'see' alternative uses, particularly when the building starts to leak and suffer from broken windows. This is where the outside view can be most helpful, and consultants have an important role to play. However, too often in my experience, limited resources are wasted on fanciful schemes by architects who pay almost no account to the potential market or funding sources. Where planners get involved they find it easier to say what they do not want, than to identify new uses that will actually be viable. There is also the problem of 'fads' as new ideas become fashionable and yesterday's art or heritage centres become tomorrow's foyers or centres for cultural industries. As with most things, it should be 'horses for courses'.

In reflecting on how URBED has come up with uses that would work in such different circumstances, a number of points may be helpful:

1. It is the location rather than the building that will influence both what types of use are feasible and the level of demand, so it is essential to start by understanding the area in historical and geographic, as well as economic and political terms. Rather than just considering what the area lacks or needs, it is more helpful to think of different scenarios for how it might develop, drawing on experience from elsewhere.

2. As local precedents are often lacking, it is important to understand what kind of place one is dealing with; this means classifying the area. In our report, *Vital and Viable Town Centres*,[15] we distinguished between metropolitan cities, suburban centres, industrial towns, market towns, historic towns and resorts. This six-fold taxonomy can be quite useful in looking for parallels. However, it is equally important to recognize whether the location is prime, secondary or tertiary in terms of demand from other uses as this will tend to set the value of the property.

3. Having understood the area, it is helpful to consider how similar kinds of building have been used. There is basically little difference between a mill, a warehouse and a malting, but factors like size and position – for example, whether the building overlooks water – can make a huge difference to the potential market. The big questions are always 'could this place ever be like some other place?' and if so 'are the right conditions in place?' for example, sympathetic owner, sources of development finance, etc. Many schemes have been driven by the availability of finance but they are often the ones that end up unoccupied. A view over water should help to make a building more attractive to live in, but not if it is hard to reach.

It is important to review other projects. My own inspiration has tended to come from visits to other countries, as well as from pioneering projects that URBED has helped or known about. There are now a number of publications that include case studies as well as new sources like the Regeneration Through Heritage website, and URBED makes extensive use of a slide library built up over the years to illustrate the range of possible uses and types of building, as 'seeing is believing'. There are a range of good practice guides available, including a number commissioned by the Department of the Environment, but many are produced by small organizations, and can be hard to track down. Conferences too have been useful in sharing experience, and it is quite common for pioneering projects in any field to create their own network, and to produce some form of guide.

Visions come from inspiration and there is nothing like a brain-storming discussion to generate ideas that would have never come through research alone. This is why in all URBED projects an action planning event is included, using the 'round table conference' method in which diverse groups of people are given particular themes or topics and asked to report back on short and longer term possibilities, having first been briefed about other projects.

While the best can easily be the enemy of the good, URBED's experience is that, given the will, solutions can be found that achieve a balance of objectives. Furthermore, the process of developing sustainable projects, while apparently more expensive and time consuming, adds value and should help to attract the funding needed for implementation. Finally, though no-one can know the precise destination and outcome in advance, by starting with a route map or chart and dealing with problems as they arise, better solutions can be found than following conventional property development practice. As the dialogue goes: 'How do you eat an elephant? Answer: a bite at a time.'

Notes and references

1 Cantacuzino, S. (1975) *New Uses for Old Buildings*, Architectural Press, London.

2 Cantacuzino, S. (1989) *Re-architecture: Old Buildings/New Uses*, Thames and Hudson, London.

3 See: Eley, P. and Worthington, J. (1989) *Industrial Rehabilitation: The Use of Redundant Buildings for Small Enterprises*, Architectural Press, London.

4 URBED, (1987) *Reusing Redundant Buildings: Good Practice in Urban Regeneration*, HMSO, London. Research was funded by the Gatsby Charitable Foundation and subsequently the Department of the Environment.

5 Timpson, J. (1997) *Timpson's Adaptables: Travels Through England's Hidden Heritage*, Jarrold Publishing, Norwich.

6 Falk, N. (1987) 'From Vision to Results: Devising Strategies to Revive Run-Down Areas', in *The Planner*, June 1987.

7 These formed the 'action research' for a doctoral thesis on Planning and Development in London Docklands partly described in Falk, N. (1993) 'Turning the Tide: British experience in regenerating urban docklands', in Hoyle, B. (ed.) *European Port Cities in Transition*, Belhaven, London.

8 More details of these two schemes can be found in Falk, N. (1995) 'Regeneration and sustainable development', in *Urban Regeneration: Property Investment and Development*, Berry, J. et al (eds) E & F.N. Spon, London. Further information is in other chapters in this book.

9 See Appendix in URBED, (1987) *Reusing Redundant Buildings: Good Practice in Urban Regeneration*, HMSO, London.

10 URBED, (1994) *Vital and Viable Town Centres: Meeting the Challenge*, HMSO, London.

11 URBED, (1997) *Town Centre Partnerships: Organisation and Resourcing*, The Stationery Office, London.

12 Falk, N. and Rudlin, D. (in preparation) *Building the 21st Century Home*, Architectural Press, London.

13 English Heritage, (1997) *The Value of Conservation*, English Heritage, London.

14 Eley, P. and Worthington, J. (1989) *Industrial Rehabilitation: The Use of Redundant Buildings for Small Enterprises*, Architectural Press, London.

15 URBED, (1997) *Town Centre Partnerships: Organisation and Resourcing*, The Stationery Office, London.

My business is called the SPACE Organisation ... and I blush somewhat to confess that 'SPACE' is an acronym for the Society for the Promotion of Artistic and Creative Enterprise – which is, roughly speaking, what we try to do.

SPACE now runs eleven projects – including the Custard Factory in Birmingham – which, altogether, provide workspace, warmth and comfort for about 1,000 small start-up companies. Actually, I'm not sure it's right to call them companies, because quite a lot of them consist of just one or two people. In fact the total number of people at work under the SPACE umbrella is not much more than 2,000. But even so, I guess that's quite a lot of jobs for a small private organization to create, especially when you compare it with the sad statistics of the much heralded and highly spun £3.5 billion New Deal and Welfare to Work programmes!

In their different ways, all the SPACE projects are based upon the principle of creating coherent 'working communities' – and then helping to release and nurture the tremendous energy that always seem to flow from them in order to bring about urban revitalization. At the same time, most of the SPACE projects involve the recycling of old buildings.

So to begin with, this chapter runs through some general 'how to do it' principles. Then it recounts the story of the conception, gestation and birth of a few typical SPACE projects. But to repeat – the purpose of every one of them is to bring about regeneration through the creation of 'working communities' of one sort or another.

The role of

the entrepreneur:

seeing the opportunity

and ensuring success

– an edited transcript of a talk given by

Bennie Gray ▌

The SPACE Organisation ▌

The seven steps

Broadly speaking, there seem to be seven crucial steps to all the SPACE projects. However, before running through them, it is worth issuing a warning about the way in which the accumulation of uncontrolled professional fees can sink all but the largest of tight budget projects. Each one of the seven crucial steps is simple enough, but they all demand a degree of specialist knowledge. So beware of spending too much time in smoke-filled rooms taking advice from solicitors, planners, surveyors, architects, bankers, marketing people, accountants and tax experts, interior designers, politicians, graphic designers, energy consultants etc ... for each of the hundreds of hours spent they will be hitting you for something between £20 and £200 an hour. And not many of these specialists speak the same language. It is only a slight exaggeration to say that many of them know so much about so little that they end up knowing everything about nothing – which is a fat lot of use to you when you are trying hard to work within what is usually an almost impossibly tight budget and an equally tight programme.

In practice, to get things done well and economically, of course you need lean and mean access to the best advice. But you also need a really good generalist to co-ordinate this advice – a 'jack of all trades' who can talk to specialists with confidence and make decisions on the run. As things stand, there is no formal training for the would-be urban regeneration generalist. The obvious professional to take on that role is the architect and I believe that the sooner architects are trained to do so, the better it will be for the whole area of regeneration. Meanwhile, you must glean what you can, inadequate though it be, from the few people like me who are already active in the field.

But let us return to the seven basic steps necessary to mount a project. These are: the initial concept or Big Idea; finding the money; getting the permissions; doing the design; construction; marketing; and last, but not least, managing the project.

The Big Idea

The first step is the big idea – your vision of the project-to-be, half-closing your eyes and imagining and thinking through what it is that you're going to achieve. Usually the big idea comes first and then you find the place to do it. Occasionally it's the other way round: you find a neglected building, sometimes old, sometimes less old, but always potentially interesting and atmospheric, and you figure out 'how can I bring this place back to life and fill it with interesting people and activities?'

Finding the money

Finding the money is usually the most difficult step. To get to first base you need to define your goals, complete your designs and costings and establish some sort of business plan. Bankers tend to ask inconvenient questions like, 'What market research have you done?' Very often, with an innovative project, you are in uncharted waters. This means that you are asking people questions about a concept or commodity of which they may know nothing. Sometimes, you simply have to bluff your way through while you work on instinct.

Most of the time you have to borrow the money from financial institutions of one sort or another – sometimes supplemented by public funds or grants. The trouble is that most banks dislike mixed-use development almost as much as they dislike old buildings, short leases and start-up businesses – in fact all the necessary ingredients in the sort of urban revitalization that makes a difference. They can take an awful lot of persuading.

The public funding process, when it is needed, can be just as bad – endless and impenetrable bureaucratic rituals lasting for months on end, form-filling, artificial criteria and, worst of all, the seemingly inevitable need for the new breed of public funding consultants. They can charge up to £1,000 a day, and I believe that they often make public funding inaccessible to the local groups and other people who might make the best use of it. And of course linked to this are the millions of pounds which, in the last few years, have been wasted on absurd feasibility studies for doomed lottery projects. 'Oh to be a big name architect now the lottery's here...' Thankfully (but sadly for the big name architects) this particular fat fee-feeding frenzy has almost come to an end.

One of the most important things that the government could do to encourage urban regeneration is to lubricate the pathways to public funding. It would certainly result in much more efficient and effective targeting. And, by way of a spin-off, it would give private sector lenders more confidence in the funding of regeneration projects.

Getting the permissions

Once you have found the building and lined up the money, you have to get planning permission and all the other approvals for a project which does not always chime with the local plan for the area. All of this has to happen more or less simultaneously. It's tough, but not as tough as it used to be. Since the 1960s and '70s most planning authorities have emerged from the dark age doctrines of Corbusian zoning and all the rest of the Utopian post-war ideals. These days they do tend to recognize some of the virtues of dense and diverse mixed-use inner city development and of a flexible collaborative approach to regeneration. In fact, at SPACE we have enjoyed a remarkably energetic and creative relationship with planners, particularly in Birmingham. I like to think that received planning wisdom now takes into account the destructive absurdities of the planning strategies of the recent past.

Doing the design

Now, you have reached the stage of detailed design and the pattern of eventual management is very much in your mind – and so are the costings. Given the fact that regeneration projects frequently involve the reconstruction of existing buildings, you also have to strike a balance between the logistical advantages of settling every single design detail upfront and the alternative advantages of keeping things flexible and being able to exploit the possibilities that often emerge when you open up an old structure. You will certainly need a highly accomplished, experienced and VERSATILE architect to help you sustain this balancing act. Maybe you do it yourself; at any rate it needs to be someone who can think on their feet. You will also need an excellent and thoroughly thought-through and well documented relationship with an intelligent contractor who will not try to make a financial killing on every design variation. Again, this is a huge subject and one that I can hardly begin to cover here. One thing I can tell you though – on no account assume that all will be well if you merely take the conventional route and employ a squad of highly qualified specialist professionals and leave the whole thing to

them. You must delegate only with great shrewdness and sensitivity. And you must be able to hold your own with the 'Arthur Daleys' of the building trade. That is something they don't teach you in architecture school – but they should!

Construction

With most regeneration projects the cost of construction is critical. You will almost certainly be working in marginal areas with low rents. But construction costs will be not much less than they are in the West End of London, so cost engineering becomes a crucial factor. How can you make every penny look like a pound? It's not a good idea to rely entirely on your quantity surveyor. If you are the architect, and especially if you are the generalist, you must be highly cost-conscious – not so much 'hands-on' as 'fingers-on'. You must know today's price of '2 by 2' timber and plasterboard and all the other materials you specify. You must know how many doors a good 'chippy' should hang in a day. You must make the fullest use of recycled and second-hand materials. You must know if there is some cheap copper tubing available at the bankrupt plumbers' merchant on the other side of town.

Of course, very few good design architects deign to know such things. It's not dignified. But if you are to prosper in the gritty brown mud of the urban regeneration game you must cast your professional dignity to the winds, and do so without a second thought.

Marketing

So far, so good. You've refurbished your building. Now you have to fill it – and appropriate marketing is crucially important. How do you do it? In my experience, established estate agents are the last people to market projects like the Custard Factory (*see page 111*). There, as the reconstruction works of phase one drew to a close, we were on a roll to success. So we decided to eschew the agents and do the marketing ourselves. We wrote, designed and published an elaborate and fulsome manifesto, singing our own praises. It cost thousands but by the time it arrived from the printers we had let every square inch of the 80,000 square feet project simply by word of mouth. Somehow the spirit of the Custard Factory had broadcast itself in the right way. And I had the distinct feeling that people positively enjoyed by-passing the conventional routes to finding the spaces they wanted. Perhaps there are lessons to be learnt from that experience. Perhaps people who want to become part of a 'working community' tend not to look for it in estate agents' windows.

But marketing doesn't stop at the launch – with all of our projects to date it has gained momentum as the emphasis has moved from marketing the project itself, to marketing the people that work within it. At SPACE we are shameless advocates of what we do – we can never resist the chance of haranguing any audience that cares to listen about the power and the pleasures of working communally.

Management

Now you have a project on your hands. You've done your marketing, allocated the space, it's full of interesting people doing interesting things. And you have to run it – to plan the management. In an ideal world there will be continuity of responsibility – the development of the project will merge seamlessly into the process of managing it. In a very real sense, if you've done it in the right way, you will be midwife to the birth of a lusty working community. In the early months you will attempt to nurture and also to guide the anarchic infant. But as people get to know each other and as they develop all sorts of fertile relationships, the project – like any new born creature – will begin to establish a spirit, an identity and a direction of its own. Meanwhile, however, you must engender and maintain discipline and structure of a high degree – but you must do so without a smidgen of the appearance of bureaucracy. It is a tall order indeed.

Those are the seven characteristic steps leading to the creation of a working community in the inner city. You might think that all this seven crucial step business is rather formulaic and, in a way, I suppose, it is. But you must remember that flexibility within the formula will be the key to your success. After all, you will be dealing with and needing to please large numbers of creative and independent people who by definition dislike formulae and bureaucracy.

So, now let us move on to see how things work in the real world by looking at five of the SPACE projects. It's all anecdotal, but instructive to see what actually happens as you go through the process of identifying the projects, trying to make them happen and finally bringing them to maturity. If nothing else, you will get an insight into the fevered mind of one entrepreneur.

Alfies Antique Market

I suppose Alfies Antique Market is a particularly unlikely example of how the establishment of a working community can lead to urban revitalization – all the more so because this is a working community of antique dealers. But antique dealers are people too. And Alfies cost not a penny of public money. So I will tell the story anyway.

Alfies occupies an ex-department store – in fact a rather beguilingly tatty terrace of Victorian and 1930s buildings at the eastern end of Church Street in Marylebone, north-west London. In recent years, Church Street and the area around it has changed quite a lot. Until the early 1950s a fairly coherent traditional working class community lived there but then it all began to go downhill. The commercial and shopping focus of the area has always been Church Street itself, which is enlivened by a 150 year old Saturday street market and a large number of local shops that line both sides of the street.

For nearly a century Church Street's commercial flagship was Jordans, a rambling department store encompassing a sales area of more than 30,000 square feet, which had been run by the Jordan family for generations. People remember it having an evocative atmosphere of post-war 'make do and mend', with a strong emphasis on things like haberdashery and knicker elastic – which was

6.1
Alfies Antique Market,
Church Street, London.

6.2
Interior of Alfies
Antique Market.

hardly part of the throwaway swinging Sixties. Unsurprisingly, by the early 1970s Jordans went 'bust' and the terrace of old buildings it had come to occupy fell into disrepair. At the same time, and I don't really know why, the entire eastern end of Church Street also fell on hard times. Shops were boarded up and many of the buildings were vandalized. Certainly, the gathering social problems of the nearby Lisson Green, a giant 1960s housing estate, didn't help.

In 1976, with money borrowed from a high street bank, the SPACE Organisation took over the derelict Jordans' premises. The idea was a modest one – to turn the terrace of buildings into a no-nonsense unpretentious antique market with very low overheads and a no-nonsense unpretentious name – Alfies. It worked like a dream – and within a matter of weeks nearly one hundred antique dealers had been recruited to the project. To begin with we used the ground floor and opened only on market day Saturdays, but we were so successful that within a couple of years Alfies had grown to fill all four floors of the building and expanded trade to five days a week. Since then we have built two major extensions to accommodate the demand for space and quite a few of the antique dealers who started off with a stall in our market have moved into the once disused neighbouring shops. Now the eastern half of Church Street has become one of the best enclaves for antiques and collectibles in London. Moreover, since Alfies was launched, the whole of the immediate area has become revitalized in a very interesting, unyuppified and organic manner. Old buildings have been renovated, all sorts of small businesses have sprung up, there is now a healthily diverse mix of people living and working in the area – and many people think that Alfies Antique Market has made an important contribution to the process. Naturally, I like to think they are right.

Just to round off the story of Alfies, I must point out that among the 200 or so dealers there is a sprinkling of tenants from the neighbouring Lisson Green estate, some of whom have made the transition from being unemployed and 'on the dole' to becoming self-sufficient antique dealers – following a trade that they seem to enjoy.

All in all, Alfies represents a splendid, albeit rather unusual, example of the way in which the birth of a dynamic working community can make a real difference to a run-down inner city neighbourhood.

Danceworks

Danceworks occupies a rather awkwardly shaped but elegant listed nineteenth-century building in central London. In 1981 it lay empty and derelict and the owners had no ideas of what to do with it; they approached me, knowing that I had had some experience of dealing with 'difficult' buildings. I looked at it and liked it but, initially, I had no ideas for it either. The planners said that office use was out of the question, nor was it right for housing.

In the end my proposal for the building was influenced by my young daughter Rosie's passion for dance and movement. In the early 1980s the whole world seemed to be in the grip of John Travolta and *Saturday Night Fever*, Baryshnikov, *Fame*, the Bee Gees and all of that. So I thought – why not turn this building into a school of dance? I did some sums, looked at the likely costs of reconstruction and decided to go ahead. Over a period of about eight months we virtually gutted the building – it had to be threaded with steel to withstand the rhythmic impact of hundreds of dancers jumping up and down at the same time – and fitted it out.

Danceworks opened to a full house on April Fool's Day in 1982 and has been there, buzzing with energy, ever since – not that it's ever made much of a profit, I'm sorry to say. Nevertheless, from the beginning Danceworks has provided accommodation for more than thirty teachers of dance and movement, and subsequently another eighteen or so healers and teachers of natural therapies. A strong working community has built up. We give over 100 dance and movement classes a week, hold lots of professional auditions and rehearsals and provide complementary medicine for a large and growing number of people. In fact Danceworks has become something of an icon in the world of dance. The project is sustained by a flourishing working community of forty or fifty self-employed teachers, healers and choreographers – and enjoyed by upwards of 2,000 members.

6.3
Entrance to Danceworks, London.

6.4
Dancing class inside Danceworks.

In the first two or three years of running Danceworks I came to know a lot of people working in television and film, people who came to rehearse shows and hold auditions. In the 1980s Channel 4 was beginning to act more as a publisher than a producer. The company was encouraging commissioned work from outside, in contrast to the BBC and other major television companies who produce much of their own material. This led to a proliferation of small production companies as people working for the BBC or ITV decided to set up on their own. This phenomenon leads me to the next project I want to discuss – Canalot Production Studios.

Canalot

The mid-1980s saw hundreds of little production companies and facility houses hunting for somewhere to work. But, unhappily, it was also the time of the great property boom and there was very little affordable space to be had in London's Covent Garden or Soho or Camden Town – the places where such enterprises traditionally operate. As a result, these little companies were reduced to setting up in Potters Bar, Morden, Brixton and 'Metroland' – and all sorts of exotic places in the London suburbs! That was all very well, but film making is a linear process: objects and information move from one place to another and, despite the information superhighways, film and television people prefer to be in close proximity. Many of the new companies that were banished to the suburbs felt uncomfortable – they were too far flung.

It seemed clear to me from the people I was talking to that a major focus was needed for their activities – a large building with a good feeling, not too far from the West End, where a large number of small film and TV enterprises could work. In fact another working community. I began to look around for such a building, but it wasn't easy. In the end I found it purely by chance.

One misty spring morning in 1985 I was jogging along the Grand Union Canal towpath in North Kensington when I was confronted by

a very small and aggressive man with two even more aggressive Rottweilers. They went for me. I had two options: one was to jump into the canal, which was filthy; the other was to scramble over the towpath wall – which I managed to do, the dogs snapping at my heels. I found myself in a vast and derelict factory. A tramp approached me and with great courtesy demanded to know what I was doing. We fell into a rather 'Pinteresque' but very friendly conversation and he ended up gravely and with great dignity giving me a conducted tour of his 70,000 square feet home. He was probably the first of London's loft dwellers – ten years ahead of all the 'trendies' who now pay a fortune to live in old factories. That morning I knew that I had found the building I was looking for. It was to become Canalot Production Studios.

6.5
Canalot Production
Studios, London.

In those days North Kensington was a designated 'Taskforce Area', of which there were perhaps twenty up and down the country. These were the urban areas considered to be Britain's most deprived, both socially and economically. In 1985, the 15-acre Kensal Basin part of North Kensington, between the canal and the elevated motorway, certainly lived up to its reputation – it was like a moonscape. It was, and still is, dominated by vast 1960s social housing estates and there was, and still is, a great deal of violent crime, vandalism, drugs, unemployment and all the other unrelieved misery that disastrous post-war planning policies left in their wake.

Even so, it seemed to me that the Kensal Basin part of North Kensington held great potential for positive change. It had a number of virtues. First there was Erno Goldfinger's Trellick Tower – a wonderfully gaunt concrete block of council flats – one of the highest in the country. There was also a sprinkling of amiable run-down older buildings of which the red brick turn-of-the-century Canalot factory was probably the most interesting. Then there was the Grand Union Canal – water is always a good and soothing presence in inner city areas. In addition there was a run-down little park – and although its only use at that time seemed to be as a dogs' lavatory, it was not hard to visualize it as the pleasurable green space it has now become.

So – what to do with the Canalot project? The building was big enough, it was affordable, it was ten minutes from Marble Arch, it was on the Grand Union Canal and it sat opposite a park. Plus there was the extremely cosmopolitan local population. Although it was all too evident that some of the young people living around and about were heavily into petty crime, many were also highly talented, fascinated by film and television and full of energy. It was an irresistible mix and I decided to go for it.

At that time the building was owned by a publicly funded organization called GLEB – the Greater London Enterprise Board. They had acquired it two years previously to turn it into managed workspaces. But, serendipity of serendipities, they had just come to the conclusion that it couldn't be made to work. I, on the other hand, believed that it could and after a lot of sleepless nights, and to my bank manager's consternation and to accusations of madness all round, I managed to buy this huge empty derelict building.

Originally built as a chocolate factory, Canalot (my name for it) has had a varied career. It had been used as a textile and clothing factory in the 1930s, then during the war it was used to produce light armaments and eventually it became a laundry. More recently it was occupied by a company called Oliver Toms who made kitchen catering equipment. They left in the 1970s and it stayed empty and fell derelict.

The use I had in mind was something the planners disliked because I couldn't say exactly what it was, other than 'studios'. It wasn't really offices and it wasn't really workshops. Those two terms were too specific to describe the diverse facilities that people in the film and television industry wanted. Happily we

6.6
Design for the atrium at Canalot Production Studios, London.

managed to obtain planning permission because it was the year when the government changed the use class categories and introduced category B1. As a result, there was no longer a distinction between offices and workshops, and that allowed a much more flexible use of space. Subsequently, I might add, the planners were delighted with the Canalot project.

We then started to design. One of the interesting things about designing a big building and dividing it into lots of small spaces is that every space has to be a winner. Give most architects a big building to design and certain spaces will be second class – 'that's where the post room can go', or something similar. Usually that's okay because, when a big company takes on a building, it accepts the inevitability of a mix of good and bad spaces – the post room is lousy and the board room is terrific. But if you are dividing a building into a hundred different units for individual occupation, every single one has to be good and desirable because someone has to be charmed by it and decide 'I want to work here'. There is no room for lousy space in any SPACE project. In addition, as part of any working community, it is really important to have a place where people can get to know each other. Apart from anything else, this strategy is commercially fertile. Therefore in Canalot we have a fairly glamorous canalside atrium with a very popular restaurant and bar.

In the end the 70,000 square feet Canalot reconstruction job – and it was a thorough going one – cost about £12 a foot. That wasn't much money, even in 1986. We had to be fairly crafty, though, and prepared to flout many of the conventions of the British building industry to get the product we wanted for a price that made sense. For example, our services engineer told us that to put in a central heating system for the whole building would cost £2.50 a foot, a total of £160,000 in a building of that size. But we figured out that if we put in nine domestic systems instead we could do it for a third of the cost, and that's what we did – with the added advantage that if one system breaks down eight-ninths of the building remain heated. The other advantage was that our stick-in-the-mud services engineer resigned in disgust.

The pressure to economize was all the greater because Canalot was completed without any help at all from the public purse. It was all done with private finance borrowed from the National Westminster Bank – and to tell the truth we only managed to borrow it from them because we had a good track record on other projects. I think that someone coming in for the first time might have had trouble with funding.

Once the reconstruction works were nearing completion we started the marketing. We staged a terrific on-site party one Sunday afternoon to which we invited everyone who was anyone in the film and television industry. It worked. Within twenty-four hours – with one or two exceptions – we had signed up nine-year leases on every space in the building.

That was more than ten years ago. Ever since – and throughout the recession of the early 1990s too – Canalot has been a great success, with seventy small companies generating over 200 jobs. Many politicians, including Kenneth Clarke and Michael Portillo, have come to visit, always trailed by a carefully primed media entourage.

Another thing that I should like to emphasize about Canalot – and this applies to all inner city projects – is the importance of making a positive intervention to integrate activities with the local community. We go to great lengths to encourage local people to take jobs and also try to provide local facilities – a children's theatre, to give one example. These linkages are a vital part of making a permanent contribution to the well-being of the neighbourhood.

In the wake of Canalot, something like four or five hundred little arts and media companies have now set up in the Kensal Basin area – it's really taken off. And Canalot gained an instant reputation as a pretty hot place – a 'media centre'. Of course that was the phrase that gained so much currency in the late 1980s – probably because of the way in which local authorities developed a kind of civic megalomania, a desire to become known as the city of media or the city of culture or whatever it might be. This was probably sparked by Glasgow's success in establishing a reputation at that time as a place full of creative activities. Anyway, because of Canalot's instant reputation we were bombarded with enquiries from various people saying 'come and show us how to do it here'.

The Custard Factory[www]

One of the enquiries came from Charles Landry who worked for the Joseph Rowntree Foundation. He had been commissioned by Birmingham City Council to advise on the generation of arts and media activities in the city and, in turn, he asked me if I would go and take a look. I did – and in the process I was hooked. To me Birmingham was a fascinating place because there were so many question marks and contradictions about it. First, why was it there at all? Most cities have at least one obvious reason for existence: a port or a major river, a mountain or a mine, some amazing architecture or at the very least, a setting of natural beauty. But Birmingham has none of these things. I suppose Birmingham exists simply because it is a crossroads ... the gravitational centre of the United Kingdom ... well placed for commerce and communication.

Its *raison d'être* has always been trade and Birmingham has long been proud of its reputation as the city of a thousand trades – a place where things are made.

But in the slump of the early 1980s Birmingham almost lost that *raison d'être*. It was really tough – at one time 30 or 40 per cent of the commercial space in the city was empty, with no takers at any price. Deep civic depression ensued. I believe it was because of the slump of the early 1980s that Birmingham decided in effect to pull itself up by its bootstraps. New thinking and new projects were encouraged, cultural activities were imported in a big way, ideas for the National Exhibition Centre and the International Convention Centre took shape. The new approach culminated in what I think of as one of the most significant events in the history of planning and urban affairs in this country: the 1988 Birmingham Symposium. I always think of it as 'Whither Birmingham' although the official name was the 'Highbury Initiative'. And it was fantastic. 150, maybe 200, eminent people were invited from all over the world: planners, thinkers, philosophers, journalists, architects, politicians and so on. For two or three days they were shown around Birmingham and the discussion was of what might be done to lift Britain's second city. The proposals that came out were tremendous, perhaps iconoclastic in the eyes of some of the more entrenched city planners, but the really wonderful thing was the Council's readiness to listen to new ideas. Ten years on and the results of the Highbury Initiative are already in evidence. Birmingham is a transformed city.

It is important to understand the milieu of Birmingham at that time – and the reasons that I and many others became fascinated by what was going on and wanted to become involved. To begin with, my involvement consisted simply of attending the Highbury Initiative, getting to know Birmingham and (in partnership with architect Ian Ritchie) writing a report on how to use arts and media activities to revitalize a badly run-down inner city suburb called Digbeth.

One day, during one of my frequent visits, I read in the *Birmingham Post* that a building in the middle of the Jewellery Quarter had just been sold at a price which seemed to me to be absurdly small. I knew the building quite well – a vast 100,000 square feet, eight storey flatted

factory built by the Norwich Union insurance company in about 1969. It was partly derelict and three quarters empty. Several terraces of small-scale Victorian buildings had been torn down to make way for it. I fantasized about bringing the building back to life as a sort of belated apology for the desecration of twenty years before.

So I called the estate agent who'd sold it. 'Why speak to me? I've just sold it so it's not for sale,' he said. I replied that I wanted to buy it from whomsoever he had sold it to. Eventually he produced a local property dealer who, after much discussion, said, 'OK, I will sell it to you for a profit, but only on condition that you also buy a pile of old rubbish that I happen to own down in Digbeth.' That satisfied me because the price he wanted for both lots of property was more than justified by the Jewellery Quarter building alone. In fact I was almost ready to do the deal without even looking at the 'pile of old rubbish' in Digbeth – I'd simply assumed that it was some old sheds with asbestos roofs. To my

6.7
Scott House, the Custard Factory, Birmingham.

6.8
Devonshire House, part of the Custard Factory built by Sir Alfred Bird (*see Plate 5*).

6.9
The Custard Factory building as it was first found.

excitement and astonishment the 'pile of old rubbish' turned out to be the magnificent collection of buildings (some listed) now known as the Custard Factory. I would like to discuss the Custard Factory first and come back to the building in the Jewellery Quarter later.

What we now call the Custard Factory Quarter consists of 200,000 square feet of buildings at the point where Digbeth High Street crosses the River Rea, Birmingham's only river. It stands about 800 yards from the Bull Ring on the exact site of the prehistoric settlement where Birmingham was founded. One of the main buildings, a beautiful terracotta affair, was built by Sir Alfred Bird in celebration of his knighthood, given in recognition of his success in marketing custard powder. However, in the early 1980s, after more than 100 years of production employing up to 1,000 custard makers, custard seemed to lose its glamour. Bird's was taken over by a conglomerate and Sir Alfred Bird's proud custard factory fell derelict.

Derelict or not, I was stunned by this so-called 'pile of old rubbish' in Digbeth. To me the beauty and charm of the Custard Factory was irresistible. It had a marvellous sense of urban place – a feeling of being at the centre of things. I even convinced myself that this was where the ley lines met in the West Midlands. It was a good place to sit and think and watch the clouds go by.

However, as with the Danceworks building, I had no idea what to do with it. Oddly enough the solution to the problem arrived in the shape of *Hamlet*. One summer afternoon, as I was sitting by the river admiring the jumbled roof lines of the Custard Factory silhouetted against the magnificent Digbeth railway arches, I was approached by three intense, bearded and beaded youths who said that they were actors. Without ceremony they asked if they could have space in the building. I asked them to *prove* that they were actors – and they did. The following night they played *Hamlet* for an audience of one. It was a fine performance and I gave them the space.

They set themselves up as 'The Custard Factory Theatre Company'. Since then, amongst much else, they have won an *Observer* national prize, toured Italy, and gained excellent reviews at the Edinburgh Fringe. Meanwhile, the word spread that you could get free space at the Custard Factory and out of the woodwork of the West Midlands crept hundreds and hundreds of people, mainly young, mostly wanting space to do creative things. Within weeks about seventy small enterprises were working away. We were deluged with applicants but it soon became impossible to give away so much free space – when the roof leaked we had to pay for repairs ... and there was no money coming in. Clearly it was time to do a proper job.

Because the Custard Factory is so big we couldn't work on it all at the same time so we began with Scott House, the large building at the rear of the site. We turned the loading bay into a lake around which, on the ground floor, we installed dance studios, shops, art galleries, a café, a bar, a 220-seat theatre and the reception area. The rest of the 100,000 square feet was turned into workshops, studios and offices.

We completed the work on Scott House for just over £1.8 million, which isn't at all bad at £18 per foot. And it was thoroughly and properly done. The overall cost was roughly £2.4 million against which we obtained a gap funding City Grant of £800,000 (the system is now administered through English Partnerships). Currently 500 people work in that building and over the years literally thousands more have applied to come in – but until the next phase we have no space for them.

I discussed marketing at the beginning, and I would like to stress the importance of moving seamlessly from development to management. It would not have worked nearly so well if a developer had refurbished the building and then turned it over to the local authority or to some Arts Council sponsored body. A major attractant of the Custard Factory, which our people like, is precisely that it does not have upon it the dead hand of bureaucracy. With the best will in the world, this is something that public sector organizations find it very difficult to avoid.

The Custard Factory has kept its original grittiness, it has created hundreds of jobs, and we have tremendous links with local schools and colleges and with organizations such as the Birmingham Royal Ballet and the D'Oyly Carte Opera Company. It has been a huge boost for the surrounding area and Digbeth itself has now become a focus for Birmingham's civic ambitions. It is to be the site of Millennium Point, an educational project with a new campus which has been granted £100 million of public money. Partly as result of the Custard Factory project, Digbeth, once falling headlong into decay, is now enjoying a renaissance.

The development of the Custard Factory has not been without its problems. One of them is our rather confused relationship with Birmingham City Council. Since we do both for-profit and not-for-profit things, people understandably get confused. It's a marvellous thing to be able to balance commercial discipline with cultural potential (as we do at Danceworks) and we are lucky at the Custard Factory to have the space and the place in which to do it. As with Canalot, the politicians like it. I remember the day when Michael Portillo came bearing the £800,000 City Grant cheque. He had come to Birmingham to dole out more than £20 million to various schemes. Some of these were for large council estate projects. But despite the fact that ours was by far the smallest grant, the Custard Factory was used for the televised ceremony.

The 1998 G-8 summit, held in Birmingham, helped to bring the Custard Factory to the attention of many international politicians, some of whom were keen to create similar projects in their cities. For example, in Spring 1999 we were invited to Italy by the Mayor of Milan to make a presentation about the Custard Factory.

To begin to address the seemingly unquenchable and unsatisfied demand for space at the Custard Factory, the next step in the development will be a new building around a public courtyard. It will be called the GreenHouse. The ground floor, like that of Scott House, will comprise shops, cafés, bars, and art galleries and upstairs there will be 100 new studio workspaces to let. The centrepiece of the new courtyard will be a 12-metre high statue of the Green Man, which is already attracting a great deal of interest.

Other future projects at the Custard Factory include a block of seventy live/work spaces. For this we are working with Focus Housing Association. The flats will be rented to people generally working in arts, media, cultural, and

6.10
Design for the Green
Man in the second phase
of the Custard Factory.

design activities. More live/work spaces are
planned for a triangular site currently named
'the village'. The idea is to create an area
resembling a medieval town with a random
street plan on a intimate scale around a square.
The new buildings will be designed by a group
of innovative young architects and built with a
variety of materials ranging from brick to straw
bales to concrete to steel to timber.

The Big Peg

The large building that first caught my
attention in the middle of the Jewellery Quarter
is the 100,000 square feet, eight storey, 1960s
flatted factory which rises like a concrete hat
box to tower over the low-rise Victorian
buildings all around. As part of its
transformation we have renamed it the Big Peg
because in that area in the nineteenth century a
'peg' was a small workbench supplied for the
use of itinerant tradesman and craftsmen.

In the last year or so the Big Peg has become
almost an annexe to the Custard Factory. People
who can't get space to work at the Custard
Factory go to the Big Peg which is less than a
mile away.

By a gradual process we have done quite a lot
with the building, all without subsidy – at least
so far. In a funny way, since we took it on about
ten years ago, the 1960s 'Brutalist' architecture
of the Big Peg has become quite admired in
certain quarters. The building also has some
practical advantages – industrial floor loading,
good floor to ceiling heights, superb
daylighting, amazing views, a floorplate ideal
for subdivision, and it is very close to the city
centre with plenty of car parking space.

On a space by space, floor by floor
programme, we have so far reconstructed
internally about two thirds of the upper floors of
the building – producing lots of attractive self-
contained studio workspaces, most of which
have been taken by arts/media/jewellery
related start-up enterprises. On the top floor we
have built seventy 'artist's penthouse studios'
and as we say – 'in the Jewellery Quarter you
can't get closer to God than the Big Peg Artist's
Studios'. They cost about £20 per week to rent.
We have installed a glamorous new entrance
and reception area and more recently have built
a restaurant and art gallery in the basement,
both of which are much used by the people
upstairs in the building.

In 1997 we gave a section of the car park to
the Prince of Wales's Institute of Architecture for
their summer project. Each year, its students
design and construct a small building within a
six week period. There was great excitement
when HRH The Prince of Wales came to
Birmingham to open the building. To coincide
with the visit we staged an exhibition of the
work of local young craftspeople and artists and
of course the Big Peg gained lots of publicity.

The 150 or so small enterprises at the Big Peg
are now really beginning to coagulate into an
energetic working community. In common with
the Custard Factory and other SPACE projects,
people now want to be there for reasons way
beyond the mere occupation of space. They
want to be part of something bigger, to gain
identity, to become part of the spider's web of
inter-trading and to enjoy it. This is all quite a
good result for what was, not so long ago, a
decrepit and despised eyesore.

There are many more SPACE projects that I
could discuss but I will close with a story that is
a sort of parable, showing the hiatus in
communication and understanding between the
rulers and the ruled.

6.11
Entrance to the
Big Peg, Birmingham.

About a year ago some people from a government sponsored agency came to see me saying that they would like to talk to all the people in the Custard Factory about finance and expansion. I agreed for them to do it so they went and knocked on 150 doors and said, 'We would like to advise you about VAT and Euroland, about finance and other important things so that you can expand and make more money' – or words to that effect. In almost every case, the answer was polite but unprintable. What characterizes the people at the Custard Factory is that they enjoy what they are doing NOW and they don't distinguish very much between making a living and enjoying living. When they finish work – which can be at midnight or at three in the afternoon – they go down to the lake and have a drink and meet like-minded people. Sometimes they will be there for seven days a week because that is what they most enjoy. And that is what a good working community is all about. Think about it.

Introduction

During the last quarter of a century, there has been a burgeoning of popular interest in the recent past.[1] One of the most remarkable aspects of this trend has been an enthusiasm for visiting and studying machines, buildings and landscapes associated with the Industrial Revolution. This chapter will consider popular support for industrial museums and heritage centres, approaches to interpretation, and their potential in educational terms. Particular attention will be given to the Ironbridge Gorge in eastern Shropshire where many key developments in iron production and engineering occurred in the eighteenth century; the maritime museum at Albert Dock, Liverpool, one of the finest examples of British industrial architecture; and the Museum of Science and Industry in Manchester housed in the world's earliest surviving passenger station.

Britain has pioneered much of the growth in industrial tourism. It is now a cause that gains support across most of the developed world. Historic ports and mill towns, from Lowell in the United States to Norrköping in Sweden and Volos in Greece, either have, or are planning, some form of museum, interpretation centre or tourist area. These projects, often seen as part of regeneration initiatives, can combine striking architecture, innovative museums, and opportunities for recreational retailing and eating. Visitors are offered a cocktail of self-improvement and indulgence. In the case of Norrköping, museum provision is complemented by the re-use of other mills by the university, as an art school and by computer firms, while a paper mill has been re-worked as a concert and congress hall.

At best, industrial heritage projects can present challenging and important concepts relating to technology, industrialization and urban life. At worst they can pander to the worst foibles of Middle England, offering history and culture in its most trite and flavourless form.[2] Some harbourside projects, as at Victoria & Alfred, Cape Town, South Africa, are primarily heritage honeypots for tourists rather than initiatives in conservation and interpretation.

Why and how do docks, mills and workshops strike a chord with so many and with such a broad range of visitors? What are

Chapter seven

Tourism and the industrial heritage:

new uses as museums and heritage centres

Michael Stratton ▮

The University of York

1 Gryt's Mill: ProNova computer centre

2 Berg's Mill: Expansion zone for ProNova
   (Ericsson & Solectron companies)

3 Drag's Mill:
   Temporary premises for the university

4 Kåkenhus: Main university building

5 Täppan and Spetsen:
   Expansion zone for the university

6 Skvallertorget square and Bergsbron bridge

7 The Town museum

8 "The Flatiron": Museum of Work

9 "The Ironing Board": Art school, museum

10 "The Heating Church":
    Former heating plant, now empty

11 The Cotton Spinning Mill:
    University premises

12 Louis De Geer Concert & Congress Hall:
    Former Holmen pulp and paper mill

13 The Holmen Tower:
    Erected 1750 for the Holmen Company

7.1
The industrial landscape
of Norrköping, Sweden
showing the location of
three museums.

(Photo: Per Wichmann)

the criteria for success in attracting tourists and
school groups and in generating repeat visits?
Little systematic research has been undertaken
into the benefits of tourism and museum
development in promoting employment and
morale across local communities blighted by
industrial decline and dereliction. As will be
seen, most industrial museums are not
developed primarily to serve the communities
that mills and foundries once sustained, but
successful projects may help to turn round local
attitudes and create a positive image for
attracting commercial investment.

The appeal of
the industrial heritage

Cultural tourism has become highly popular in
the late twentieth century. Holidaymakers and
day trippers expend large amounts of money
and energy to study aspects of history and
architecture, from cathedral cities and country
houses to battle re-enactments and ghost trails.
Enthusiasm for the industrial past attracts
tourists to dockyards and mill districts that less
than a generation ago were the no-go zones of
many cities.

   The Grand Tour was an important aspect of
gentrified life in the eighteenth century, but
cultural tourism really took off in the 1960s and
'70s. Shorter working hours and rising incomes

were matched by greater mobility and a broadening of interest in history and the arts, promoted by television and colour supplements. Traditional museums and art galleries, with objects safely encased and captioned, were slow to respond to this growth. Instead a new breed of museum emerged, its instigators being motivated by the decline of traditional industries such as coalmining, ironfounding and textile production. Professionals and amateurs alike saw industry as a legitimate subject of study and worthy of preservation. The writings of L.T.C. Rolt and the photographs of Eric de Maré presented canal aqueducts and huge warehouses as objects of grandeur.[3] Grimy brick and black cast-iron created a legacy to be revelled in rather than reviled. To planners and politicians industrial museums could give an identity to otherwise bland new towns, while allowing redundant buildings to be relocated out of the way of new roads or shopping centres. Mines, factories and mills became a source of public nostalgia, admiration for the energies of miners and potters and the close-knit communities in which they lived out-weighing associations of hard graft and danger.

The most successful museums – Ironbridge,[www] Beamish, and the Black Country Museum – were established on derelict land, their staff and volunteers conserving the in situ industrial monuments and re-erecting redundant structures and machinery brought in on flat-bed lorries. Others were set in redundant works: for example, the Gladstone Pottery Museum[www] at Longton, Staffordshire and Quarry Bank Mill[www] at Styal, Cheshire. All depended on the enthusiasm of volunteers, many of whom had many years experience in industry, and a skeletal staff who hadn't, but quickly learnt the art of drawing funds into the capital budgets of their trusts.

The full story of how these museums developed, with steam engines being saved from the scrap merchant and archives being plucked from skips is yet to be told, but all have had to adapt to changing demands from the public and to shifts in conservation philosophy and governmental policy.[4] Museums housed in redundant factories rather than open-air sites have had the more chequered history, finding the need to draw in large numbers of visitors incompatible with their prime *raison d'être*, to conserve and interpret a particular works and its processes. All too many mills and pumping stations are cluttered up with interpretative panels and objects irrelevant to the site.

During the 1970s and 1980s, museums were established at closed coal mines in Blaenavon, Caphouse, Chatterley Whitfield, and two sites in Lothian; and in the last steam-powered cotton mill in Burnley in Lancashire. Government-funded labour schemes provided

7.2
The reconstructed coal mine with the town street in the distance, North of England Open-Air Museum, Beamish, County Durham.

free and, often, highly skilled labour. More radically, an old soap factory at Widnes was transformed into a museum of the chemical industry – using bright modern displays and interactives to give a grossly polluting industry a more environmentally sensitive image.

Museum visitor figures to individual sites flattened in the 1980s, due to the opening of new museums and competition from more popular visitor attractions such as Alton Towers theme park and Granada Studio Tours. After an upturn, peaking for most museums in 1988, the recession of the early '90s caused more major dips and even slumps, numbers of day trips being closely influenced by levels of real disposable income and the cost of petrol.

Admissions to historic buildings and monuments in England strengthened again in the mid 1990s, rising by 2 per cent over 1995–6 to reach a 30 per cent increase since 1982. There were about 58.4 million visits to 1,131 historic properties in England in 1996, and 65 million visits to museums and galleries.[5] A recent regional survey recorded a threefold increase in museum visits since 1960. But many museums have recorded reductions in numbers of around 5–7 per cent per annum over the last couple of years, a downward drift blamed on dry warm summers and new competition including shopping on Sundays. A worrying weakness is the inability of many museums to attract the 16–24 age group, who have to be wooed with dramatic and expensive audio-visuals and interactives.[6]

Industrial museums or centres have taken something of a back seat in terms of new initiatives, only one, Gants Mill, Bruton, Somerset being opened for the first time in 1996. Worse, there have been several closures, most notably Chatterley Whitfield Mining Museum (which has recently been rescued by English Heritage), and Abbeydale Industrial Hamlet in Sheffield, the latter housed in one the world's few surviving eighteenth-century steelworks. Industrial museums in Birmingham and Cardiff have been closed with their collections put in store. The survival of mining museums is likely to continue only with some degree of national funding.

Tourist motivation

Why do old buildings, old objects and redundant machinery appeal to the public? Professionals and academics justify the preservation and interpretation of a particular site in terms of historical and archaeological significance, and ranked against others in terms of its rarity and completeness.[7] Visitor surveys provide more general and softer justifications: wish fulfilment, escape from a mundane environment, pursuit of relaxation, play, education, and opportunities for speciality shopping. The late Raphael Samuel examined in detail the popular appeal of the recent past – sufficiently close to our own memories of steam trains, Meccano construction kits, playing in the street and warm beer.[8] Such nostalgia has been fuelled not only by exhortations from Margaret Thatcher for a revival of 'Victorian values' but by advertisements for brown bread, and by television classic drama and soap operas set amidst the mills and cobbled streets of northern England.

Most visitors to Ironbridge are not studying specific technologies and structures but are, according to visitor surveys, seeking 'an authentic representation of nineteenth-century life and industry'.[9] Motivation varies between different types of visitor, often classified into organized tourists on a package holiday, individual or family tourists, day trippers from home, and children coming as a school party.[10] The majority of those who visit sites of working class labour are professionals, though shortage of time is testing their commitment to cultural activities.[11] Surveys at Ironbridge show that 45 per cent are professional and non-manual workers (classified as ABC1) and 30 per cent retired. Apart from those in organized groups, they are most likely to come as couples, with older and retired visitors becoming increasingly important. Curators and marketing managers have to accept that the decision on whether to visit is often a marginal one, made at short notice.

Beamish, a major open-air museum near Newcastle-upon-Tyne, presents a slight contrast, being more of a family destination with manual workers being better represented. A third come from the northern region. Meanwhile Ironbridge gained only 21 per cent of their visitors from within Shropshire and West Midlands; visitors from London and the South-East making up a remarkable 39 per cent.[12] For both museums, visitor patterns are highly seasonal, rising from March to a peak in August then falling off in September.[13]

Education and the industrial heritage

Industrial museums have furthered their educational aims, reinforced their political credibility and aided their finances by responding to the demands of school groups. Of the 300,000 visitors to the Ironbridge Gorge Museum, 20 per cent come in educational parties. The long-established tradition of schools making virtually unplanned visits to their local museums was transformed by the introduction of nationally defined key stages and, for secondary schoolchildren, of GCSE examinations based on tightly defined curricula. Museums found that they could charge schools if their displays were oriented around appropriate coursework and projects, and especially if handbooks provided sample exercises and projects based on buildings and artifacts in their care.

National Curriculum guidelines for 6–14 year olds, brought out in the early 1990s, encouraged curators to tackle issues relating to environment and heritage. Education officers in museums have to be agile in responding to each new initiative in school education. When science became a core area in primary schools, several industrial museums introduced interactive science centres.[14] When the National Curriculum was introduced, both history and geography were mandatory subjects at Key Stages 1–4, but now only 1–3 remain. Local history is not a part of the National Curriculum but does provide a way of illustrating general themes and encouraging powers of observation.[15]

The Museum of Science and Industry at Manchester has an education service that can provide a complete teaching package, the themes on offer including 'The Way we Were: Queen Victoria to the Beatles', and 'Slums, Bugs and Diseases'. Other education services, such as

Ironbridge, have focused on developing high quality publications, which present case-studies on how teachers can best make use of the museum. Schoolchildren can then gain experiences that will build on their understanding of the world, teach them new skills and introduce them to environmental, moral and human issues.[16] Younger parties can use a reconstructed classroom and are encouraged to don Victorian-style costume. Groups are encouraged to stay for longer than a day, two youth hostels having been opened in historic buildings within the Ironbridge Gorge.

In the early 1990s many museum directors perceived a major market in self-funded activities for adults, in the belief that many were seeking more engaging and satisfying visits than the one day whistle-stop tour. While hands-on workshops in ceramics and day classes in driving steam locomotives are often fully booked, this area is unlikely to develop beyond a side-line. Two further areas of formal education should be noted. Industrial archaeology was born as a subject of study in the sphere of adult education. Many adult education groups or societies became closely linked with local industrial museums and have undertaken a remarkable range of historical research. A number of universities have developed links with museums to further research and training at postgraduate level, basing a department or institute on site, and so making the museum's buildings, collections and expertise available to the students. The Ironbridge Institute, founded by the Museum and the University of Birmingham has developed pioneering courses in industrial archaeology and heritage management and undertaken extensive research on the museum's monuments and collections, and into issues concerning their management.

Interpretation initiatives

British industrial museums have embraced and in some cases pioneered innovative approaches to interpretation. They have extended their remit beyond that strictly dictated by their collections to interpret landscapes, towns and

7.3
Replica of Ford's
Mack Plant of 1903–5,
Greenfield Village,
Henry Ford Museum,
Detroit.

regions through broad themes that are likely to appeal to the British public – working and living conditions, the relationship between manager and worker, and even the lure of the public house. The challenge has been to generalize, encapsulating the flavour of the age in a populist way, often using reconstructions, actors, dark-rides or audio-visual shows.

The concept of using museums to save and interpret buildings was drawn from the movement to preserve aspects of folk life, developed in Scandinavia during the last decades of the nineteenth century and imported to the United States in the inter-war period by John D. Rockefeller at Colonial Williamsburg and Henry Ford at Greenfield Village. The theme of Ford's Greenfield Village, located on the edge of Detroit and dedicated in 1929, was to encapsulate the resourcefulness of the American people, including great innovators such as the Wright brothers, Henry Heinz, Thomas Edison and, of course, Ford himself. Ironbridge, Beamish, and other British open-air

museums adopted the same formula of re-erecting redundant structures or creating replicas. By the early 1970s many conservationists expressed disquiet over the removal of buildings from their original setting. With more extensive protection of industrial buildings through listing, attention came to focus on in situ preservation, rather than dismantling and re-erection. The open air museum, meaning a collection of buildings which have been demolished and re-erected, is now a discredited concept in Britain. Planning permission is unlikely ever to be given again for the removal of any structure of real merit. A similar shift in conservation philosophy has occurred in Scandinavia – many Swedes regret the plunder of Old Linköping in Sweden, whereby the best buildings were moved to a museum on the outskirts.

Meanwhile, industrial museums quickly discovered that the key to attracting paying visitors was to present their buildings and objects in more dynamic and appealing ways. Audio-visual shows, furnished interiors and

had to combine stage sets, computer interactives and visitor facilities such as shops and restaurants. Several industrial museums introduced 'experiences' – for example the 'Annie Mcleod' time-car ride at New Lanark and the 'Into the Thick' walk-in coal mine experience at the Black Country Museum which culminates in a mock explosion. Neither have become 'cult attractions' and most museums now accept that such high-tech extravaganzas are best left to the likes of Madame Tussaud's or Alton Towers who can invest millions of pounds each year. Low-tech, costumed interpreters, either talking with visitors or acting out a role, have proved both affordable and durable in their appeal. They typically occupy reconstructed buildings as at Beamish or Ironbridge, or stage sets as with the 'Emigration Experience' at Merseyside Maritime Museum.

Industrial and science museums located within towns and cities have evolved to be at the forefront of innovative interpretation and, in some cases, to act as agents of inner-city regeneration. They have cleared or reworked formal galleries to create hands-on exhibits covering popular themes – in the case of London's Science Museum including flight, food and the exploration of space. Some science museums and science centres are located in run-down industrial and dockside areas. The Power House at Sydney was opened in a generating station in 1988. Bristol's 'Exploratory' was established in the same year; the simple 'string-and-sealing-wax low tech approach' suited the use of an adapted building, Brunel's Temple Meads station. Around the same date, hands-on interactive centres were established by National Museums on Merseyside within their large objects store, and by the Museum of Science and Industry in Manchester. More recently the *Cité des Sciences et de l'Industrie* was developed at La Villette in a dramatic new building on the site of one of Paris' cattle markets. The *Cité* has few objects, focusing instead on 'new interactive exhibit methods and advanced museum technology'. The aim is to present the social impact of science and technology, decisions which confront us relating to science and technology in our everyday lives, and such French technological achievements as the Renault Espace and the TGV.

costumed interpreters were widely adopted. The interpretative and commercial stakes were raised in the 1980s as heritage centres latched on to public taste for animated history. Jorvik Viking Centre in York, the Oxford Story and the Tales of Robin Hood in Nottingham featured 'dark rides' in electric cars. At Wigan Pier, the interpretation centre was titled simply 'The Way We Were' and comprised a stage-set coal-mine, schoolroom and pub – all to be brought alive by actors in Victorian costume. Museum directors struggled to keep up with ever-rising public expectations. Their new-look museum

Museums, area interpretation and regeneration

Since many industrial and science museums are located in historic buildings and landscapes, it seems logical that they should provide some interpretation for their surroundings as well as their own collections. The French developed the concept of the *ecomusée*, applied most notably in the 1970s at the industrial town of Le Creusot. The museum addressed issues embracing heavy industry, urban life and agriculture to help the community confront the trauma of industrial decline and social change.[17] Similar philosophies have been adopted by several community museums in Britain, most successfully by the Springburn Museum in a district of Glasgow which used to be dominated by railway engineering workshops. America has led the way in terms of the formal interpretation of industrial landscapes, as exemplified by Lowell, Massachusetts conserved as the first urban National Park in the United States from the 1970s. Groups of visitors travel to various mills by foot, tram car and boat, meeting costumed actors who consider such themes as industrial and race relations, power and manufacturing technology (*see Plates 12, 13 & 14*).

Traditional industrial museums, who need visitors to pay and see their collections, are more ambivalent about encouraging visitors to spend too much time considering the broader landscape. At Portsmouth Historic Dockyard, there is clear tension between the need of the trusts looking after the *Victory*, the *Warrior* and the *Mary Rose* to attract visitors to their ships, and the value of interpreting the naval base, for which there is no entrance charge. All too many industrial or maritime museums can become victims of their own success. Visitors drawn to Portsmouth, Ironbridge or New Lanark for a rewarding 'day out', are happy to spend their few leisure hours walking in the restored surroundings and browsing in tourist shops rather than paying admission charges and concentrating on formal displays.

Industrial tourism

Working factories have also become tourist attractions. Cadbury's of Bournville in Birmingham found that factory tours had been hugely popular back in the 1920s. The firm built on their appeal in the 1980s by developing a visitor centre called Cadbury World, to bring in revenue and to promote their chocolate. For many years Cheshire County Council co-ordinated public visits to local firms such as Rolls-Royce in Crewe and municipal undertakings including the sewage works. Where industrial areas are associated with the decorative arts, firms have been able to develop tourist trails, combining commercial, educational and regeneration aims. The Sunderland Glass Trail was launched in 1992, with a guided bus tour linking factories and the town's museum. A National Glass Centre has now been opened in a radical, glass building at St Peter's Riverside, as part of an urban regeneration programme.[18] More recently, in December 1998 the Industrial Trust was established with the support of the National Trust, to encourage access to factories and public and educational interest in industry.

'The Birthplace of the Industrial Revolution': Ironbridge Gorge Museum

The Ironbridge Gorge[www] has been a site of pilgrimage from as early as 1781, when the Iron Bridge itself was completed and became a symbol of new industrial technology. The iron industry became established in the West Midlands and South Wales in the following century and the Shropshire coalfield gently declined. Most of its blast furnaces, iron bridges, and ceramics works survived. A museum was established in 1967 to preserve these monuments. An open-air site was developed at Blists Hill to house, according to early plans, reconstructed buildings, locks and even a railway marshalling yard. It was believed that, by displaying the wondrous achievements of the Industrial Revolution,

7.6
The Great Warehouse,
Coalbrookdale,
Shropshire, built 1836
with the cast iron clock
tower being added in
1843. Now housing the
Museum of Iron, part of
the Ironbridge Gorge
Museum.

7.7
Pouring iron into
castings at the
reconstructed foundry,
Blists Hill Open Air
Museum, Ironbridge.

passionately by the great architectural writer, Reyner Banham, back in 1973:

It has been a lowering experience for over 20 years to watch the Iron Bridge going from simple neglect in the early fifties when it passed into the un-safekeeping of the county council, and began to be vandalised to its present condition of embalmed municipalisation... the gardenesque devastation of everything around it is relentlessly eroding its visible and tangible meaning. It is hardware and brickwork, water and iron, that matter. Grand general statistical overviews mean nothing here; everything is specific, local and peculiar – because of the landscape. The prime need is to convey the excitement of those eighteenth century visitors (who) went out of their tiny enlightenment skulls on viewing it in the original flaring colours preserved for us in de Loutherbourg's pictures, while the risk is of failure to respond to the physical presence of the scene and its buildings and artefacts.[19]

Banham would weep if he could return a quarter of a century later to see the centre of Ironbridge cluttered with 'heritage' cast iron

society would be encouraged to rediscover the inventiveness and entrepreneurship of Thomas Telford or the Darbys. This vibrant message (the original plans for the open-air site including a helipad) caught the imagination of the local development corporation, the visiting public, and industry who donated most of the capital for development projects during the 1970s and '80s.

The tally of buildings preserved and of innovations in interpretation is highly impressive. A particular feature of Ironbridge has been the revival of out-moded technologies, such as tile-making and wrought-iron manufacture. But throughout the thirty-year history of the project there has been an underlying tension. Does and should Ironbridge explain the broad generalities of industrialization for a broad audience and risk giving a glib and over-sanitized view? Or should it focus on the singular and remarkable collection of monuments set in the unique setting of a river gorge? The dangers of generalization were presented most

bollards and kerb stones, and traffic bobbing over sleeping policemen to landscaped car parks and vernacular-style lavatories. But the museum has had to live with such 'heritat', not having control over the urban landscape outside its boundaries. The museum has achieved high standards of conservation for many of the buildings in its care and historical credibility in its displays. Some of the reconstructed buildings on Blists Hill, such as the candlemaker's shop and the squatter's cottage, do succeed in conveying a suitably tough, even squalid atmosphere. Curators have sought to relate their collections and buildings with the landscape, through trails, superbly detailed models of the Gorge and audio-visual programmes. Yet the latest visitor surveys show that the visiting public are still, after thirty years of interpretation and marketing, unsure of the nature of the museum and the significance of Ironbridge – is Ironbridge a bridge, a museum, several museums, a landscape or a symbol of the Industrial Revolution across the western world?

The Ironbridge Gorge, now designated as a World Heritage Site, is currently the subject of research towards a management plan to conserve the 'industrial heritage in its distinctive semi-natural landscape' and 'interpret it as a whole for a wide public' while preserving its character, nurturing a sustainable economy and avoiding the alienation of the local community through traffic congestion. It is too early to tell whether this plan will nurture excellence and originality in interpretation or result in heritage planning by bureaucracy and compromise, posterity being compromised by short-term local interests.

The building as an exhibit: Merseyside Maritime Museum, Albert Dock, Liverpool

Albert Dock, Liverpool[www] exemplifies the ways in which building preservation and museum development can complement each other; the connection gaining added significance through its location in the most self-destructive and yet

7.8
View from Albert Dock, Liverpool, showing the vessels preserved by the Merseyside Maritime Museum and, beyond, the Pierhead.

most haunting of Britain's industrial cities. The dock warehouses became recognized as the ultimate expression of the bold, functional use of brick, iron and granite in industrial architecture in the 1950s.[20] During the early 1980s Merseyside Development Corporation and a firm of developers, Arrowcroft, devised a re-use project largely of offices and apartments, but propelled in its early stages by two major cultural attractions – a maritime museum and an art gallery. Within an overall scheme co-ordinated by Holford Associates, Sir James Stirling designed the Tate Gallery of the North, and Brock Carmichael the Maritime Museum. Block D, housing the Museum, was conserved in a purist manner, so that Jesse Hartley's Grade I listed masterpiece could form an exhibit in itself. The startling roof of wrought iron ties and galvanized iron plates is preserved, whereas it was replaced in most of the other warehouses. The most complex and potentially intrusive displays were set in the basement, with more traditional galleries being located under the brick-vaulted roof. Services were designed as exposed and removable insertions, and new staircases in the form of steel gang-planks.[21] The museum combines ship models, pictures and reconstructions with real ships, actors, videos and computers. It succeeds in tackling major themes of maritime and naval history while retaining a strongly Liverpudlian flavour.

A trail round the warehouse, highlighting its features and former use, was written but has not been published, one suspects because the agenda has moved on and most visitors almost inevitably take the building for granted. There is an interactive area for children called 'Shipshape' and a suite designed for corporate hospitality. The museum has succeeded in making visitors more aware of the dock itself. It has moored up a series of historic ships beside cranes, crates and barrels, and refurnished the piermaster's house and offices. Two of the museum's most successful displays – the 'Emigration Experience' and the 'Slavery Experience' – are related to the city through trails which lead visitors past shipping offices, memorials and sailors' lodgings. The staff of the museum have nurtured a wide range of research into the docks on either side of the River Mersey, leading by example through their own publications and organizing adult education classes.

'The oldest railway buildings in the world': Museum of Science and Industry, Castlefields, Manchester

A maritime museum has an obvious compatibility with a dock warehouse. It has proved rather more challenging to develop a museum embracing diverse strands of science and industry in and around the world's oldest railway station. The Liverpool Road terminus, Manchester, combining a goods warehouse and a passenger station, was opened in September 1830. The complex evolved with more warehouses and survived albeit neglected, to be fêted on its 150th anniversary.[22] The station gained an exhibition on rail travel and the booking hall was populated with costumed figures to present the flavour of an early station. It was decided to relocate the North West Museum of Science and Industry to the station, the warehouses becoming furnished with galleries on gas, electricity, power and transport. An adjoining market hall housed aircraft and displays about space flight. The latest gallery, 'Fibres, Fabrics and Fashion', interprets Manchester's textile industry, past and present, and the museum prides itself on its special events and exhibitions angled primarily towards children but also celebrating the city's multi-racial culture.

Although a replica steam train occasionally chuffs in and out of the station, the museum came to dominate its historic buildings, arguably its most important exhibits. Part of one warehouse lost its internal structure and new access ramps were inserted into later buildings. The scale of growth, and the use of innovative display techniques to draw in paying visitors, inevitably resulted in the museum becoming somewhat divorced from the dramatic landscape of Castlefields,[www] with its canals, railway viaducts and great cotton warehouses. A new interpretation centre was opened opposite the museum, and urban trails published by other organizations.

The museum has now returned its attention to the railway buildings and, specifically, the 1830 warehouse, the oldest railway building in the world. It undertook a detailed recording project and has just completed meticulous conservation works. The brick and wood

7.9
The 'Fibres, Fabrics and
Fashion' gallery, inside a
railway warehouse, at
the Museum of Science
and Industry in
Manchester.

structure was given a very mild clean,
preserving the rich collection of painted signs
and carpenters' marks. Hydraulic machinery,
internal wagon bays and taking-in doors are
being retained and the services needed for
museum displays are being designed in a
discreet but honestly modern idiom.[23]

The future outlook
for industrial museums

The public expect working exhibits to be
operating when they visit, demand high
standards of catering, and dislike the aura of
dereliction so beloved by Reyner Banham and
by pioneering industrial archaeologists. It may
be that industrial museums are trying to offer
too much. Most visits are made as part of a day
out, not of a stay-away holiday, and families
and couples do not want to be spending hours
choosing between displays, restored buildings
and sites that are effectively competing for an
almost given number of visitors. According to

one of the most recent surveys, visitors now
demand that museums should be 'fun' and
'children-friendly,' a far cry from the earnest
educational aims of Victorian institutions.[24]

Every museum director is pre-occupied with
drawing in money from the European Union
and the Heritage Lottery Fund and it is difficult
in many cases to be certain of the educational
and interpretative justification. In all too many
cases the aim seems to be create dramatic new
buildings and galleries, or to finish half-
complete capital projects. What is clear is that
museums, and perhaps especially industrial
museums, are at a threshold. Some feel as
though the Britain of New Labour is cherishing
new technology and new design rather more
than history and conservation. English Heritage
has pinned itself to the mast of promoting new
design as well as conserving that of the old. The
most prestigious Millennium projects are not
for museums but for eco-centres and arts
centres. The Millennium Dome contains few
objects and no historically-angled displays.
Meanwhile the Heritage Lottery Fund is set to
devote less than £50 million a year to museum
projects in the future, a dramatic fall from the

peak figure of £100 million per annum. During its first eighteen months the Fund had allocated no less than £65 million to 'industrial, transport and maritime' projects.

This shift does reflect, in part, a changing public mood. A survey in December 1996 asked people to say which categories of heritage project were the most important to preserve. National parks were ranked first, then historic buildings, rivers and canals, and inner city parks. Industrial heritage was ninth on the list.[25] Industrial museums are having to work increasingly hard to stand still – through marketing campaigns, improving visitor facilities and introducing interactives and other forms of innovative exhibits to broaden and up-date their appeal. Ironbridge is spending heavily on capital projects but its estate is so vast that it is difficult to avoid the ongoing march of decay let alone keep up with rising visitor expectations.[26]

The turn of the century will be a time as much for re-evaluation as celebration. A major research report on England's preserved industrial heritage has confirmed fears concerning the financial implications of maintaining large-scale sites amidst increased competition for visitors and static if not declining levels of support from volunteers.[27] Leading figures in the museum world are quietly retrenching from the populist ideal of combining education and entertainment (gruesomely nicknamed as 'edutainment'), and speaking of being in the business of 'life-long learning'. The directors of industrial museums have a record of remarkable success over the last quarter century, both in strictly museological terms and in promoting urban conservation and regeneration. One hopes that in the New Millennium they will be able to hold true to, or return to, their historical and educational remits, and work to relate objects in their collection to the historic buildings and landscapes in which they are located.

Notes and references

1 I am grateful for help from Glen Lawes, John Powell, Sue Spicer and Katie Foster at Ironbridge, Ian Jarvis and Paul Rees at Liverpool, and Patrick Greene, Diane Harris and Kathryn Wolstencroft at Manchester.

2 Several critics and academics have voiced such concern. See Hewison, R. (1987) *The Heritage Industry*, Methuen, London; and Lowenthal, D. (1985) *The Past is a Foreign Country*, Cambridge University Press.

3 Rolt, L.T.C. (1977) *Landscape with Canals*, Allen Lane, London.

4 See Stratton, M. 'Open and Industrial Museums: Windows onto a Lost World or Graveyards for Unloved Buildings?' in Hunter, M. (1996) *Preserving the Past: the Rise of Heritage in Modern Britain*, Alan Sutton, Stroud.

5 The top paying attraction was the Tower of London with 2,539,272 visitors. The best performing industrial or maritime attractions gained around 250,000 to 350,000 with Portsmouth's dockyards being the clear leader. Hanna, M. (1997) *English Heritage Monitor*, BTA/ETB Research Services, London, 44.

6 East Midlands Museum Service (1990) *Knowing Our Visitors*, EMMS, Nottingham, 7, 35–37.

7 English Heritage use a series of criteria to evaluate the importance of sites through their Monuments Protection Programme.

8 Samuel, R. (1994) *Theatres of Memory*, Verso, London.

9 Ironbridge Gorge Museum (1992) *Business Plan*, IGMT, Telford, 9.

10 Page, S. (1995) *Urban Tourism*, Routledge, London, 27.

11 Prentice, R. (1993) *Tourism and Heritage Attractions*, Routledge, London.

12 Ironbridge Gorge Museum (1996) *Annual Review*, IGMT, Telford, 11.

13 Johnson, P. & Thomas, B. (1992) *Tourism, Museums and the Local Economy: the Economic Impact of the North of England Open Air Museum at Beamish*, Edward Elgar, Aldershot.

14 Butler, S. (1992) *Science and Technology Museums*, Leicester University Press.

15 Prentice, R.C. (1995) 'Heritage as Formal Education', in Herbert, D.T. *Heritage, Tourism and Society*, Mansell, London, 146–169.

16 Ironbridge Gorge Museum (1992) *Primary Schools and Museums: Key Stage 2*, IGMT, Telford, 3.

17 Alfrey, J. & Putnam, T. (1992) *The Industrial Heritage*, Routledge, London.

18 Long, P. & Robinson, M. (1994) 'Industry Tourism in the City of Sunderland', *Insights*, (ETB) Case Study C-15–23.

19 Banham, R. (1973) 'Ironbridge Embalmed', *New Society*, 6 September, 587–8.

20 On the warehouse see Ritchie-Noakes, N. (1980) *Liverpool's Historic Waterfront*, Merseyside County Museums.

21 Thorne, R. (1986) 'Nautical Milestone', *The Architects' Journal*, 23 April.

22 Fitzgerald, R.S. (1980) *Liverpool Road Station, Manchester*, Manchester University Press.

23 Greene, J.P. (1995) 'An Archaeological Study of the 1830 Warehouse at Liverpool Road Station, Manchester', *Industrial Archaeology Review*, 17, no 2, 117–128.

24 EMMS op cit, 35–7.

25 (1997) *Museums Journal*, 97, no 10, 5.

26 Ironbridge Gorge Museum Trust (1997) *Business Plan and Budgets*, IGMT, Ironbridge, 1–7.

27 PLB Consulting (1998) *Public Access to England's Preserved Industrial Heritage: Research digest prepared for English Heritage*, PLB, Malton.

Part 3

International Initiatives

8.1
The former Eriksberg
shipyard in Gothenburg,
now with hotels,
restaurants, exhibition
halls and new housing.

Chapter eight

Old buildings for

new enterprises:

the Swedish approach

| Bo Öhrström

| Chalmers University of Technology

Background

West Sweden is a vital centre for Scandinavian trade and industry. Gothenburg, founded in 1621 as a free-port, is the node upon which a great deal of this industrial development has been focused during the nineteenth and twentieth centuries. The years after the 1960s became, however, a period of industrial decline in some sectors, most especially in the textile and shipbuilding industries.

Researchers from Workspace Design at Chalmers University of Technology in Gothenburg made attempts during the late 1970s to establish new knowledge about the terms and methods for regeneration of old industrial buildings and obsolete urban industrial environments. At the same time practitioners such as myself, mainly planners in the public sector, became engaged in the matters of new local economic development. Since then, in west Sweden progress in this field has been to a large extent characterized by a close interaction between practice and theory.

Research in this field of knowledge in the Gothenburg region was largely inspired by experiences from abroad, mainly due to direct personal contacts in Great Britain.[1] The examples inspired and created new objectives for our work. But the solutions and the modes of operations were further developed in an interplay between practice and theory. This chapter, based on a Licentiate Thesis[2] published by the author in 1997, aims at discussing some aspects of the findings of this work so far.

Learning in practice –
development of new knowledge

New practice was mainly developed through two cases, the former textile mills at Nääs 30 km east of Gothenburg and the shipyard areas on the north bank of the river Göta älv in Gothenburg *(see Figure 8.1, page 131)*.

The aims were to find methods to manage workspace development and regeneration of old industrial buildings through stimulation of new entrepreneurial enterprises and, at the same time, development of social activities in the local urban areas. As a result, the theme of this chapter is twofold. First, it is concerned with the nature and the terms of growth and localization of new, mainly knowledge-based enterprises. Secondly, the intention is to show how management of the buildings and specifically management of the planning, design and construction phases can be organized in order to support the origin and growth of enterprises and development of the local social system.

The initial phases of the regeneration of the former spinning mill at Nääs took place in the years between 1981 and 1986. The developer was the community of Lerum helped by researchers from Chalmers as well as Swedish management consultants[3] who added vital knowledge during the process. Later during the 1980s and 1990s a similar action was taken within the regeneration of the former Götaverken shipyard in Gothenburg. More recently experience has been gained through the restructuring of the major roller bearing manufacturer SKF's former production sites in Gothenburg.

The author, formerly a planning officer in Malmö in south Sweden and in Lerum near Gothenburg where the factory of Nääs is situated, acted from 1982 as a manager in the two projects that are discussed. From 1986 the practical part of the work has been organized as a private enterprise. My role as project manager required a great deal of co-operation with the researchers at Chalmers and in 1994 it became natural to join the University and as a researcher try to evaluate the experiences gained in practice.

The projects in Gothenburg also led to advising in development projects in small places in mid Sweden, which to some extent have lost their natural growth due to structural changes in the old industrial sector. The strategic issue in these places is to try to develop a new local economy, most often inspired by possibilities to re-use redundant buildings. But interest in dynamic development areas for new and small enterprises also resulted in my engagement in the early phases of the planning and construction of an incubator for university spin-off enterprises, the Stena Centre of Innovation at Chalmers, located in a former hospital on the outskirts of the campus area.

The key theme discussed in this chapter is that these, as it seems, very disparate projects, have a lot in common. They are all about transforming an old industrial society into a new knowledge-based economy using modern IT-based tools. But they also involve a focusing on the strengths arising from the development of a local arena for new economic and social initiatives based on new uses for the old buildings. Given the fact that the new content in some ways can be considered entrepreneurial, it seems that the methods of planning, design and construction of these new nodes of development require new working methods. Falk has for example suggested that there might exist a difference between what he calls institutional and entrepreneurial approaches.[4]

Many of the new economic activities are driven by communication in a wider sense, from the vital, personal dialogue between different actors, to computers, telephone systems and arrangements for IT. It is also reasonable to believe that methods for planning, design and construction are being reformed by the relatively recent introduction of these new aspects of the modern economy.

When the spinning mill at Nääs, formerly a major local employer, closed down in 1981, it was logical for me as a planning officer in the community of Lerum, to contact Chalmers for consultation. There was an urgent need for new and reasonably feasible methods to regenerate not only the old buildings, but also the entire surrounding urban structure, mainly built in the nineteenth century. In Sweden during the early 1980s there were hardly any examples showing systematic new ways to create an interaction between economic development and the handling of the physical environment. The examples from Great Britain provided new outlooks, stimulated inspiration and convinced local politicians that they were not alone in trying to find new ways to solve the problems. The existence of successful examples abroad, and the meeting with key persons in this process, gave confidence to try a new approach.

But the matter of 'how to do it' was not explicitly presented from the examples. It was obvious that it was the process of planning and carrying the project through that had to be reformed. At Nääs such new approaches were tested by the developer, the community of

Lerum, with support from the research team and the consultants.

The development of new working methods took place in an intense interaction between practice and theory. This arrangement has been of vital importance because it has highlighted the central research questions.[5] The research is based on cases conducted over many years and on terms defined more by reality than a research agenda. Reflection and conclusions have emerged subsequently.[6] Further discussion about different theoretical implications follows after a brief description of the cases.

In this chapter the development of knowledge chronologically starts with Nääs and continues with the shipyard areas in Gothenburg. The following discussion, however, takes its point of departure in the later, and more developed project. Some basic discussions of methodology will, however, be presented in the light of the Nääs project, where they were originally developed.

Local economic development based on urban regeneration

In the mid 1960s the world's largest production of tanker tonnage took place on the north bank of the river Göta älv in Gothenburg, in three (from 1965 four) shipyards, which faced the city centre to the south. In the mid 1980s there was hardly anything left of this production. Two of the four shipyards – Eriksberg and Lindholmen – had been closed down. At Götaverken a reduced repairing activity continued. The most modern shipyard, Arendal, still had limited production, mainly of platforms and equipment for the off-shore oil industry. Parts of the harbour between the shipyards were also exposed to the pressure of change, mainly due to the introduction of container traffic.

The situation called for a new approach, aimed at creating new urban life in the vast, redundant premises. The owners of the four shipyards – the Swedeyard Corporation – together with the city of Gothenburg, decided to initiate a new urban development programme within the area. The approach varied between different sites. At Eriksberg a huge new

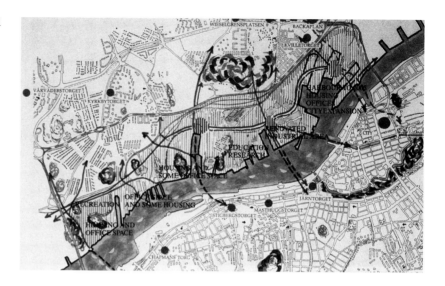

8.2
Master plan for part of Hisingen, Gothenburg.

(City Planning Authority, June 1989)

development with mixed offices, housing and visiting services took place. In Lindholmen the shipyard area was regenerated as a 'hotel' for different kinds of vocational training, within the concept of 'lifelong learning'. At Lundbystrand, the former Götaverken shipyard, a balanced incremental development strategy was implemented as a complement to heavy industrial production.

At Götaverken only small sections of more than 150,000 square metres of buildings were engaged in the shipyard's core production activities in the mid 1980s. Götaverken, with 5,000 employees in the 1960s, now had only 800 workers, a number to be further reduced in the early 1990s. Many of the buildings were empty or only partly in use. The area had been closed to the public since the Second World War. From the city's point of view, re-use of the area should be used to foster a new, sustainable economic structure, mainly in the 'third sector' of information industry, support services for production and small, creative enterprises.

The idea of 'balanced incremental development' has been described by URBED[7] after an analysis of more than ninety regeneration projects in Great Britain. They noted that successful regeneration has to go step by step, fulfilling the needs of local people in order to create a social balance and, as in gardening, taking care of all the opportunities of the place. This contrasts with the so called 'Big Bang' approach where the entire neighbourhood is reconstructed in one big step, often resulting in social alienation and the creation of isolated living areas with little or no connection with the surrounding society. Furthermore, this large-scale approach only seems to be able to create solutions within the area of new dwellings and to some extent large-scale commerce. Handling the field of new, sustainable economic life seems to be a much more complex task.

The approach of 'balanced incremental development', as it was implemented in Gothenburg before URBED's final formulation, was largely based on the ambition to establish a dialogue between users, facility managers, property owners and planners and to carry the project through step by step, taking care of quality issues when deciding the mix of new users. The on-site development organization became a key function as facilitator between practice and the planning and real estate system. Furthermore, the organization could become a powerful support function for the customers – the new enterprises.

Experiences from Nääs

The approach at Lundbystrand was a succession and a further development of experiences obtained in 1981–6 during the Nääs project, where an old spinning mill was used as a tool

for urban and economic regeneration of an industrial village in the countryside east of Gothenburg. Inspiration was found in the British examples of working communities, managed workspaces and re-use of redundant buildings.[8] This 'movement', as it could be described, was focused upon finding a new paradigm for arranging workplaces for knowledge-based small scale industry within the framework of existing resources.

The Nääs project thus aimed at an integration of the regeneration process with a management structure to foster a new spirit of entrepreneurship in the area. The buildings were used as a focus for the dialogue between the new users and planners. The work tried to give an answer to the questions of how to link planning, design and construction processes to neighbourhood development. After more than a year of preparations involving the local and regional administrative systems, a project could be formulated where the community could involve local creative persons and enterprises in an incremental development process, managed by an on-site project team working in the mill. The project manager was employed by the community. Most of the other persons were engaged specifically for the project or parts of it. The link between the ordinary political and administrative functions in the community and the local market was, to some extent, delegated to the local project management team.

The reason for this complex pattern of organization was the idea of user-involvement in the design brief of the individual workspace. The dialogue between the user and the development team, conducted directly on the 'factory floor', became the vital creative design method which conveyed the nerve of the project and secured its position in the market under the period of implementation.

In order to allow for this high degree of user involvement, the programme for the building was organized into four different layers: strategic, programming, layout and a customization level. This made it possible to run a locally initiated step-by-step process with a high degree of user-involvement in later stages of the process, whereas 'higher levels' of layers could be treated in a more traditional way. This approach was briefly formulated in a modified feasibility study, aimed at settling the borderlines between individual action and

responsibilities in the administrative system. This feasibility study in turn, was used as a basis for the building permit, postulating a purpose-designed organization for decisions during the period of phased construction, running over 3–4 years.

The problem, however, was the matter of how to activate the resources of the buildings among new users and potential entrepreneurs in the environment. In order to create this interplay with the surrounding society, people living in the village, together with a selected group of experts and artists, were invited to a creative workshop in the premises. The primary aim was to establish a social interaction and to foster a commitment among key persons.

A vital purpose of the meeting was to ask people to help the planners and the project management to establish a target picture for the future use of the area. Approximately 150 people worked together to create a bank of new and often radical thoughts about the future. Even the former director of the spinning mill – in 1982 he was more than 90 years old and the fourth generation of the original founders of the mills – took part in the event. A majority of the sixty-seven statements which could be formulated at the end of the evening were all very realistic and probably most of them were grounded in the participants' own visions and judgements of existing possibilities. The proposals were classified into different groups of interest – industry, small enterprises, arts, tourism etc. – and the audience formed working groups within each of them.

The project office was established in one of the former production spaces – an area of 1,500 square metres. In total the entire works of Nääs consisted of 15,000 square metres of floor space and 63,000 square metres of beautifully located land, by the shore of the lake Sävelången and facing the castle of the first mill owners on the other side of the water. The project office was open for visitors at any time of the day and the people who took part in the first event were invited to visit the project group whenever they wanted.

A self-aid programme for unemployed young people was developed as one part of the project. Part of the group grasped the opportunity to work with cleaning and fixing up the premises. Gradually this involvement developed into servicing the new enterprises, which sometimes had the effect that the young people developed contacts leading them into employment. The self-aid scheme influenced the set-up of the whole project.

The practice of taking part in the urban development activities on many levels, from the opportunity to design and sometimes even build a workspace under guidance from the professionals in the development team, to the action of, for example, arranging an arts exhibition in the vast premises or to discuss a project for new housing, created a sense of local mobilization.

Four years after the first creative action planning workshop the results were monitored. The factories were by this time housing more than sixty new enterprises or social activities and employing more than 150 people. 80 per cent of the enterprises had been established under the project period, mainly by people living up to 15 km from Nääs. Many of the enterprises were based on handicrafts, for example sewing, carpentry and furniture repairing. But there were creative professions as well, such as artists, photographers and video studios, working close to engineers, salespeople and mechanics. A great deal of the enterprises had customers or suppliers within the area. Others co-operated in more informal patterns. The main reasons for being at the place were of course low rent and other practical aspects. But a majority also mentioned the social environment, the 'spirit of Nääs', as a vital factor for business success.

Of the sixty-five ideas originally presented in 1982, forty-seven could be stated as completed when the project was monitored in 1986. This had happened without conscious checks. It was primarily, we believe, a result of an open process where ideas became common goods, to be conducted by the most suited or motivated people.

The process described has on one hand a highly institutionalized structure, represented by the project owners' management routines and the organization of decisions within the local administrative system. On the other hand it has given an unusual freedom for individual entrepreneurs to influence the outcome of the design and construction processes, primarily via work on their own premises, secondarily via the social process this engagement resulted in.

8.4
A textile handicrafts
workshop at Nääs.

The project was rooted in the political and administrative management of the local community, with on-site representation through the project manager and the development team. With specified routines of how to manage change, it was possible to delegate much of the development force 'down' in the system in a highly informal process, based on a dialogue with people who really cared about the future economy within the local region. Thus, local entrepreneurs could use regeneration as an opportunity to start their own enterprises, or to initiate other collective activities such as show-rooms for art and enterprises or training courses.

Today, fifteen years after the project was initiated, the village around the factories is again a lively community. The factories themselves have gone through different stages of commercial development. Younger families, largely with a modern 'working market and educational code' have moved into new or refurbished housing in the surroundings.

So far, the process described has been presented as more or less unproblematic. However, conflicts arising from the different approach have been part of the daily work. The political discussions were lively during the early stages of the project. Later on the entrepreneurial approach challenged different groups. However, on the whole, the project could be brought to a successful realization in 1986, mostly due to massive support from local enthusiasts, customers and the local political and administrative system.

After this initial build-up phase, the community of Lerum had an ambition to establish a more formalized organization for the project. Somehow, these contrasting, more institutional ideas of how to operate the site almost jeopardized the venture. After a couple of years the project was sold to a private real estate company, which gradually learned how to manage this kind of entrepreneurial project. Today, they seem to be able to pursue the role as a locally-based driving force. The transition indicates that the problem is not the artefact. It is rather the process.

Lundbystrand

At Lundbystrand, the former Götaverken shipyard – on the north bank of the river Göta älv and facing the city centre of Gothenburg on the south bank only 300 metres away – methods inspired from Nääs were applied. Because of the magnitude of this project and a radically different commercial situation, the approaches had to be further developed and adjusted.

Götaverken was, like many other enterprises in the early history of Gothenburg, founded by the Scots, in this specific case by the Kieller and Gibson families. Originally the shipyard was situated in today's city centre, but around 1860 they moved over the river to vacant land on the

island of Hisingen on the northern bank. More
than 800 ships were built in this location. In
1965 a new and very modern shipyard,
Arendal, was constructed further out along the
river. After that, Götaverken's old site was only
used for boat repairs.

In the mid 1960s Gothenburg was a leading
producer of tankers, organized in four
shipyards located within sight of each other
along the riverside. During the 1970s demand
for big tankers fell and, at the same time,
competition from Asian producers increased.
One after another the shipyards closed down
and one of the most significant industries in
Gothenburg was largely lost. Roughly 17,000
people lost their jobs and the city had
enormous amounts of vacant land to fill with
new activity. In total, more than 250 hectares of

centrally located land (approximately 625 acres)
was exposed to pressure for regeneration.

Initially, the city and the landowner together
produced target documents and images
showing a new town at the waterfront having
room for approximately 20,000 people. After
that, the different sites were developed
individually, with specific profiles, expressed in
individual ways of finding new users. Each part
of the area set up their own development
organizations and had to make results and
finance these, normally in separate or
subsidiary companies.

Götaverken is perhaps the shipyard with the
greatest amount of buildings that could be re-
used. But because of their size many of those
buildings required specific attention.
Lundbystrand, however, was originally just a

marginal part of the shipyard, located in the south-west fringe of the huge area. Initially the project consisted of four buildings of understandable proportions with about 18,000 square metres of floor space in total. The buildings had been used for service functions, such as metalwork, carpentry and stores. The more complicated buildings have been, or will be, regenerated in later stages of the process.

A renewal process was initiated in 1987. The process aimed at refurbishing the buildings step-by-step, considering the new users' individual needs and desires, but checked against a masterplan which defined structures, technical solutions and finance. The idea of the Lundbystrand project was to meet the top-down formulated targets with a bottom-up development perspective. The focus was on new, small enterprises and the aim was to open up the area to the market and to attract bigger projects in the later stages.

In 1987, when the project started, the shipyard area had a range of declining enterprises related to ship building, all of them stemming from Götaverken shipyard. The impression was that many of those had severe economic problems, all concerned with the need to find new markets for their highly skilled technicians and 'high tech' products. On the site, only one company existed without connections with the shipyard. It was a small firm specializing in repairing roofs. For natural reasons they had a major local market.

Having established the first office for the Lundbystrand project – two small rooms and a coffee area – in one of the buildings, in August 1987 a creative evening was organized with people related to the shipyard, planners, the real estate company and some old friends who were curious about the project. This early creative event was used as the starting point of a process aiming at marketing the area and creating new contacts.

One early result was that a new enterprise with four enthusiastic marine engineers was established. They wanted to rent the project office, mainly because of its nice coffee area. Very soon colleagues joined them in adjacent offices, many of those refurbished as new project rooms. Soon artists found their way to the interesting shipyard and 'squatted' in some rougher parts of the buildings with the result that the area became more well known in the

city. Altogether, the project office had to move more than ten times under the period of regeneration, every time caused by new tenants, wanting to rent the premises. All activities were supported by simple information materials, telling about the successful new inhabitants.

Still however, the area had severe access problems. The old ferry crossing the river between the city and Götaverken was scheduled to serve shipyard workers at times when no artist and hardly any consultant would go to work. The area had for security reasons been shut off from the rest of the city since the Second World War and ordinary people had long ago forgotten the joy of approaching the riverside. Public transport, to the extent it existed, was oriented parallel with the river, and hardly ever made contact with the frontages.

There was a demand for an entirely new solution to the transport problem. The entrepreneurial directors of the land-owning companies started on their own initiative a new shipping company with two fast-going smaller ferries connecting the two sides of the river in a zigzag pattern (see Figure 8.6). Today these ferries are being operated by the public transport authority of Gothenburg.

Having opened the area in this way, it was easier to convince office-people to move into the premises. As a landmark and a symbol for the new era, an old warehouse, close to the former main entrance, was converted into an exclusive office for one of the remaining shipyard related companies. Altogether, the project resulted in an inflow of new companies, most of whom were newly established. In 1992 more than ninety new activities had moved into the area, representing a range from artists and rock groups to rapidly expanding high-technology companies.

In order to find solutions for one of the really huge buildings, a former Plate Shop of 14,000 square metres and 14 metres interior height, a programming activity was launched, supported by DEGW and URBED from England. The aim was to develop a new user-oriented programme, partly via a dialogue with the industry about modern production concepts, mainly focusing on the possibilities of joint localization of different subcontractors for product design. In two workshops about

8.6
The new ferries
between the city and the
north bank of Göta älv.

*(Photo: Eriksbergs
Förvaltnings AB)*

seventy people representing bigger companies like Volvo, Swedish Telecom and the banks, came together with representatives from the community, the planning system and the universities, in order to work with new ideas for the building and the area.

Later, and related to this process, a major part of the building was found suitable for a handball and sports arena. The adjacent Lindholmen shipyard, converted into a school, played a vital role, and, together with the handball clubs and the community of Gothenburg, they successfully managed to create a package of finance which made the project feasible.

Today, many years after the programming activities and after the financial crisis that shocked Sweden in 1992, it is obvious that industry is beginning to find the area of value. Among others, different support functions in the Volvo sphere have been established at Lundbystrand, often finding the specific characters of the buildings appropriate for

different highly-specialized functions. For example the IT-intense, but also space-consuming production of spare-part catalogues for Volvo Trucks, has been located in the area. Recently the communication company Ericsson has decided to establish itself on one of the old quays near Lundbystrand.

Altogether the first stage of the regeneration process, focused on four medium sized buildings, generated more than ninety new enterprises employing 150–200 people. The new enterprises were mainly engineers, consultants, some specialized handicrafts, IT and media. Ten years after the start of the regeneration programme 2,000–2,500 people have their daily work in the former Götaverken area. Some buildings have been refurbished, while others could be used as they were. The shipyard Cityvarvet is once again successfully running its business as repairers. Other parts of the former shipyard, like the motor works, and the steam technology division, are developing well in new economic constellations. One of the new small entrepreneurial companies has grown enormously and is today European head office for an American corporation. Many others have developed in quality or organized their growth in networks based on joint locations in different parts of the buildings.

The example shows that, although IT theoretically makes it possible to locate activities far away from each other, the strength of the visible urban area, almost as a contradiction, seems to be even more outspoken. This phenomenon is most obviously expressed in the interior layout in the buildings designed for small and entrepreneurial enterprises. First, the layout is 'transparent' in the sense that it is always possible so see what happens inside the offices when using the corridor. Secondly, the area is equipped with jointly-used coffee areas and meeting rooms, one on each corridor, forming the infrastructure needed to support the growth of an intense interaction between different companies and professionals. Actually, this structure has formed the basis for an intense network activity between smaller units, all working with different aspects of information.

Of the original 150,000 square metres of floor space in the former Götaverken shipyard, mostly vacant in 1986, approximately 40,000 square metres has been rebuilt. More than 85 per cent of the premises are now in use again. In 1987 there were only nine trees in the whole area. Today 1,200–1,300 new trees have been planted. The subsidiary company of Eriksberg that owns and runs the Lundbystrand area has a high turnover and is giving profit to its owner.

8.7
The coffee-areas form a base for co-operation.

Changed conditions for production as input for work space planning

In Nääs and other urban regeneration areas approached via these methods, the result has been the development of new activities and employment which supports the change of the areas from run-down and declining industrial districts into 'Post-Fordist' activity. The new economy is often based in a local and information-dependent structure, sometimes in co-existence with up-graded industrial activities, new housing and new services. Particularly in the early stages, the on-site development organization has been the driving force in facilitating the urban development process. The tasks in the group are defined to cope with the whole range of issues, from local co-ordination of urban planning and development strategies to building and construction services, supporting the growth of new economic and cultural activities, and, most importantly, to managing a new kind of workplace, specifically designed for the new locally-based knowledge industry. Partly due to the participation in the creative processes, related to the planning and design activities, a spirit of co-operation and entrepreneurship has emerged.

This issue of urban development raises the question of whether we can see a growing new planning and development paradigm, connected with the need for new types of production environments as a result of changing production methods and the use of information technology.

Product innovation and new development is becoming an increasingly important factor for competition under the pressure of economic globalization. The demand seems to have become even more individualized and increasing parts of the production are organized in so-called 'batches of one'. Competitive advantages are connected rather with the collective knowledge of how to develop new products, than with the products themselves. The Swedish managing director of ABB, Percy Barnevik, has said that products can be imitated, processes can not. So-called dynamic systems give not only the answer to a problem, but they also create possibilities for learning, and raise the organization's ability to solve problems. To see the production as a process, rather than as the sum of a series of isolated actions, could actually be the difference that brings in quite new development dynamics. In complex systems, the steps have to be smaller and more of the development has to be customer-oriented.

Altogether, these changes are related to, or have major effects on, the pattern of communication. The more complicated the issues of production tend to be, the bigger is the need for dialogue. The Swedish geographer Gunnar Törnqvist claims that it is not the flow of information that is the strategic issue, but rather the ability to combine pieces of information in new patterns.[9] In this way, it is possible to create what he calls an 'administrated holism'. In contrast with mass production, big scale does not seem to solve the problems of efficiency in the knowledge-based economy. The terms of progress are participation and dialogue. This naturally excludes large groups and large-scale organizations. The solution to this problem is breaking down the organizations into smaller units.

All these changes affect the way people think about the environment. As a cause for high productivity in urban regions, 'external economies' are sometimes mentioned as a vital factor. It explains how companies can gain advantages by being close to other activities. Industrial districts like Manchester in the nineteenth century or Silicon Valley today are well known examples of this phenomenon. Törnqvist[10] has even pointed out that competitive advantages are gained if competing companies are located within sight of each other.

Production units also tend to be more dependent on external partners and subcontractors. For reasons of efficiency, those companies tend to strive for closer, geographic links. In Japan, for example, the average distance between the main factory and the sub-contractor is about 30 kilometres. In Sweden it has been up to 500 kilometres.[11] This pattern is now about to be changed. Volvo's new subcontractors' village at the former Arendal shipyard, just around the corner from their own main industrial location, is an example on this tendency of spatial concentration.

The discussion of spatial aspects of productivity, mainly conducted by geographers

and economists, is the starting point of a discussion of how we arrange the workplace. New concepts like 'science parks', 'working communities' and 'managed workspaces' occur. Most of these new concepts represent a change in the market following the shift of needs from rational large-scale production sites to dynamic and creative, knowledge processing workplaces.

In fact, studies of places well known for their creative capacity, for example Vienna between 1870 and 1930, show interesting characteristics also pointed out by Törnqvist.[12] Much of the dynamic in such places is dependent on the ability to create new interesting contacts. In order to do so, you have to be in a place with accumulated, interesting competences. This space should be organized in a way that raises the chances for unexpected meetings so that specialists can collaborate in each other's work. The examples from Nääs and Lundbystrand indicate that these mechanisms are a vital imperative for development today, at least concerning the small, information dependent enterprises.

The arena perspective as a planning paradigm

The main issue of the work with new economic development nodes is the focus on the 'place'. This implies a somewhat different approach from the planning issue. Again, the Swedish geographers Hägerstrand and Törnqvist[13] give us guidance, with their ideas of an *arena* as the basis for local action, as opposed to the traditionally used *systems* point of view.

The difference is, in short, that the systems view is based on the assumption of the professionals as experts with a 'global' range, each one within a defined field of knowledge, no one taking full responsibility for the whole in the local context. This way of looking upon things, merely governed by abstract thinking, has dominated the social sciences since the 1950s.

The arena-perspective for action on the other hand, is based on the idea of the old landscape-oriented concept of knowledge. Within the boundaries of a local place, a defined arena or meeting-place, the whole range of questions – global as well as local – can be handled or at least discussed together with the users and the dwellers. Planners, designers, architects, facility managers, property owners, as well as building workers and interested tenants or local people, can utilize their insights both as professionals and 'human beings' within a process defined by its space and its target.

While the systems approach is connected with the notion of human 'range', the arena perspective instead should be connected with the idea of human 'reach'. Range should then be understood as the ability to grasp all aspects of a specific matter globally, whereas reach should be seen as a person's ability to understand a local, sometimes complex context, historically, socially and as an expression of a specific culture. Most people today integrate both these aspects of life, but normally the former is used in the professional life and the latter in private. The issue for development projects is to unite the two perspectives, with focus on a specific place.

This way of looking at things has connections with the Norwegian planning theoretician Tore Sager's proposal[14] of combining the ideas of synoptic planning with those of incremental planning, under the influence and guidance of *reflection-in-action*.[15] Sager's point of view is that neither synoptic or 'blueprint' planning, nor incremental planning, defined as 'the science of muddling through' seems appropriate. The first one because it represents an idealistic view of how changes happen, the latter one because of the risks of lack of direction. Instead Sager proposes a combination of the two, where the dialogue between users and planners works as a joint instrument and a tool to keep direction under continuous re-formulation, or adjustment of the goals in the project. Often, these methods assume the presence of a facilitator who is able to organize the process of dialogue between different levels in the system. Thus, the already mentioned concept of 'balanced incremental development'[16] also could be understood within a theoretical framework familiar to the research groups at Chalmers.

Construction consequences of balanced incremental development

This process of phased, small-scale and user-oriented re-development, with a series of limited construction projects within the frame of a larger urban development programme, postulates a high degree of local decision making, integrated within a superior system of real estate economy, planning and authorities' decisions. Local IT systems are a vital instrument to govern this kind of process, with an increasing number of participants the longer the process continues.

In the late 1980s a research project in the School of Economics at the University of Gothenburg studied different designs of information systems. It was then possible to distinguish between the traditionally centralized information systems, whose main role is to feed top management with information, from local information systems whose role mainly is to support the actors. The introduction of small personal computers in the mid 1980s made it possible to handle and process large amounts of information in small batches on the floor of the workshop, virtually by carrying the computers around on the working site. The information system used applications of standard programmes, designed to support the management, the users and the real estate company in easy ways, under the sometimes turbulent process of user-involvement in designing serviced spaces for new enterprises.

The advantage of these decentralized information systems is the possibility to link all individually designed, specific issues with an overall structure of the construction activities. It is also possible, and even easy, to relate professional information about economic and technical issues with questions concerning enterprises, people and the social aspects of the development process. The notion of 'administrated holism' mentioned earlier suddenly becomes a very practical and necessary tool to control a complex and fast moving process. The idea of creativity seems to demand a high degree of local information processing in order to satisfy the need for decision making in the de-centralized process. The information must not only provide the local actors with information, but it should also be congruent with the need for information at higher levels in the system.

In a sense, the IT-equipped focal point apparent on the site also serves as a window to a 'new world' in old industrial areas, and a living illustration of possible new ways to work. IT is a vital service for project management, but in a wider sense it also promotes the use of new technologies in the area, and thereby project management methods, at least initially, have secondary effects, showing new techniques for new kinds of locally based enterprises.

By co-ordinating a wide range of activities under the overall ambition to create a locally-based learning process, the on-site development group serves as a kind of a general purpose organization for local development, based on the fact that sustainable development strategies should be grounded and manifested in changes in the physical infrastructure.

The knowledge producing system

Local development management, as used in the described ways, is a field of knowledge running vertically through established structures. Vital parts of the discussion have their origins in an urban planning perspective, but central issues come from the fields of management, architecture, economy and construction. Furthermore, the research at Chalmers has in these cases taken the approach of action-research, based on existing projects.

The work has to pay attention to matters on several levels in the system at the same time – planning, design, architecture, construction and finance to mention some – and to bring these different worlds of action to co-operate in harmony under a long period of development and under conditions that from time to time change, due to circumstances arising in the dialogue with customers. The conception of an arena for the action is thereby helpful in order to understand the approach and to discuss it in relation with other system oriented views of urban planning.

The ambition to work under a continuous design dialogue with the users has a social side-effect, which in the long run could be shown as one of the main means. The users have been trained via the design activities into a new social context, where it seems natural to continue to co-operate. The development management organization also serves as a training group for this new pattern which is necessary for those new enterprises competing in the market of knowledge and information to adopt.

The idea of taking part in the projects as a professional, and then to reflect on them as a researcher, has been practised in many disciplines. As an example it has been discussed by the Swedish economy-researcher Einar Gummesson.[17] His point is that the access to the field of knowledge in development projects is intensely linked with the inner circles of decisions. The role as an external researcher does not satisfy this need. This way of trying to generate theory from practice has similarities with Glaser and Strauss' discussions of grounded theory.[18] They argue that theories should be grounded on data from the reality, rather than being governed by traditional theories or theoretical ways of thinking. Donald Schön[19] as well, claims that the knowledge of professionals can be developed first if it is made interpretable to them. Gummesson uses the term 'action research' to be considered as a variant of case studies. These processes, he argues, are teleological, that is they aim at guiding companies or processes in specific directions.

The discussion so far has aimed at pointing out some common factors behind the re-structuring process in parts of the economy, leading us to question whether there exists a broader need to create a new type of workplace, some sort of new infrastructure, to support our wishes of a growing new economy. It has already been discussed that the terms of production in many of our new information based companies creates new demands concerning the workplace product as well as concerning the processes under which these new workplaces are created. The links between urban and economic development seem to be very close and, in order to gain best effects, focus has to be on both at the same time. In contradiction with our tradition to become specialized in segments and parts of problems, we now seem to need the capacity and the skills to handle a broader spectrum of matters, expressed within the framework of a territory which can be understood and reached by individuals.

Continuous work

These insights have led us to act in different fields in Sweden, all based on the same tradition of knowledge. For example, key-people from innovative re-development projects recently have been interviewed under the assumption that there is a need for some sort of national network which supports the development of knowledge between projects with similar points of departure. The network activity, aimed at creating a 'learning link' via IT, is conducted with financial support from the Swedish Council for Building Research. So far it has resulted in a number of action-planning events in different places in Sweden, all focused upon the role of redundant physical structures, for example barracks and old industrial areas, for local economic development.

University spin-off activities, mainly as part of regional development strategies, are another field of interest. Recently we have conducted a forum for discussions between different parties interested in this specific field, in order to better understand the links between the development of the physical environment and the organizational growth of new ventures.

The Chalmers research environment, connected with urban economic development and management of facilities, has a long tradition. Different people have individually developed specific angles within the field.[20] The links with practice are traditionally strong. However, the Swedish tradition of local co-operation and adult education forms a base for the action, combined with a new view of workplace concepts. This tradition can easily form a base for a development influenced by international scientists such as Patsy Healey[21] or John Forester[22] in their discussion of dialogue and user participation as a concept for local development. Continuously, new projects are initiated where researchers from Chalmers form 'facilitating teams' in difficult planning situations where users, real estate representatives and planners together try to create a breakthrough for new ways of working. For this purpose we use the support of design theory to form methods and processes for reflection in action. The intersection between theory and the practice of planning and design within the discussed field can and will open new views of how different parts of the system can be brought to co-operate with and influence each other in synergetic ways.

The projects discussed have all focused on small scale step-by-step solutions within a framework of larger development projects. Thinking about these projects today it would be wrong to claim that all the results occurred in this kind of process. On the contrary, it is obvious that sustainable development requires a combination of different approaches. In the early stages, small and new enterprises including artists and voluntary organizations are a vital and easily mobilized force. Later in the process however, it is the more established and bigger interests that form the structure of the projects. There is not a single formula. It is more about the ability to work with both worlds and not to lose the multi-dimensional aspects of the field of successful regeneration. As one of the managing directors of the north bank project pointed out, in order to conduct a sustainable new urban environment the tools have to be both tweezers and bulldozers.

To establish a further understanding of these complex matters of urban and economic development, the aim is to continue the studies of the north bank regeneration project in Gothenburg, in an intense co-operation between the owners, the planners and the research at Chalmers.

Notes and references

1 The researchers were Professor Joen Sachs, Jan Åke Granath, Lisbeth Birgersson and Trad Wrigglesworth in the Department of Workspace Design at Chalmers. Since the early 1980s the London-based researchers and consultants Nicholas Falk, URBED and John Worthington, DEGW have had frequent contacts with the group in Gothenburg.

2 Öhrström, B. (1997) *Building Enterprises. Planning, Construction and Workspace Management Supporting Entrepreneurship*, Chalmers University of Technology, Gothenburg.

3 The management consultants were KRESAM and The Fore Sight Group, specializing in learning processes and so-called 'intra-preneurship'.

4 Department of the Environment (1987) *Managing Workspaces. Case Studies in Good Practice in Urban Regeneration*, HMSO, London.

5 Clark, P.A. (1972) *Action research and organisational change*, Harper & Row, London.

6 See for example Scriven, M. (1969) 'The Methodology of Evaluation' In: I.R.W. Tyler (ed.) *Perspectives of Curriculum Evaluation*, Rand McNally, Chicago.

7 Falk, N. (1992) *Industrial Renaissance. A Practical Strategy for Regenerating Gothenburg's North Bank*, URBED, London. Also in Swedish: Öhrström, B., Riise, J., & Törsäter, T. (1993) *A Program for Regenerating the Plate Shop at Lundbystrand*, Industriförnyelse, Göteborg. (English summary).

8 See Department of the Environment (1987) op. cit. and Department of the Environment (1987) *Re-Using Redundant Buildings. Good Practice in Urban Regeneration*. HMSO, London.

9 See for example Törnqvist, G. (1991) *Svenskt näringsliv i ett geografiskt perspektiv*, Liber, Stockholm. (In Swedish).

10 See for example Törnqvist, G. (1989) *Kreativitetens geografi*, SNS Företag och samhälle nr 2–89 and Törnqvist, G. (1996) *Sverige i nätverkens Europa*, Liber Hermods, Malmö. (In Swedish).

11 Vedin, B.A. (1993) *Nätverk för produktion och kunskap*, Liber Hermods, Malmö. (In Swedish).

12 Janik, A. & Toumlin, S. (1973) *Wittgensteins Wien*, Doxa, Lund. (In Swedish). See also Törnqvist, G, *Kreativitetens geografi*. (In Swedish).

13 Hägerstrand, T. & Törnqvist, G. (1980) *Om behovet av helhetssyn i forskning och planering*, Svensk geografisk årsbok 1980. (In Swedish).

14 Sager, T. (1994) *Communicative Planning Theory*, Avebury, Aldershot.

15 Schön, D. (1983) *The Reflective Practitioner: How Professionals think in action*. Basic Books, New York.

16 Falk, (1992) op. cit.

17 Gummesson, E. (1985) *Forskare och konsult – om aktionsforskning och fallstudier i företagsekonomin*. Studentlitteratur, Lund. (In Swedish).

18 Glaser, B.G. & Strauss, A.L. (1967) *The Discovery of Grounded Theory: Strategies for Qualitative Research*. Aldine de Gruyter, New York.

19 Schön, (1983) op. cit.

20 Most of this work has been conducted by researchers in the Department of Workspace Design under Professor Joen Sachs. See for example Birgersson, L. (1996) *Att bygga mening och rum*, Chalmers University of Technology, Gothenburg. (English summary).

21 Healey, P. (1992) 'Planning through debate. The communicative turn in planning theory'. *Town Planning Review* 63 (2) 143–162.

22 Forester, J. (1989) *Planning in the Face of Power*, University of California Press, Berkeley.

Further reading

DEGW & Technibank (1992) *The Intelligent Building in Europe*, DEGW, Milan.

Worthington, J. (1992) *Workplace Design for the Knowledge Industry*, DEGW, London.

Chapter nine

The adaptive re-use of industrial buildings is becoming increasingly validated as the debate over sustainability and brownfield versus greenfield development moves higher up the European political agenda.

The Ruhrgebiet, Germany's industrial heartland, has reflected this trend with many inventive examples of this phenomenon: the Emscher Technology Park, Duisburg; the Essen design museum and the Oberhausen retail centre. The Ruhrgebiet, an economically depressed area, has nevertheless benefited greatly from the proximity of cities such as Düsseldorf, Essen and Cologne, cities that had significant critical mass of commerce and culture to underpin such regenerative schemes.

The fall of the Berlin wall brought with it the inheritance of another industrial heartland in the East and very different problems. Several years after German reunification, it is easy to forget the sheer scale and pace of the regeneration of East Germany and its transformation from one socio-political system to another.

In the early 1990s, West German scepticism about *Deutsche Einheit* was perhaps fuelled by new federal government legislation, such as the *Solidaritätszuschlag*, a 5 per cent income tax surcharge (payable in the West only), to help fund its DM 90 billion annual investment plans for the East. At the time, the daily roll-call of bankrupt East German industries, environmental catastrophes, corruption and rising unemployment (beyond 17 per cent), meant that many Germans could have been forgiven for questioning such an enormous undertaking.

As more new federal government incentives were introduced, such as a 50 per cent tax reduction on all new construction completed in the East by 1995, initial scepticism gave way to a vigorous sense of urgency and new-frontierism. East Germany soon became the 'Klondike' of the late twentieth century and, in the subsequent boom, a burgeoning free market system was thrust upon the largely unprepared people of the *Neue Bundesländer*.

Whilst much attention was focused on grandiose plans in Berlin, the city of Jena, although outside the mainstream arena, had a nonetheless impressive agenda.

Regeneration in the *Neue Bundesländer*:

Carl Zeiss, Jena (1991–6)

Philip Tidd ▮

DEGW

Economic, social and historical background

Jena had become synonymous with the names of Carl Zeiss and Ernst Abbe, the two founders of the renowned optics manufacturing firm established in 1846. In the late eighteenth century Zeiss and Abbe did much more than turn Jena into the 'centre of nineteenth-century high-tech'. While their microscopes, binoculars and rifle sights were earning German precision mechanics a high reputation around the world, Zeiss and Abbe were pioneering the welding of social welfare to free enterprise. They wrote into the corporate statute their work force's rights to adequate pensions, paid vacations and the eight-hour working day.

This industrial and intellectual legacy managed somehow to survive over time. Prosperous under Prussia, Imperial Germany, the rise of National Socialism, and the Second World War, ownership of Carl Zeiss Jena was eventually divided up by the Allies at the end of the War. Under the division of Germany by the four powers act, the State of Thuringia was initially to find itself in the American sector, only in 1945 to become occupied by the Russians. Carl Zeiss Jena was then divided up by the ensuing political realities of the Cold War. The Americans established *Zeiss Hohenkocken*, near Stuttgart, which benefited from post-war Marshall Plan investment, whilst the Russians retained the remnants of the company. In this process, the *Kombinat* Carl Zeiss Jena was largely stripped of its skilled workforce and best machinery by both the American and Russian forces, but was reassembled as a state enterprise or *Volks Eigene Betrieb (VEB)* by the German Democratic Republic (GDR). In 1989, Carl Zeiss Jena employed 27,000 people in a city with a population of 100,000 – the city *was* Zeiss.

Through forty years of East Germany's command economics and rigid centralism, Carl Zeiss Jena, despite continued under-investment, had tenaciously managed to survive to become universally acknowledged as one of the largest and best precision-optical manufacturers in the world. It was the GDR's jewel-in the-crown and became a high technology benchmark of the Eastern Bloc countries.

Following German reunification, Zeiss Jena found itself living on borrowed time. The sudden collapse of the Soviet Union's *ComEcon* system meant that the company lost 80 per cent of its sales overnight. The divergence of Zeiss Jena's technology was soon identified to be irreconcilable with that of the Carl Zeiss Group in the West. The former *Kombinat*'s traditional optics products and exclusive rights to the Zeiss trademark were once more transferred to the West. Jena was subsequently left with now redundant factories awash with toxic waste and few marketable products left to its name. As a consequence, most of the Jena *Werke* were to be quickly decommissioned.

Upon re-unification, the German privatization trust, the *Treuhandanstalt*, took over Carl Zeiss Jena, and a new company, JenOptik AG, was formed in December 1991, assuming ownership of all the Jena plants and their workforce. Dr Lothar Späth, the former high-profile Prime Minister of Baden-Württemberg, was handed the difficult stewardship of JenOptik as its newly appointed chairman. On 31 December 1991, Späth was left with little room for manoeuvre and had to shed 17,500 of the workforce.

Fortuitously for Jena, the deal with *Treuhandanstalt* also included a federal government dowry of DM 3 billion and a clear social commitment by JenOptik to create 10,000 new jobs over five years. Government subsidies quickly evaporated however, as DM 1 billion went in writing off the old debts of the *Kombinat*, DM 900 million covering redundancy and pension costs of laid-off Zeiss employees, leaving DM 1.1 billion for rebuilding the company. JenOptik's aim to re-engineer the main industry and create a 'High-Tech Centre in the heart of Germany' included a re-engineering of the city itself; such was the extent of Zeiss land ownership.

Perhaps the most important challenge facing the *Treuhandanstalt* was how to transform former East German *Kombinate* – where everything was produced by the organization itself – into businesses that could compete in an open and free-market environment. One solution was to transform *Kombinate* into technology parks. Jena, a community that was always half *Kombinat* (Carl Zeiss Jena) and half Technical University, was designated as a technological city. The approach for regeneration was based on research capabilities that could generate revenue through new products and create jobs for a highly skilled local workforce.

Späth's high media-profile brought valuable airtime to many in the East who viewed Carl Zeiss Jena's regeneration as a test-case for the social and economic potential of reunification.

DEGW's introduction and first steps

9.2
The *Hauptwerk* occupied a 3-hectare block bifurcating the old city centre.

In July 1991, Dr. Späth invited DEGW to inspect Carl Zeiss Jena's *Hauptwerk*, its main production facility. The site occupied a

3-hectare city centre block with 125,000 square metres of production space, bifurcating the old city centre. It was the most prominent of Zeiss's four production facilities in Jena.

The *Hauptwerk* was the site where Zeiss had been founded some 150 years previously and is situated at Jena's epicentre. Of the four main Zeiss plants in Jena, the *Hauptwerk* was the oldest and least modernized. While it defined Carl Zeiss Jena's character and represented a tangible source of civic pride, the site was destined not to survive the intensive restructuring plans that JenOptik was having to force through. The site had grown over a 140-year period by accretion rather than to any defined plan, yet contained many fine examples of early German reinforced concrete industrial architecture. Part of DEGW's preliminary work was to undertake an extensive appraisal of the entire building stock, evaluating each building in turn.

The buildings on the *Hauptwerk* were assessed initially using three broad criteria:

▌ *Condition* – many older buildings on the site had suffered extensive war damage and forty years of a scant and neglectful maintenance regime. Structural integrity had also been compromised in many buildings by deleterious chemicals used during the glass-making process.

▌ *Heritage* – the entire *Hauptwerk* was under a *Denkmalschutz* (conservation) order. This was a 'blanket' order however, and had not been objectively assessed or challenged as is possible under the German planning system.

▌ *Adaptability* – the key to assessing the refurbishment/new-build potential was to evaluate the robustness of the existing buildings and how they could accommodate changes of use.

In beginning to evaluate the buildings' suitability to accommodate new uses and users, it became increasingly apparent that an ill-defined and changing pattern of supply and demand was emerging in the new markets of East Germany.

Testing, researching, 'inventing' the brief

DEGW's work began by gaining a comprehensive understanding of the building stock and site conditions of the *Hauptwerk*. Fortunately, all the Zeiss *Werke* had enormous archives of construction drawings, specifications, photographs and data covering the entire estate.

While the general appearance of the *Hauptwerk* was one of a large factory, the site actually comprised many different types of buildings abutting each other but clearly sub-divided with party walls. The archive department had meticulously catalogued every building and each was named according to its year of construction, hence *Bau* 10 & 13 were built in 1910 and 1913 respectively, for example.

A comprehensive building appraisal document was then drawn up to assess each building in turn. The same criteria of condition, heritage value and adaptability were applied to evaluate the proportion of the site that could accommodate adaptive re-use against that which would require demolition and rebuilding.

DEGW's work then began in earnest on two parallel fronts: to produce an initial 'masterplan vision' and to establish a redevelopment brief. The intention of both studies was to rapidly produce a regeneration strategy for the entire site that could be used to attract investors, involve the public, local planning authorities and, significantly, the City Mayor. The Mayor and Späth became the driving forces behind a project that was to be undertaken very quickly, as the despair at losing the city's principal employer began to grow.

The 'masterplan vision' was regarded very much as a quick snapshot view of the site's redevelopment potential over a ten-year period. This took into account the preliminary condition survey of the site, which attempted to find a balanced approach to complete redevelopment against preservation of an impressive architectural heritage of Carl Zeiss. This study comprised preliminary sketches, aerial perspectives, rudimentary phasing diagrams and sketch models.

Establishing a redevelopment brief was made more necessary due to the evolving and

9.3
Fabrikstraße, which became *Goethestraße* in the finished scheme.

somewhat unknown territory of 'demand' at the time. German reunification revealed stark contrasts between East and West. Jena, like many other East German cities, had ostensibly developed around a single manufacturing base – in the command economy of the former GDR, social amenities and service sector industries were well provided by the State, whilst entrepreneurism and the free market were actively discouraged.

To expedite the process of matching supply and demand, DEGW offered to appraise the city in its broader context. This was done by a comparative analysis study, whereby Jena was compared and contrasted with a number of cities of similar size. After narrowing the field, Erlangen and Koblenz were chosen as cities comparable in size and profile to Jena. Erlangen's population was approximately the same as Jena's, was dominated by a single industry (Siemens) and also had a long established technical university. Unsurprisingly, Jena was found to be suffering from a significant deficit of retail, leisure, and business support service industries, while telecommunications and basic utilities also were completely sub-standard.

This study helped provide JenOptik with a profile of commercial and amenity facilities that Jena lacked and to give a target for what the city might aim to achieve in order to redress the balance. While JenOptik was sitting on a prime tract of city centre real estate, an under-developed commercial market meant its true potential asset value was not clearly understood at the time.

Combined, these two initial studies became an effective tool for creating a framework within which JenOptik could articulate loosely defined objectives in five key areas, to:

I realize the employment potential of the site

I create a development strategy for short, medium and long term action

I highlight key implementation problems

I create an agenda for preliminary discussions with the local planning authorities

I frame a change of use strategy.

A key document to be developed during this phase was the ten-year implementation strategy which, some eight years after it was first devised, remains remarkably close to the actual building programme. The diagram centred on a three tier development strategy that involved:

I short-term uses: re-training centres

I medium-term uses: temporary car parking/decant space and an investor/exhibition centre

I longer-term uses – such as major refurbishment and new buildings.

Developing a masterplan framework

On the strength of the first two studies, DEGW were given the contract to undertake a detailed comprehensive masterplan study of the *Hauptwerk* and they established a joint venture with Stuttgart-based engineering firm, IFB Dr Braschel & Partner. The joint venture, called JenProjekt, had a remit to procure all project

9.4
The *Hauptwerk* after redevelopment.

management, design consultancy and construction services for JenOptik over all former Carl Zeiss sites, with the added social dimension of employing local skills, wherever possible.

The masterplanning was undertaken in two tranches of work, by dividing the *Hauptwerk* into two sites – the south and north site. Although the *Hauptwerk* occupied an entire city block, it was itself bifurcated by an old public right of way, long since closed off and turned into an internal service road during the Cold War years.

DEGW's first action was to recommend a re-opening of the street, known as *Fabrikstraße*. The Mayor held his annual Christmas address in this street, symbolizing the importance placed on keeping the public informed of the redevelopment proposals as they were progressing and, at key stages during the project, allowing public consultation. *Fabrikstraße*, later to be poetically surpassed and renamed *Goethestraße*, was to become a key transitional zone between the quite different character of the developments on the south and north sites.

Of both the sites, it was the south that, from the outset, was earmarked for more demolition. The buildings here were of far less architectural significance than those on the north site, proved difficult to subdivide and almost unfeasible to access at certain points. Above all, however, up to 80 per cent of the buildings' structure and fabric was ruinously corroded by industrial lubricants and chemicals. Thus, having the most new-build potential, the south site was viewed with keen interest by several private sector investment groups and commercial developers. JenOptik, the landowners, saw the potential sale of the south site as an opportunity to cross-subsidize the less commercial development already being anticipated on the north site.

The north site, by contrast, contained many buildings of architectural significance that in their plan form were inherently more flexible to adapt. The Technical University of Jena, in a reversal of fortunes to Zeiss, was actively expanding and expressed a keen interest in the north site as an opportunity to extend its campus and facilities. This helped give a new impetus to the redevelopment, which had as its centrepiece the concept of a new public square

9.5
Looking down over the *Goethegalerie* development – a shopping street along *Goethestraße*.

that would link a number of old routes across the site from the old city centre, permeating the perimeter buildings of the *Hauptwerk* at various junctures. The proposal to extend the city's tram network through the site with a stop at the new square also began to enliven the debate on striking the right balance between the ostensibly commercial direction that the south site was taking on and the more public sector oriented north site.

The detailed masterplan of the south site formed a strategy for a mixed-use commercial development, comprising retail, leisure, office and hotel facilities. DEGW presented results of the study at a series of 'investor workshops', modifying the proposals to the changing requirements. Included in the workshops were key members of the city planning authorities and this proved to be crucial in enabling JenOptik to sell off the land with outline planning consents. At its centre, the masterplan developed the concept of a main covered 'street' linking, on its northern side, a 200-metre long five-storey façade of refurbished industrial buildings with, on its southern side, an almost entirely new-build redevelopment. The masterplan of the south site developed generic planning guidelines which set a framework for architectural design, but was very detailed in

previous page
15
Carl Zeiss Factory, Jena,
Germany; now a mixed-
use commercial
development.

(Photo: DEGW)

this page
16 *(top)*
Bass Maltings,
Sleaford, Lincolnshire.

(Photo: Michael Stratton)

17 *(bottom)*
Oxo Tower Wharf,
South Bank, London.

(Photo: Timothy Soar)

opposite page
Ancoats, Manchester.

18 *(top)*
Blossom Street as it
is today showing the
Ice Warehouse on the
left and the recently
renovated St Peter's
Church.

(Photo: Ian Finlay)

19 *(bottom)*
Concept illustration
showing Blossom Street
which will link the
Urban Village to the
Northern Quarter and
the City Centre.
Architect: Ian Finlay.

this page
**Landscape Park,
Duisburg-Nord,
Germany.**

20 *(top)*
(Photo: Michael Verhoelen)

21 *(bottom)*
(Photo: Andreas Molingen)

opposite page
22
Bluebird Garage,
Chelsea which now
houses a café, restaurant,
food store and a branch
of the Conran Shop.
Architects:
CD Partnership.

plot and building sizes, building height restrictions, set backs, car parking provision and phasing strategy for demolition and new construction work.

DEGW progressed the south site masterplan to the *Bebauungsplan* (land-use development) stage which formed a significant component of the city's legally-binding urban development guidelines. After the initial period of master-planning, DEGW were retained by JenOptik and Berlin developer Grundag AG, to design key buildings within the new development.

Key buildings

Investor Centre

DEGW's first design commission was the fit-out of JenOptik's new 'investor centre'. Situated in the Carl Zeiss's former fire station along the main street frontage, the investor centre was intended to attract inward investment and involve the public in viewing plans for the site as they developed. As a simple double-height volume, the design comprised a mezzanine level at one end and three huge arched fire tender bays, fully glazed with a single cruciform post and mullion detail. A common enough concept in the West, the design of the investor centre reflected the new openness of the city and became a 'shop window' for regeneration and development in the Jena region.

The *Hochhaus*

The *Hochhaus*, built in 1929 and one of Germany's earliest examples of reinforced concrete tall buildings, was the landmark building of the *Hauptwerk* with fifteen storeys; it was earmarked to become JenOptik's new headquarters building.

A stringent preservation order on the building meant that major refurbishment was confined to the interior only and detailed consultation with the *Denkmalschutzamt* was necessary. The building's envelope did not comply with present day insulation regulations, therefore non-compressible insulation board and

self coloured GRC render were 'invisibly' added to the façades. Windows were replaced with thermally efficient models, to the original 1920s configuration, and their elegant original stone surrounds were replaced. A series of intricate stone 'zodiac' tableaux above the entrance to the building were removed and faithfully restored by local masons before being reset into the new stucco façade.

The original plan form of the Carl Zeiss Jena administration building was too narrow and inflexible for sub-letting. The richly decorated core was over-sized and contained a delightful, if non-compliant, paternoster hoist to the fifteenth floor. Internally, the building was all but stripped back to its original structure, a new core inserted and the plan reconfigured to produce a more efficient and flexible office environment. At ground floor, a double-height foyer was created by the removal of one third of the first floor. This new generous volume created a much more appropriate space for a building of its height and would later house the JenOptik investor centre relocated from the old fire station, as JenOptik's original intention was to occupy two thirds of the building only.

Buildings B10/13

In parallel with its work on the *Hochhaus*, DEGW undertook an extensive feasibility study on buildings B10/13 to evaluate their potential. The five-storey buildings, comprising some 30,000 square metres of space, were fine examples of early German industrial architecture and even included an original Carl Zeiss rooftop observatory and dramatic arched concrete beams (cast in situ) in the main roof spaces.

The initial findings of the study soon revealed the buildings to be robust enough in plan form and structure to accommodate a number of different uses. The 200-metre length of the building proved more problematic, however. In its day, B10/13's main access was strangely via the adjoining buildings, the *Hochhaus* and B15, at either end of the main run of building.

As DEGW were developing ideas for B10/13's refurbishment, the sale of the south site had already been agreed and its masterplan concept signed-off by the client and designated in the *Bebauungsplan*. This resulted in the

southern façade of B10/13 becoming the
boundary line between two ownerships and
subsequently, two different construction
contracts. The south site masterplan had
already proposed that the centrepiece of the
new development would become a covered
Einkaufspassage (shopping street) and the lower
two levels of B10/13 given over to retail usage.

To provide separate and multi-tenanted
access points, DEGW decided early on that the
entire building should be accessed and serviced
via externally-placed cores situated on its north
side, facing the proposed new public square. In
the study, DEGW identified different plan
forms and tenancy demises for potential uses
such as small to medium offices, business
support space, re-training centres, library space
for the university, business apartments and
even a proposed JenOptik 'teleport' situated in
the old rooftop observatory.

The feasibility study progressed to DEGW
being awarded the contract to refurbish the
entire building. Four new glass and steel cores
at the north side contrast with the solidity of
the building's reinforced concrete frame and
provide an elegant backdrop to the central
space of the north site.

The *Goethegalerie*: Hotel and the *Galerie*.

DEGW, working together with joint venture
partners IFB Dr Braschel GmbH, took the south
site masterplan through to the concept design
stage. A Berlin developer, Grundag AG, was
spurred on by the government tax breaks to
develop the entire site in one complete phase
before the end of 1995.

Grundag actively promoted the concept,
developed in DEGW's masterplan, of a mixed-
use development comprising retail, office,
leisure and hotel uses. The entire development,
known as the *Goethegalerie*, became a
shopping street along *Goethestraße* – the
former service spine road running through the
Hauptwerk. The *Goethegalerie* provided a gross
area of some 80,000 square metres, had a
contract value of DM 250 million and was
built concurrently in six separate construction
contracts.

Hotel Esplanade

As owner/occupier of the growing number of
4-star Esplanade hotels in Berlin, Grundag
intended to sell off the entire *Goethegalerie* but
retain ownership and control of the hotel.
Bounded by the *Galerie* on the east and by Carl
Zeiss Platz on the west, the site presented an
opportunity to link the public areas of the hotel
with the *Galerie*. The hotel would carry a 4-star
rating and have conference facilities, bars, a
restaurant, service business apartments and
175 bedrooms, configured around a boomerang
shaped atrium with wall-climber lifts and
bridges linking across.

The hotel was a complete new-build apart from its corner, where the listed *B12 Turm* had to be integrated within the design. The tower building had significant floor to floor discrepancies with the new hotel, and mezzanine floors were inserted at key points.

The Galerie

The *Galerie* became the centrepiece of the entire *Goethegalerie* and gave Jena a much-needed focal point, appropriately situated at the heart of the Zeiss *Hauptwerk*. DEGW developed the concept of the *Galerie* as a naturally ventilated 'covered street' and not an air-conditioned mall. To this end, the final design was to remain true to the original concept and retains the image of the central public street running through the Zeiss *Werke* as it had done fifty years previously.

Using the Milanese *Galleria Vittorio Emanuele* as a model, DEGW placed the roof at high level, containing the restored façade of buildings B10/13 beneath it and creating an enormous volume to enhance the sensation of public space. After testing a number of different structural configurations, a 'fish bone roof truss' was chosen, as it enabled the structural support system to be minimized – the truss is supported by a row of columns above the retail units and 'propped' against the façade of building B10/13 (*see Figure 9.5 and Plate 15*).

An 'anchor' for the *Galerie* – a 'rotunda' – was created on axis with the rooftop observatory of B10, as it was a natural focal point of the building and had, on its axis, an existing route through to the north site at ground level. The straight array of roof trusses turn through 180° to form the rotunda and presented the greatest structural challenge. The *Galerie* roof trusses are propped against the old façade of B10/13 along its length and exert a high lateral force through the building. The upper floor slabs of the existing building were subsequently reinforced to accommodate this loading. The rotunda presented a much greater loading problem. The entire loading of the rotunda is transferred down and back away from the building by five long 'branch' columns sitting on a 'trunk' column embedded within the *Galerie* floor slabs. The logic of this strategy is clear, and in its effect, stunning. The *Galerie* is naturally ventilated by mechanically glazed louvres at its base and head. Heating the *Galerie* during winter is aided by the dumping of exhaust air from the retail units into the central area.

In the design of the highly engineered steel and glass lightweight roof construction, the *Galerie* pays a suitable homage to the technological and engineering legacy of Carl Zeiss, Jena.

The *Goethegalerie* was completed in January 1996 and attracts an important number of visitors and clients. Approximately 20,000 people per day use its facilities – 60 per cent coming from Jena and the rest from a catchment of around 50–60 km. The Hotel Esplanade with 180 rooms attracts the business trade sector and occupies the second position in the ranking of most successful hotel in Thuringia. The *Galerie* has had a minor negative impact on some of the small shops in the centre of the town due to the

9.7

The Hotel was a complete new-build apart from its corner, where the listed *B12 Turm* had to be integrated into the design.

(*Photo: Wolfram Jänzer*)

competition and the long hours. This was very carefully considered during the masterplanning stage and a firm restriction kept on the amount of new retail space allowed.

The north site and university

On the north site, the refurbished buildings B6 and B7 are now part of the university. A new institute building, parallel to the street, connects to the former factory buildings, with three lecture halls located in the newly formed courtyards. The new 17,000 square metre site of the university is laid out in block form with the historically valuable and protected former industrial buildings and can be accessed from the inner courtyard of the *Hauptwerk*. The main university entrance leads to a glass-roofed passageway along the rear of the new institute building, ending at the library. Traffic is dealt with by a two-storey underground car park providing 320 parking spaces, and the city's tram network extends into the inner court area.

Facilities were created for the economics and law faculty of Friedrich Schiller University as well as for the higher college for social science. Lecture and seminar rooms, auditoria and a library for a total of 3,500 students as well as office space for the 500 university personnel were realized. The university occupies a number of different buildings on the *Hauptwerk* and it was important to be located centrally, to allow a concentration of students from the same faculty (4,500 students of economics) to add much needed vitality to the life of the city. The humanities and the cultural sciences department are also housed in these buildings.

Historically, the origins of Carl Zeiss Jena from the glass manufacturing expertise of Otto Schott and the technical genius of Zeiss and Abbe, inevitably resulted in a degree of sibling rivalry between industry and education. One was always trying to out-do the other and usually Zeiss came to prominence. As Zeiss Jena went into rapid decline however, the technical university grew rapidly to the point where today, Jena is regarded more as a university city. The Friedrich Schiller Technical University is a state university with 4,500 employees and an estate of 120 buildings occupying 260,000 square metres. It has increased the number of students from 4,500 in 1991 to 12,500 in 1998 – 7,000 of whom now study on the former Zeiss *Hauptwerk* – and there are plans to extend the number to 17,000 students by the year 2010. To accommodate the students, the plans include a 6,000 square metre new building occupying the 'missing tooth' slot between B6 and B59, which is now under construction and will house the linguistics department.

Conclusion

During the course of initial planning, DEGW's ideas on retaining a core of existing buildings on the *Hauptwerk* met with resistance from over-eager developers intent on wiping the slate clean with completely new development. DEGW's comprehensive analysis of the existing building stock and insistence on re-using many of the old industrial buildings has meant that the legacy of Carl Zeiss is still redolent in the *Hauptwerk* today. This concept of 'stock-taking' has been central to DEGW's approach during its twenty-five year history and has spanned many different disciplines from space planning, through architecture to urban planning. It is an approach that chimes well with the issues surrounding brownfield planning.

The lessons learned from Jena are important to this current debate. The growth and decline of industrial areas is a cornerstone of the social and physical evolution of most cities. If the success of brownfield development can be measured in terms of how well the adaptive re-use of inner city industrial areas can retain, adapt and build upon the past, then Jena has to be judged a success.

Acknowledgments to Josefina López Galdeano for assisting with research for this chapter.

Part 4

Looking to the Future

10.1
The Oxo Tower and
Coin Street area on the
South Bank of the
Thames in London.

(Photo: Iain Tuckett)

❙ Chapter **ten**

Industry and

regeneration

in a new century

❙ John Worthington

❙ Deputy Chairman, DEGW International

For over forty years there has been a gradually increasing focus on industrial regeneration. In the 1950s the symptoms of industrial restructuring were present, but the impact on the landscape of our cities was recognized by few at the time. Southampton, Liverpool and the Port of London were declining as great centres of shipping as the movement of cargo was containerized. This had a dramatic impact on the need for dock labour and the relocation to cheaper, better connected sites. Market functions moved out of crowded city centres (e.g. Covent Garden) to areas where functions could be rationalized on urban fringe locations with convenient motorway access.

Heavy industry (steel, locomotive building and textile) shed increasingly expensive labour and rationalized processes to increase productivity with a fraction of the labour force (*see Figure 10.2*) or disappeared in the onslaught of cheap overseas competition (e.g. the motor cycle industry). By the 1970s, with the three day week and the demise of trade union restrictive labour practices, it was generally recognized that the industrial economy, dominated by mass production, large organizations and a diverse management workforce mentality, had given way to a service economy. The stark separation between blue collar (manual work) and white collar (clerical, professional work) was being superseded by 'rainbow' collar work where the distinction between manufacturing and office functions was becoming blurred. Politically, this change, from the socialist ideal of the dignity of 'real work' at the blast furnace, or in the 'Fordist' factory, as distinct from the parasite nature of supporting clerical services, was hard to absorb. As the landscape of work changed, large tracts of industrial land and buildings were left vacant in the desperate hope that industrial jobs in real factories would return. Studies such as *Industrial rehabilitation*[1] aimed to show that the fine industrial Victorian heritage, which was blighting so many of the inner city fringes through dereliction, could make a valuable contribution to stimulating the growth of small new enterprises, whilst at the same time rejuvenating our declining cities. Twenty years later, the role of small entrepreneurs providing added value services and innovative thinking is recognized. Multi-tenanted buildings with shared business services have become an accepted facet of the property market. The focus

	Output (million tons)	Output per man year (tons)	No. of collieries	Employees
1950	219.5	298.0	901	688,600
1970	144.7	471.0	292	286,000
1993	60.0	2,692.0	16	7,400

10.2
Changes in the UK coal and steel industries between 1950 and 1994.

(Source: BCC 1993–4 Annual Report)

is shifting from individual buildings to the multiple use of large building complexes and the comprehensive renewal of 'brownfield sites'.

There is now an acceptance by all political parties of the change from an industrial economy via a service economy to a knowledge economy. The latter, focused on intellectual capital,[2] crosses national boundaries to form global production lines, with a majority of the workforce adding value through research, product development, engineering and design, marketing and administration.[3]

Robert Reich in *The Work of Nations*[4] describes a work force composed of three increasingly separate strata. First the routine production services; second 'in-person' services, a declining sector of the workforce; and last the elite knowledge workers, a growing 30 per cent of the American labour force which comprises

'symbolic analysts' who perform problem solving, problem identifying and strategic brokering activities. In his study *The Turn to a Horizontal Division of Labour*[5] Stephen Barking shows that the information worker accounts for over 60 per cent of the total North American work force (*see Figure 10.3*). In the majority of what were once 'industrial cities', it is now recognized that it is a futile goal to recreate jobs from the past, but more fruitful to move with the trend to the future. Urban planners and conservationists need to recognize that their role will be one of managing and moderating change, in an environment where the speed of change is rapidly accelerating.[6] Today the average life of a *Fortune 500* corporation is forty years, and the product life of computing appliances is less than three years. As we enter the next millennium the context for renewal is changing and the approach to planning and design is maturing.

Successes in regenerating many of our fine redundant industrial complexes such as Dean Clough Mills, Halifax; Salts Mill, Saltaire; the Custard Factory, Birmingham; and Camden Lock in London, have not been the result of grand plans, institutional investment and bureaucratic organizations. The success has been achieved through:

▌ individuals with tenacity and vision (Sir Ernest Hall, Jonathan Silver, Bennie Gray and Eric Reynolds);

▌ entrepreneurial ambition, coupled with a willingness to achieve the grand scheme through incremental stages;

▌ low cost investment attracting non-institutional users who, often with the same commitment as the initiator, have made the venture succeed;

10.3
The changing profile of employment.

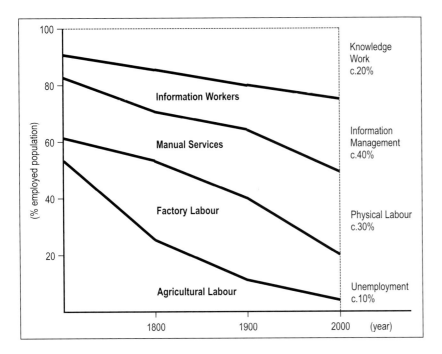

1. Twenty-five acre park

A new, large-scale urban park at the heart of the King's Cross site follows the precedent of other London parks and makes a major addition to the total stock of London's public open spaces. It is a natural way of integrating the existing features of the site and will help meet the needs of the community for recreational space.

2. Retained features

King's Cross and St Pancras stations are Grade I listed buildings and will, of course, be retained. The site also contains other Victorian buildings from the same period, all located to take full advantage of the interchange between road, rail and canal transport systems.

3. Gateway building

Nineteenth-century engineers – like Brunel, Telford and Stephenson – welcomed new technologies in a way that was often controversial. In the design and structure of railway station architecture this manifested itself in the widespread use of the glazed, vaulted roof.

The May proposal for King's Cross is for the new passenger interchange between the two historic stations to be spanned by another great glazed vault, conceived in the same spirit as Cubitt's at King's Cross and Barlow's at St Pancras.

4.

Proposed square – a shopping square – increased in size.

5.

New square – a commercial square – added in the north-east.

6.

The pinching of the park produces a smaller area of open space than the September masterplan, but in conjunction with the realignment of the rail tracks into King's Cross, the gains are significant. The additional space created allows for an earlier start to construction to the east of the park, in areas that avoid the need for building over tracks.

7.

Another variation for the southern end of the site, showing a repositioned gas holder acting as a light and ventilation shaft to the low-level station.

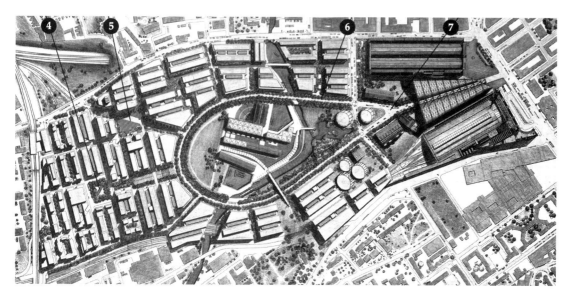

10.4

Master Plan proposals for King's Cross, London, 1988.

Top: existing railyards;

Bottom: London Regeneration Consortium proposals (not executed).

■ high profile exposure, through events and functions that include the wider local community;

■ immense patience, concern for the detail and a recognition that the development period can be a twenty-year time frame.

The lesson from these achievements should be a realization that the centrally generated comprehensive development plan, so popular since the 1960s (e.g. the London County Council's plans for Covent Garden or London Regeneration Consortium's plans for King's Cross in the 1980s[7]) may not be the most effective approach for the future (*see Figure 10.4*). The reality has been successful regeneration at the fringes, where loft developments are booming, creative firms have moved into the converted warehouses along the canal, and short-term entertainment and service uses have moved into the historic buildings on disused railway sites. The last ten years through the recession have seen development and confidence growing and an emergence of mixed-use economy of living, working and leisure. Instead of following rigid frameworks, development has been more organic and opportunistic. The recession saw a relaxation of dogmatic planners' expectations, with the overriding need to retain businesses and grow the economy.

As we enter the twenty-first century, four trends can be identified in planning that will have a considerable impact on our future expectations for the industrial heritage. First, the recognition of a need to use more effectively what we have already is forcing planners and architects to consider ways of using space and time with greater intensification. There has been a realization that to leave expensive buildings vacant or underused for over 80 per cent of the total time available makes bad business sense. Similarly, traffic engineers are recognizing that to continue to take up land use with new infrastructure is a vicious circle. New technology and improved logistics can improve capacity within the existing systems. Moreover, public opinion is realizing that to continue to demolish existing buildings does not make good ecological sense. Much of our existing stock is sturdy, has generous capacity, is well located, has character and with time will be cherished for its memories.

Second, planners are recognizing the need to accommodate a greater diversification, with both the formal and informal sectors, public and private investment and a variety of business types from the institutional corporation to the young entrepreneur (*see Figure 10.5*). Redundant industrial complexes such as at Saltaire and the Herlitz complex at Tegel, Berlin have shown the dynamism and

10.5

The specialization of accommodation reflects business maturity.

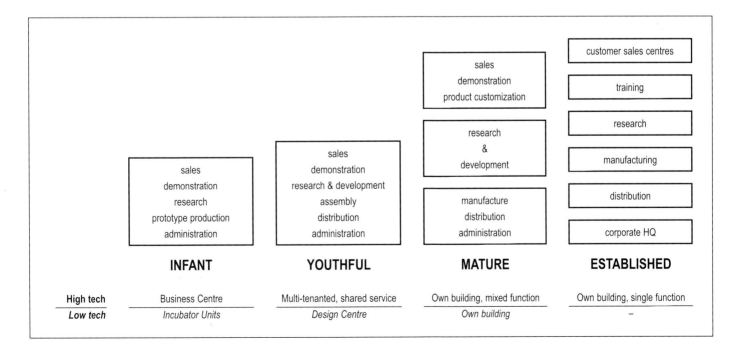

	INFANT	YOUTHFUL	MATURE	ESTABLISHED
High tech	Business Centre	Multi-tenanted, shared service	Own building, mixed function	Own building, single function
Low tech	*Incubator Units*	*Design Centre*	*Own building*	–

economic vitality that can be generated by mixing uses to create a heterogeneous community of interests. Third, one can recognize a trend towards the city of paradox where plans are no longer conceived as being either this or that, but for the plurality of both this and that. Using the past does not preclude the use of the latest technology to improve functionality nor to accommodate high technology businesses.

The success of many of the industrial building adaptations of the past such as those at Lowell, Massachusetts or in Emscher Park, Duisburg have succeeded through lateral thinking and a willingness to change the paradigm. The brilliance of Lowell was to designate the area an Urban National Park and at one stroke change the perception of the areas from a 'standing joke' to a *must* on the tourist itinerary (*see Plates 12, 13 & 14*). Fourth, planning is slowly recognizing the folly of the grand slam, comprehensive single phased development strategy. Since the comprehensive redevelopment mania of the 1960s and the development bonanza of the 1980s, there is an understanding that comprehensive visions can be incrementally developed. Meanwhile, in the last ten years the initial stimulus has attracted loft living, creative firms and the weekend youth culture and, by adapting the existing buildings, established a thriving economy.

As communities and individuals become more concerned and vocal about the quality and development of their neighbourhoods, we may expect to see more gradual and incremental development. It is recognized that planning needs to manage the demands of investors to build rapidly to achieve a return and minimize cash flow on expensive infrastructure, but communities need time to reflect and assimilate proposed change. The King's Cross redevelopment reflected just such a conflict which was articulated by the King's Cross Action Group and their alternative proposals. In the early 1980s the Coin Street community group, brilliantly marshalled by Iain Tuckett, won the right for the community to develop a large area of the South Bank, Waterloo adjacent to the National Theatre. Fifteen years later, time and a gradualist approach have resulted in a world class piece of urban regeneration with high quality uses in the renovated Oxo Tower, a community

boulevard and a genuinely mixed-use environment (*see Figure 10.1, page 157, and Plate 17*).

The trend to urban refurbishment is now globally well established. Waterfronts such as Capetown, Darling Harbour, Sydney, Toronto and the Calls in Leeds (*see Plates 23 & 26*) have been rejuvenated. Warehouse districts from Covent Garden, London to Minneapolis are the generator of entertainment, retailing and creative industries. The next step is the far greater challenge to renew the vast tracts of space left over by the declining industries of coal mining, steel, shipbuilding and the utilities. The issue of brownfield sites has been given political authority with Lord Rogers' Urban Task Force. It is an exciting challenge for the next decade.

Industrial regeneration in the last thirty years has moved from tentative steps to reusing individual distinctive buildings for community uses and small enterprises to the large canvas of urban regeneration. We cannot afford to discard what we have already: the challenge is to grow on the past.

Notes and references

1   Eley, P. & Worthington, J. (1984) *Industrial Rehabilitation: The Use of Redundant Buildings for Small Enterprises*, Architectural Press, London.

2   Stewart, T. (1997) *Intellectual Capital The New Wealth of Organisation*, Nicholas Brealey, London.

3   DEGW (1985) *Meeting the Needs of Modern Industry*, Stanhope Properties, London.

4   Reich, R. (1993) *The Work of Nations: Preparing for 21st century capitalism*, Alfred A Knopf, New York.

5   Barking. S. (1994) *The Turn to a Horizontal Division of Labour*, Office of Educational Research and Improvements, US Department of Education.

6   Warren, J, Worthington, J & Taylor, S. (1998) *Context: New buildings in historic settings*, Architectural Press, Oxford.

7   London Regeneration Consortium, (November 1998) King's Cross Proposals for Redevelopment, London. Sir Norman Foster's plans, with the uncertainty of the Euro Rail Link and declining real estate demand, were never realized.

Part 5

Regeneration Through Heritage Database

(http://www.bitc.org.uk/rth)

(Photo: Borough of Rossendale)

(Photo: Wood & Co)

(Photo: Michael Stratton)

Conservation and regeneration projects in Britain and Ireland

I **Michael Stratton & Sue Taylor**

I The University of York

The Regeneration Through Heritage database constitutes a gazetteer of industrial buildings, many of which have been successfully restored and converted for contemporary economic uses. It includes projects that are currently underway, and examples of major redundant buildings that are awaiting conversion as well as numerous links to other relevant organizations. The database is part of the Regeneration Through Heritage initiative (*see Chapter four*) and is intended primarily as a resource for specialists, community groups, and local partnerships seeking new uses for industrial buildings.

Throughout the book the projects included in the database are marked with the ʷʷʷ symbol; they will not necessarily be included in this chapter. The examples shown are just a selection of the data available. Further information including contact details and more of the 200 or so projects can be freely accessed on the internet at www.bitc.org.uk/rth.

This is an on-going initiative which will be updated as projects develop and evolve. It includes already some examples from Continental Europe, and the USA, which limitation on space does not allow to be included here. This section of the database will continue to be expanded.

This chapter concentrates on projects in Britain and is organized on a regional basis as illustrated in the map below.

A   London

B   South East

C   South West

D   Wales

E   West Midlands

F   East Midlands

G   Eastern*

H   North West

I   Yorkshire & Humberside

J   North East

K   Scotland

L   Northern Ireland

M   Republic of Ireland

* No Eastern region selections appear in this book.

Bankside Power Station – London

(Photo: The Tate Gallery)

History and former use

Bankside Power Station was built as an oil-fired power station; it replaced an older coal-fired station on the same site. Designed by Sir Giles Gilbert Scott in 1947, the building was completed in 1963 and decommissioned in 1981. The central chimney of this massive and imposing structure was limited to a height of 325 feet in order to be lower than the dome of St Paul's Cathedral, which is on the opposite side of the river. The massive turbine hall, which runs right across the full width of the building, is approximately 115 feet high and 500 feet long.

New use

The Tate Gallery of Modern Art (Tate Modern) opens in May 2000. In 1994 Bankside was selected as the site for the new gallery because of its prime location, vast space and accessibility (*see Plate 10*). The cathedral-like windows in the building open up views of St Paul's Cathedral and central London. Glass is used throughout to make maximum use of light. A series of top-lit and side-lit gallery spaces have been created for the display of works of art. A covered street has been created in the former turbine hall with a large, gently sloping ramp bringing visitors down into the building. Other facilities include: information centre; facilities for families and disabled visitors; auditorium for conferences and film screenings; education centre with workshop and seminar space; gift shop; café with outdoor terrace; restaurant with views across London.

Community issues

In May 1996 an office and visitor centre was established at the site. This provides a direct link between the Gallery and the local community. It will remain in operation for the whole of the development period and will act as a focal point for information and other activity until the Gallery opens.

The Tate aims to: develop partnerships with local authorities, businesses, residents and community groups; create opportunities for participation in the development of the gallery; be a resource for the community; promote Bankside as an attractive area in which to live, work and visit. The Gallery aims to develop a programme of activities that caters for the needs of all in the community and that will increase understanding and enjoyment of modern art. These will involve: outreach programmes; partnerships with schools, colleges, local residents, employers, community groups; collaboration with artists.

Employment

The Tate Gallery of Modern Art aims to ensure that the economic benefits of the regeneration process are experienced by local people. Employment and training initiatives focusing on the surrounding area have been developed for the duration of the construction programme. The Gallery has initiated and piloted the development of the Bankside Arts Training Trust to create, with partners, customized training packages geared to employment opportunities in cultural industries in the area.

Sources of funding

In 1995 the Tate Gallery of Modern Art received £50 million from the Millennium Commission as one of its fourteen Landmark projects for the Millennium, £12 million from English Partnerships to acquire the site and remove all machinery, and £6.4 million from the Arts Council. With significant donations from other public, private and charitable sources, £120 million had been raised towards the target of £134 million by March 1999.

Conservation issues

The architects had intended to keep the concrete roof of the turbine hall but surveys revealed that it had serious carbonation and therefore it had to be replaced.

Location
Bankside, London

Architect
Herzog & de Meuron

Cost
£134 million – first phase

Bluebird Garage – London

Location
Chelsea, London

Listed status
Grade II*

Developer
**Harris & Webber/
Conran Restaurants**

Architect
CD Partnership

General contractor
Wallis Ltd

Total floor area
50,000 sq. ft

Cost
£6 million

(Photo: CD Partnership)

History and former use
It was Europe's largest motor garage when built in 1923.

New use
Restaurant, food store, café, club, shop with a forecourt market (*see Plate 22*).

Community issues
On the King's Road in Chelsea, it was a famous local landmark but one that had attained a bad reputation. Its use as a clothes market had attracted occasional undesirable visitors and there was a problem of drug dealing in the building (and on one occasion a shooting!). Local groups were keen to see high quality use and sensitive restoration. It was a difficult building to find a use for as it had very few windows on the sides and rear and a very deep plan.

Employment
The new use has provided several hundred jobs.

Construction schedule
March 1996 – May 1997.

Sources of finance
Private.

Conservation issues
Faience was restored. Lights and railings that were removed during the Second World War were reinstated. Façade was restored including the copperlite glazing. The unusual roof structure was preserved.

Future prospects
The famous local landmark which had become run down has been transformed to a sound commercial business which enlivens the area.

Butler's Wharf – London

History and former use
Warehouses.

New use
Apartments, restaurants, shops, offices and The Design Museum.

Community issues
The former docks area which had become derelict was brought back to life by a development team led by Terence Conran. It has now become part of a series of major regeneration projects on the South Bank including the new Tate Modern, the Globe Theatre, the South Bank Complex, and the Oxo Tower.

Employment
The new use has provided several thousand jobs.

Construction schedule
1985 to present.

Sources of finance
Private.

Conservation issues
The strategy taken was to preserve the good buildings and replace the poorer ones with interventions of high quality. There have been long and complex negotiations with English Heritage and the Royal Fine Art Commission about the appropriateness of this but the result has been many award-winning projects.

Future prospects
The recession in the property market caused the strategy to be only partly implemented. Since the sale of the site, new projects have been of disappointing design quality with a loss of the earlier mixed-use vision for the area.

Location
Shad Thames, London Docklands

Listed status
Range of buildings both unlisted and Grade II

Developer
Butler's Wharf Limited

Architect
CD Partnership

General contractor
McAlpine

Total floor area
Several million sq. ft

Cost
In excess of £100 million

(Photo: CD Partnership)

Michelin Building – London

Location
**Fulham Road,
London**

Listed status
Grade II*

Developer
**Hamlyn Publishing/
Terence Conran**

Architect
**CD Partnership
(formerly Conran
Roche) & YRM**

Total floor area
120,000 sq. ft

Cost
£9 million

(Photo: CD Partnership)

History and former use
Built in 1909–11 the building housed the
Michelin head offices, a tourist office selling
maps and guides, and on the ground floor was
a tyre-fitting bay. Michelin left the building in
1985 when it was immediately taken over by
Sir Terence Conran for the Conran Shop. The
building was restored and additions were
made.

New use
Conran Shop, restaurant and oyster bar, offices
for Hamlyn Books.

Community issues
A famous local landmark which had fallen into
a poor state of repair.

Employment
The new use has provided several hundred
jobs.

Construction schedule
1986–7.

Sources of finance
Private.

Conservation issues
Faience was restored and glazing and lighting
reinstated. The unusual structure was retained.

Awards
The conversion has received an Award from the
English Tourist Board, an RIBA London
Regional Award, a Europa Nostra Award and a
Civic Trust Commendation.

Museum in Docklands – London

History and former use

Warehouse No 1 was part of a half-mile long range of nine warehouses built along the north quay of the vast West India Dock enclave, completed in 1802–3 for the handling of sugar, rum and coffee. The warehouses were once a veritable fortress, surrounded by a moat, high walls and patrolled by armed militia to protect the valuable goods stored there. During the Second World War the range of buildings suffered bomb damage and seven of the warehouses were demolished. The remaining warehouses are now described by the Royal Commission on the Historical Monuments of England (RCHME) as 'one of the great monuments of European economic power'.

New use

The warehouses are to be converted into the Museum in Docklands, scheduled to open in January 2001, which will tell the fascinating story of London's river, port and people, from Roman times to its recent regeneration. The new museum will occupy five floors of Warehouse No 1. Besides its main galleries, the Museum will provide a temporary exhibition gallery and an extensive library and archive, together with educational facilities, a shop and a restaurant.

Community issues

Since Roman settlement, London has been a centre of maritime trade. By 1939 the Port of London employed around 250,000 people; however, with increasing mechanization of cargo handling and processing by the mid-1970s, modern facilities were focused further downstream and much of the historic port area fell into disuse. During the 1980s a programme of oral history was recorded producing 260 hours of taped interview material from men and women who were once dependent on the port for their livelihoods. The voices form an important part of the museum galleries. By offering auditorium and temporary exhibition space the Museum intends to become a vibrant arts and cultural focal point for the whole of Docklands and East London.

Education issues

In 1986, the Museum of London acquired the Port of London Authority's Library and Archive together with primary source material dating from the mid-eighteenth century. Since 1987 educational outreach programmes have been operated that have benefited thousands of pupils/students as part of the National Curriculum. The new Museum hopes to attract an estimated 32,000 pupil/student visits per annum. Facilities will include three study rooms, a refectory and a schools exhibition area. The Children's Gallery will be integrated into formal education programmes within the National Curriculum.

Sources of funding

The project has secured a grant of £11.525 million from the Heritage Lottery Fund. London Docklands Development Corporation (LDDC) provided a capital grant of £3.5 million. In addition the Museum has raised a further £1 million by way of gifts and sponsorship.

Conservation issues

The LDDC has recently completed an extensive repair and restoration programme throughout the historic buildings and the adjoining quayside.

Future prospects

The new museum offers the opportunity to bring together a large amount of historic archives and artifacts under one roof, to be used as an important educational resource, and to play a central role in the physical and cultural regeneration of the Docklands area.

(Photo: John Nelligan)

Location
West India Quay, London Docklands

Listed status
Grade 1

Architect
Purcell Miller Tritton & Partners

Environmental Engineers
Fulcrum Consulting

Structural Engineers
The Morton Partnership Ltd

Exhibition Designers
Haley Sharpe Associates

Quantity Surveyors
Franklin & Andrews

Total floor area
110,000 sq. ft

Cost
£16.025 million

Oxo Tower – London

Location
South Bank, London

Architect
Lifschutz Davidson Ltd

Project Management
Turner and Townsend Project Management

Cost Consultants
Turner and Townsend Quantity Surveyors

Engineers
Buro Happold/ Cundall Johnston & Partners

Main Contractor
Trollope & Colls

Total floor area
90,000 sq. ft

Cost
£20 million

History and former use

Built towards the end of the nineteenth century as a generating station for the Post Office, the site was taken over in the 1920s by the Liebig Extract of Meat Company who owned the Oxo brand. The building was developed from 1928 onwards, retaining its original frontage and incorporating the famous illuminated Oxo tower (*see Plate 17*). The building changed hands several times, used mainly for food storage until the late 1970s when it became derelict and threatened by a massive development proposal along the river from the National Theatre to Blackfriars Bridge. The subject of a huge public 'Save the Oxo Tower Campaign', the building was purchased in 1984 along with other sites in the area by the Coin Street Community Builders, a not-for-profit company established by local residents.

New use

On its rooftop is the Oxo Tower Restaurant, Bar and Brasserie and public viewing terrace, which take full advantage of the outstanding location. The residential area below consists of five floors of housing association flats with their own entrance, lifts and parking (78 flats – Redwood Housing Co-op). On the second floor is the riverside restaurant and bar. Also on the second and first floors are retail design studios for contemporary designers – a unique feature of the Wharf. A delicatessen and Coin Street Information are both located on the ground floor, together with *the.gallery@oxo* featuring regular changing exhibitions of design, contemporary art and architecture.

Community issues

The development proposals of the 1970s included a parade of large office blocks 14–16 storeys high that would have swept down the river bank from behind the National Theatre to Blackfriars Bridge. The Coin Street Action Group, formed in 1977, brought together local residents and drew up plans for social housing (to reverse the population decline of the area), a new park and riverside walkway, managed workshops and other leisure facilities. All the residential accommodation on Coin Street sites is social housing available at affordable rents to individuals and families in housing need.

Construction schedule

1988, central section between riverside building and Bargehouse demolished to allow light into the heart of the complex; 1991–2, delaminated concrete replaced, structure of Wharf repaired; 1993, refurbishment began; 1995, residents move in to Oxo Tower Wharf; 1996, commercial areas of Oxo Tower Wharf open to public.

Sources of funding

Housing Corporation, English Partnerships, private borrowing and Coin Street Community Builders' own equity.

Conservation issues

Many original features of the building have been retained: the post and beam reinforced concrete structures have been left exposed as have the large pillars supporting each floor. Where necessary, original bricks have been replaced with specially commissioned ones stamped with the Oxo letters. Other features such as the layout of the loading bays and the wind-down wooden loading platforms have also been retained or echoed in the design of the refurbishment.

Awards

The building has won the Royal Fine Art Commission/BSkyB Building of the Year Award for Regeneration and a Royal Institute of British Architects Regional Award.

Future prospects

Further design-based retail units will open off the ground floor level riverside arcade and central mall. Another focus is funding for Phase II of Oxo Tower Wharf, known as The Bargehouse, which until the end of 1998 remained derelict. In November 1998 The Museum of Collectors, the first of a series of fun, free, innovative temporary museums opened to the public. This museum project relates to the future plans for a permanent Museum of the River Thames at The Bargehouse. The temporary museums will provide a focus for critical debate, contributing to decisions about the form the permanent Museum of the River Thames will eventually take. The second phase proposals also include covering the central mall area at second floor height to provide a flexible performance space and a covered street.

The Prince's Foundation – London

History and former use

19–22 Charlotte Road is a Victorian brick warehouse of traditional construction on six storeys consisting of basement with clerestory windows to the street elevation, raised ground floor with shorefronts, and four storeys above ground. The building has timber sash windows, timber floors, cast-iron columns and exposed timber roof structure. The roof is slate which has been 'turnerised' in the past in lieu of traditional repair. Major refurbishment is necessary but, once stripped out to an open plan arrangement and restored, the building will have clean, simple and flexible spaces with excellent natural light. The building has been in mixed use as fur warehouse, storage, design and photographic studios.

New use

The Prince's Foundation is a new charitable organization formed to unite and extend HRH The Prince of Wales's initiatives in architectural design, building and urban regeneration. The Foundation encourages a more holistic and humane approach to the planning and design of our urban communities, working with a wide range of professionals and partners to help the development of places which can better meet the social, economic, environmental and spiritual needs of individuals and their communities.

This building will be a unique centre for study and learning, research and debate, and hands-on practical project work. It will house an organic café, gallery and bookshop, together with a fully equipped lecture theatre, print-room, darkroom and workshop. The Foundation will offer a continuous programme of exhibitions and activities.

Construction schedule

Stripping commenced November 1998. Main contract let 4/1/99. The building will be ready for use in early 2000.

Location
Shoreditch, London

Developer
The Prince's Foundation

Architect
Matthew Lloyd Architects

General contractor
Alsop Zogolovitch act as the client representative;

Ballast Wiltshire is the main contractor

Total floor area
19,250 sq. ft

Mistley Maltings – South East

Location
Mistley, Essex

Listed status
Listed Grade II, in a Conservation Area

Architect
Allen Tod Architects

Total floor area
10,870 sq. m.

Cost (approximate)
Demonstration stage: £250,000

Stage 2: £3.3 million

Stages 3 and 4: £10 million

History and former use

Of medieval origin, the village of Mistley developed principally during the eighteenth century as a spa town. This project failed but, with its proximity to the river, the area gradually developed in the nineteenth century as a centre for the malting industry, with several maltings buildings and related domestic architecture. Changes in working practices in the industry have resulted in the abandonment or partial demolition of several of the maltings buildings. Malting No 2 retains its original use and Malting No 1 is partly occupied by the Mistley Quay and Forwarding, a subsidiary of Trent Wharfage who own the building. It stands amongst a series of buildings located between the quay and the High Street. Terraced onto the riverbank, it provides spectacular views over the River Stour and is only a few minutes walk from the railway station for Harwich and London.

New use

The project for regeneration is in its early stages. In 1997 a working partnership was established between Essex County Council, Regeneration Through Heritage, Tendring District Council, Mistley Parish Council, Trent Wharfage, English Heritage and local residents. A Conservation Area Partnership Scheme operates in the village. Proposals are to provide a variety of uses including offices, workshops, community space and training studios. The top floor would be suitable for residential space, penthouses or lofts, which would give life to the building after normal working hours. The quayside maltings has been chosen to herald the start of the regeneration scheme and act as a catalyst for the surrounding area.

Community issues

There is a high level of unemployment in the district. Mistley, with its advantage of good communications, is seen as a location with potential for the growth of small businesses.

Construction schedule

February 1998
Appointment of consultants to examine a feasible method of developing Malting No 1.

April 1998
Start implementation of Conservation Area Partnership Scheme programme.

September 1998
Feasibility Study published.

Winter 1998 onwards
Implement recommendations of Feasibility Study. Funding applications submitted. Start on site projected for November 1999.

Sources of funding

Funding for a Feasibility Study was provided by the owner, the Conservation Area Partnership Scheme, and Essex County Council. Funding for Stage 1 was provided by the Conservation Area Partnership Scheme, English Partnerships, Essex Environment Trust, and the owner.

Conservation issues

This is a good intact example of patented maltings.

Future prospects

The proposals have attracted considerable public support and local businesses are already expressing an interest. The project will regenerate Mistley and provide a visitor destination and stopping place for tourists entering the country from Harwich.

Bursledon Brickworks – South East

History and former use
Late Victorian brickworks.

New use
Centre for the conservation of the built environment run by a charitable trust promoting enlightened conservation of the built heritage and providing an educational facility for all ages.

Community issues
Bursledon Brickworks Trust was formed to restore the historic buildings and original brickmaking machinery on this unique site in order to present the United Kingdom's brickmaking heritage to the public.

Employment
A small dedicated staff of four people along with enthusiastic volunteers.

Construction schedule
Restoration scheduled over an approximate ten-year period using site staff, specialist contractors and volunteers.

Sources of funding
Dowry from Redlands Plc
Local authority grants
Private sponsorship
Help in kind

Conservation issues
Finding an adaptive re-use compatible with the form and nature of the site, listed buildings, and surviving historic brickmaking machinery.

Location
Swanwick, Southampton, Hampshire

Listed status
Grade II*

Developer
1991–3: Hampshire Buildings Preservation Trust

1994–continuing: Bursledon Brickworks Trust

Total floor area
Approx. 50,000 sq. ft

Cost
£1.3 million (80% completion) Funding now being sought for completion

Bliss Tweed Mill – South East

History and former use
Built by William Bliss II, this unique mill stands in the beautiful landscape of north Oxfordshire. Completed in 1873, the mill produced fine tweeds and fabrics for over 100 years.

New use
Production ceased in 1980 and it lay empty for eight years until plans for a residential conversion were approved. The mill itself has been restored as thirty-four apartments, with one, two or three bedrooms. The adjoining Warping House has been converted into eight open-plan duplex apartments. Original features such as the brick vaulted ceilings have been preserved. The original windows have also been retained, ensuring that externally the building is virtually unchanged. The Wool House has been adapted as a leisure complex for the residents, with swimming pool, jacuzzi, squash court, billiard room and conservatory. The former Weaving House provides indoor parking for all residents.

Location
Oxfordshire

Listed status
Grade II*

Developer
Edward Mayhew

Great Western Railway Engineering Works – South East

Location
Swindon, Wiltshire

Listed status
Grade II*

Developer
BAA McArthur/Glen

Architect
Rawls & Co

Total floor area
200,000 sq. ft
of retail space

History and former use

In 1840 the Great Western Railway decided to build its main engineering works in fields near the small town of Swindon. The decision was so successful that a major town grew up around the works: a town created by steam, in which everyone owed their living to GWR. The BAA McArthur/Glen's Great Western Designer Outlet Village (*see Plate 1*) is situated in the Joseph Armstrong's Locomotive Works built in the 1870s. Here foundries for brass and iron, halls for the assembly of boilers and engines, painting shops and tool stores were all contained in the huge Locomotive Works. Each area played its part in the bringing together of the thousands of components in each locomotive.

New use

The historic core of the works, today known as the Great Western Village, contains the Great Western Designer Outlet Village, the National Monuments Record Centre (NMRC) and a proposed railway heritage centre. The outlet village is the largest retail regeneration project in the country. It is located on the former site of the Great Western Railway workshops at Churchward Village, Swindon. One hundred boutique-style units occupy the 200,000 sq.ft site which includes a food court, children's play area and crèche. Parking for up to 2,000 cars and twenty-two coaches is available within a state-of-the-art computerized parking system. The interior design of the village preserves its historical past, which is positively celebrated by the installation of the steam locomotive, the *City of Truro*, as centrepiece of the themed food court. In addition, pieces of machinery such as various cranes and presses, left behind when British Railways vacated the site, have been refurbished and incorporated as focal points.

Conservation issues

From the inception of the Great Western Designer Outlet Village project, and throughout its development, owners and developers BAA McArthur/Glen have been aware of the importance of the heritage of the former Great Western Railway site, not just in its physical history, but also in the hearts of the people of Swindon.

The developers have endeavoured to maximize the potential of the listed buildings in which they have constructed Europe's largest covered retail outlet village. Practical measures such as the camouflaging of heating ducts in existing roof vents have ensured the retention of the building's character from the exterior. On the inside, features such as arched walls and fretwork cast-iron beams have been retained as part of the quirky Victorian characteristics which add detail. Planners were keen to ensure that as few as possible of the immense iron columns were removed: careful and imaginative planning has meant that no columns have been removed, nor the layout of the retailing units compromised.

(*Photo: Rawls & Company*)

Leadworks – South West

History and former use
The first part of the Leadworks building was constructed for Rowe Brothers in 1884 to a design by Bristol architect Herbert J Jones. In 1900–1 the site was developed, which effectively doubled the size of the existing building. The remodelled site provided extended warehousing for storage of products, including sanitary ware, rainwater goods and raw materials. A glass works was also opened on the site probably during the 1930s. The Rowe Brothers occupied the whole site until the early 1960s, but their main business had turned from manufacturing into a builder's merchant.

New use
Bristol's landmark Millennium project, 'at-Bristol', is being developed on the harbourside. This major project will offer a stimulating, innovative celebration of nature, science and art, enhanced by world-class architecture. It encompasses the Leadworks, which will be incorporated into the exciting new building of the 'Wildscreen at-Bristol'. A visit to Wildscreen will bring you face to face with the extraordinary diversity of the natural world. There will be a walk-through botanical house with free-flying birds and butterflies and a giant screen IMAX.

Location
Bristol

Watershed – South West

History and former use
Five two-storey transit sheds on the west side of St Augustine's Reach in Bristol City Docks were built in 1894 for the storage of goods (mainly wine). The warehouses (known as E, W, U, V and T sheds) varied slightly in construction and architectural style. By the end of the 1960s they had fallen into disuse and disrepair and there were plans to comprehensively redevelop the area. This provoked a campaign to list E shed, which had a decorated gable end, stimulating an interest in retaining the sheds and finding new uses for them. W shed was used in the early 1970s as a home for the Arnolfini Gallery.

New use
T shed was demolished; U and V sheds were converted into exhibition spaces and E and W were re-used as a media centre and shopping arcade.

Construction schedule
1979–82.

Employment
50 (1986).

Financing
Public sector: £206,000
Private sector: £1,549,000.

Location
Bristol

Listed status
Listed within a conservation area

Architect
JT Design Build, Bristol

Total floor area
42,000 sq. ft

Cost
£1.75 million

Harvey's Foundry – South West

Location
Hayle, Cornwall

Listed status
Grade II

Architect
For proposed design: Poynton, Bradbury Wynter

History and former use
John Harvey, a blacksmith by trade, established the Foundry at Hayle at the end of the eighteenth century and by 1830 it was one of three leading Cornish foundries supplying mining equipment to collieries and ironworks throughout Britain, Europe and as far afield as Australia and South America. The surviving structure was built during the period of the firm's greatest prosperity from 1825–70. At the opposite end of the river estuary a rival copper smelting works, the Cornish Copper Company, was also established in the eighteenth century. Between them the two companies were responsible for the development of several buildings in the town. At the Foundry end of the town, although the engineering works and shipyard had closed down by 1904, other businesses survived on the site. Although in various ownerships and use, many of the original Harvey's buildings remain.

New use
The renovation of the Foundry is part of a programme of regeneration for the town. Hayle Town Trust, established in 1985, has renovated the Hammermill and Ropery as an amenity area. The Foundry Barn has been purchased by the Guinness Trust and grants have been obtained from various organizations to prepare detailed plans for 'Hayle Heritage/Craft/Workshop Centre'. Phase 1 of the project has begun, to stabilize the main building. Phase II is to secure funding for the completion of stabilization of the main building and to secure funding for renovation work to the stables, barns and yards.

Sources of finance
Grants totalling £6,000 for feasibility study obtained from: Hayle Town Council; Penwith District Council; Rural Development Commission (now known as the Countryside Agency); Single Regeneration Budget Challenge Fund.

Exeter Quayside – South West

Location
Exeter, Devon

History and former use
Exeter was a major port and clothmaking centre in the late-Medieval period. A ship canal was constructed as early as 1564–6, and the quayside developed to have an interesting range of structures.

New use
The oldest building (c1680) is a warehouse built on a medieval wharf and designed to handle imported raw materials and woollen cloth for export. It has now been converted into an interpretation centre run by the City Council. Nearby is the classical Custom House (1680–1) and an open market shelter and group of warehouses now housing shops. A new canal basin was opened in 1830. Commercial traffic ceased by 1965 and the warehouse came to house a boat museum; the collection now dispersed. The city has striven to draw visitors and locals into the riverside area. Following a design competition covering the 16 acre site, won by Niall Phillips architects, a new footbridge over the river was opened in 1988 and a formal square, Piazza Terracina, laid out in front of the major housing development. Just upstream a malthouse has been converted into a pub. The initiative is appropriately modest but has faltered at several stages due to the distance and gradient from the riverside to the centre of Exeter. Plans to re-use the Edwardian power station have foundered and Cricklepit Mill remains virtually derelict.

Coldharbour Mill – South West

History and former use

This woollen mill complex on the eastern fringe of Devon is notable for the extreme sensitivity with which it has been converted into a working museum. The complex was developed from 1799 by the Fox family on the site of a grist mill. Wool was spun there until 1981.

New use

Recognising its architectural qualities and the survival of both a water wheel and steam engine, a local group led by the vicar, Geoffrey Fraser, re-opened the mill in 1982 producing woollen and worsted yarns. Coldharbour Mill is now run primarily as a museum project but retains the feel of a working mill, having been spared the intrusive and over-tidy hands of museum designers and curators. A wide range of machinery is demonstrated to the public and two steam engines can be inspected.

Community issues

The project was developed by the local community, including those previously employed at the mill. The Coldharbour Mill Trust was established in January 1982.

Employment

Renovation and conversion of the mill, using the Manpower Services Commission Community Enterprise Scheme, employed twenty-seven for one year. Six permanent jobs initially created.

Construction schedule

January to July 1982.

Sources of funding

Loans: Parish Council – £3,000; District Council – £20,000; County Council – £50,000.

Matched by:
Rural Development Commission (now known as the Countryside Agency) – £73,000.
National Museum of Science & Industry – £5,000 for preservation of historic machinery.
Manpower Services Commission – £143,000 for wages and materials for renovation of mill.
National Heritage Memorial Fund – interest-free loan for 5–6 years for purchase of the mill.

Techniquest – Wales

Location
Cardiff Bay

Developer
Cardiff Bay Development Corporation

Architect
Paul Koralek (Arhends Burton Koralek)

Cost
£3.5 million

History and former use
Techniquest was designed around the frame of Bailey's Heavy Engineering workshop, a cast- and wrought-iron structure built between 1894–8. In 1993–4 the original framework was carefully dismantled and cleaned and repaired. A new mezzanine floor was constructed and the building extended beyond its original boundaries to create additional exhibition and workshop space.

New use
Science discovery centre. Techniquest was first established in 1986 and its original premises were in Cardiff city centre where there were thirty-five hands-on exhibits and 1,000 visitors per week. With the opportunity to move to the former factory site the size of the exhibition doubled and an education programme was linked. This was the UK's first purpose-built science discovery centre. It is part of a massive regeneration programme being undertaken by Cardiff Bay Development Corporation (CBDC). It is funded by the European Union and the Welsh Office. The largest project of the CBDC is the Cardiff Bay barrage.

Employment
Approximately 100 employees, full- and part-time.

Construction schedule
1993–5 (opened May 1995).

Sources of funding
European Union
Welsh Office.

Swansea Maritime Quarter – Wales

Location
Swansea

Listed status
Conservation area with listed buildings

Developer
Swansea City Council

Total area
95 acres

Cost
£117 million

History and former use
The South Dock was built in the 1850s, primarily to meet the needs of the local copper trade, around which the local economy was built. The area was once the centre of the city's social and political life, marked by Georgian houses and gardens and long promenades by the sea. The decline of the local metal industries in the mid-nineteenth century led to the closure of the dock in 1969, when it was purchased by the City Council.

New use
After resisting efforts to fill in the basin, the Council set about turning this derelict property into an asset and began rebuilding the infrastructure in 1975. Swansea Maritime Quarter today represents a complete turnaround in its origins. It is a successfully regenerated area with a mixture of residential accommodation, visitor attractions (including the historic area), and a major recreational harbour. Amongst the historic buildings, the Coastal Lines Warehouse of 1900 has been converted to Swansea Maritime Museum. The pumphouse has been converted into a pub/restaurant.

Construction schedule
1975–continuing.

Ebley Mill – West Midlands

History and former use
There is a long history of milling on this site. A fulling mill called Maldon's is recorded as working at Ebley in 1469. The long range of the present building, known as the machine blocks, was begun in 1818. In 1862, G F Bodley, the great Victorian church architect, added a new wing at the end.

New use
When the Council acquired the property its departments were scattered across Stroud and neighbouring Dursley. The building was converted to Council offices which have open-plan spaces and carefully accommodated computer systems.

Employment
300 Council employees (1990).

Construction schedule
1985–9.

Conservation issues
The Stroud Valley contains many large and grand mills. Twenty years ago they were all empty or beginning to deteriorate. Stroud District Council has taken a particularly pro-active role in trying to find new uses for them.

Location
Stroud, Gloucestershire

Listed status
Grade II*

Developer
Stroud District Council

Architect
Niall Phillips Associates

Total floor area
65,000 sq. ft

Gloucester Docks – West Midlands

History and former use
Gloucester was a site for waterborne transport from the time of the Romans at least, and in 1580 the City was granted Port status by Elizabeth I. However, the River Severn was not easily navigable and from 1793 the Gloucester and Berkeley canal was developed with the aim of bypassing the river. In 1820 the canal was linked to the network serving London, which made Gloucester an important trade link to the Midlands. By 1827 the canal was fully operational. It was the longest and widest ship canal in Britain at the time and an important centre for the trade of corn and timber.

By the mid 1860s larger ocean going vessels could no longer navigate the canal and much of the trade was taken over by Avonmouth Docks, leaving a rich legacy of warehouse buildings.

New use
The City Council now occupies one of the buildings. Other projects include museums and a shopping arcade. The National Waterways

Museum tells the story of England's extensive inland waterway system.

Construction schedule
Completed mid-1980s.

Conservation issues
The project aimed for the restoration and adaptive re-use of fifteen Victorian warehouses that line the basin of the historic harbour.

Location
Gloucester

Listed status
Conservation area with several listed buildings

Developer
Crest Nicholson Properties

Total area
32 acres

Custard Factory – West Midlands

Location
Birmingham

Developer
SPACE Organisation

Total floor area
200,000 sq. ft

Cost
£1.8 million

History and former use
A factory complex, which includes the late-nineteenth century terracotta-façaded building for Alfred Bird (*see Plate 5*). A large part of the complex is of the 1920s.

New use
Cultural centre – workspace and studios for young artists. A disused factory, formerly known as Scott House, has been converted by the SPACE Organisation into workspace for artists, musicians, craftspeople, filmmakers, designers, dancers, etc. The second part of the programme, Custard Factory Two, is to provide a new building with 100 workspaces above shops and cafes; a public piazza for performance and exhibition; a giant sculpture; open artists' studios; the restoration of an old factory to provide craft workshops; a riverside restaurant and 140 car parking spaces.

Community issues
The new use of the building filled the need for workspaces and studios for young artists at affordable prices.

Employment
300 people now working in the building.

Jewellery Quarter – West Midlands

Location
Birmingham

Listed status
Conservation area

History and former use
The jewellery industry gradually developed in this area of Birmingham from the mid nineteenth century. It grew from being a home industry, with a jewellery maker taking over a room in a house, to building a workshop behind. By 1861 7,500 people were engaged in the industry, having converted houses to workshops. A Jewellery Association was formed in 1890 by the setting up of a School of Jewellery and Silversmithing. By 1914 employment had grown to 20,000. The industry was hard hit by the recession following the Second World War and part of the area was redeveloped, including an extensive road widening scheme. Only part of the scheme was realised but by 1985 employment in the area that remained was reduced to only 4,000 in 600 firms.

New use
Since the 1980s the City Council has provided a good deal of support in the area with environmental improvement schemes. Warehouses have been converted to housing and smaller workshops in the St. Paul's Square area in particular. The Jewellery Quarter visitor centre has now been established.

Cromford Mill – East Midlands

History and former use
The first mill at Cromford was established by Richard Arkwright in 1771, where machinery was developed for water-powered cotton spinning. It became a model for factory building throughout Britain and the rest of the world. Towards the end of the nineteenth century, parts of the site were put to other uses, and from the 1920s until 1979 most of the site was used for the manufacture of colour pigment for paint. Cromford Mill is one of the major historic and industrial archaeological sites in the United Kingdom. Its importance may be considered in world terms.

New use
The buildings were under threat and in 1979 the Arkwright Society purchased a major part of the site. Since then it has gradually been transformed into a highly successful heritage and educational site, part of which is occupied by the University of Derby. Most of the buildings that have been refurbished to date are rent earning. The Society plans to refurbish further buildings, which are all committed to heritage and educational uses.

Employment
The Arkwright Society and Cromford Mill Ltd employ thirty-five staff both full- and part-time in jobs including retail, catering, visitor services, finance and administration. The Mill is open to the public every day except Christmas Day so little of the employment is seasonal.

Construction schedule
Work began on site in 1979; the programme continues.

Financing
Funding has come from various sources including (to 1998):
Architectural Heritage Fund loans £332,000
English Heritage £315,000
Derbyshire County Council £267,000
Derbyshire Dales District Council £21,000
Manpower Services Commission £870,000
Derbyshire Probation Service (unspecified amount in community projects)
English Partnerships £905,000.

Other sponsorship has come from industry, charities including The Arkwright Society, and volunteers.

Conservation issues
Before the buildings were adapted, all the original features were identified and, as far as possible, the new elements were designed around the old. In most instances, where it has survived, the original plaster has been left unrepaired so that any of the scars that may reveal the archaeology of the building remain to be seen. All the original walls have been limewashed; only on modern blockwork have modern paints been used. The external appearance of the buildings excludes as far as possible twentieth-century features to recreate an ambience of c.1800. The only exceptions are the restaurant and lavatory accommodation and Building 16, which retains its twentieth-century windows and floor levels as it is feared that the structure might be affected if these were changed.

Future prospects
The Cromford Mills have been considered worthy of World Heritage Site status. Projects planned should ensure that the unique site continues its success into the future.

Location
Cromford, Derbyshire

Listed status
Conservation area with various listed buildings

Developer
The Arkwright Society (registered charity no. 515526)

Cost
£4 million spent between 1979–98

A further £6 million expected to be spent on new projects

Torr Vale Mill – East Midlands

Location
**New Mills,
North West
Derbyshire**

Listed status
**Grade II* located in
the New Mills
Conservation Area**

Total floor area
**4,244 sq. m.
distributed through
six attached blocks,
which range in size
from 83 sq. m. to
2,360 sq. m.**

History and former use

Torr Vale Mill is a complex of gritstone buildings dating from the 1790s to the 1950s. It has a dramatic location in the deep gorge of the River Goyt where it runs through the once thriving textile town of New Mills. The building varies from single storey to five storeys in height. The complex was originally water-powered with two large water wheels in the basement of one of the three multi-storeyed mills. In the 1860s, when the mill was expanded and partly rebuilt, a large Lancashire steam boiler was installed, which was run in conjunction with the water-powered system. In the 1950s gas and electricity became the sources of heat, steam and power.

For 200 years the mill has produced cotton products and has possibly the longest chronology of continuous cotton manufacturing in England. It currently houses a towel-making business but cheaper imported products are likely to cause the closure of the business in the near future.

New use

Ideas for new uses are only tentative until a feasibility study is completed. But a mix of uses is considered appropriate including: offices, catering, training, educational, light industrial/commercial, and possibly use as residential accommodation or a visitor attraction.

Community issues

The mill complex provided hundreds of jobs in the past. It is the last mill in the gorge, others having been burnt down or demolished. There is a need for local job opportunities to be created as the town is almost without development land for industry or commerce. The mill is seen as both a conservation challenge and an opportunity to provide new local employment and community facilities. Its dramatic location and historical significance also make it a visitor attraction.

Environmental issues

The mill retains its water power supply channels and tunnels except for the two wheel pits that have been filled in. An initial study by a hydro-power consultant has shown that the site has the potential to generate enough electricity to supply the building's needs. This green asset has spawned the idea that the whole regeneration should be developed around principles of ecologically sound design. This ethos will influence the feasibility study brief.

Immediately opposite the mill complex, on the opposite side of the gorge, will be the Torrs Aerial Walkway (the Millennium Walkway), which is being built to provide the missing link in The Goyt Way, part of a long distance footpath. This dramatic facility will be cantilevered out from the gorge rockface in some places and on standing stilts in the river in others. It will add a new perspective to the mill. The possibility will exist to extend the walkway across the river into the mill yard.

Sources of funding

A partnership is being formed between the mill owners, the local authorities, community groups, businesses and statutory agencies to put the relationship on a formal basis. Feasibility studies will then be commissioned to explore practicalities, costs and funding for the project.

(Photo: Derbyshire County Council)

Kiln Warehouse – East Midlands

(Illustration: Allen Tod Architects)

Location
**Newark,
Nottinghamshire**

Listed status
Grade II*

Developer
**British Waterways
North**

Architect
Allen Tod Architects

Total floor area
2,050 sq. m.

Cost
£1,400,000

History and former use
Kiln and malting floor and warehouse dated 1857. Thought to be the earliest mass concrete building in Britain and possibly the world. In recent times it was standing derelict and burnt out.

New use
Information Centre and offices for British Waterways. Lettable office space for tenants.

Community issues
Reviving the riverside area in Newark as part of a larger regeneration project.

Employment
Providing employment for approximately fifty people.

Sources of funding
British Waterways
English Heritage
English Partnerships.

Conservation issues
Earliest example of mass concrete building in Britain. External walls kept intact by erecting a new building within a building.

Future prospects
Flexible office facility with lettable space to encourage a variety of potential users.

Lace Quarter – East Midlands

Location
Nottingham

Listed status
Conservation area

Developer
Nottingham City Council and private developers

Cost
**Up to 1985:
£3 million**

History and former use
Nottingham's lace industry expanded in the second half of the nineteenth century with the development of machine-made lace. In 1890 about 17,000 people were employed in 500 lace factories. The heart of the industry was centred on the Lace Market where massive ornate

warehouses were built with impressive centrally placed entrances that resembled huge town houses. The lace industry fell into decline after the First World War and many of the warehouses were subdivided and let to small textile firms paying minimal rents. Lack of maintenance led to very run-down conditions by the 1960s.

New use
In 1969 the Lace Market was designated one of Nottingham's first conservation areas. It took considerable time and effort to get regeneration under way but between 1976–85 over 100 buildings had been renovated with mixed use including housing and commercial premises.

Construction schedule
1976 onwards.

Awards
Europa Nostra 1983.

Etruscan Bone Mill – East Midlands

Location
**Etruria,
Stoke-on-Trent**

Listed status
Grade II* and a Scheduled Ancient Monument

Developer/Architect
City of Stoke-on-Trent Council

General contractor
City Council Direct Works and external consultants

History and former use
A former potters' mill built in 1857 by George Kirk of Etruria, the complex comprises a flint calcining kiln with a truncated chimney, and a two-storey mill housing two bevel gear trains in the lower floor to drive ten grinding pans on the upper floor. Original machinery is intact and in use including an 1820s steam-powered beam engine in the engine house and in the boiler house a 1903 Cornish boiler. The mill was used commercially until 1972.

New use
Industrial museum.

Employment
Four full-time staff, two part-time and a licensed blacksmith.

Construction schedule
Restoration began in 1975 and is continuing.

Financing
City of Stoke-on-Trent Council; grants; sponsorship; private donations.

Conservation issues
The historic machinery is still used regularly for demonstration purposes.

(Photo: City of Stoke-on-Trent Council)

Gladstone Pottery Museum – East Midlands

History and former use
A nineteenth-century bone china tableware factory, including a steam engine, four bottle ovens to fire pottery, and workshops.

New use
Gladstone Working Pottery Museum – a museum that preserves and presents the way of life of the North Staffordshire pottery worker past and present.

Employment
The museum currently employs eighteen full-time equivalent staff.

(Photo: Gladstone Pottery Museum)

Location
Longton, Stoke-on-Trent

Listed status
Grade II*

Developer
Originally Staffordshire Pottery Industry Preservation Trust;

now Stoke-on-Trent City Council

Architect (Current)
City of Stoke-on-Trent, City Architect's Department

General contractor (Current)
City of Stoke-on-Trent Council

Quarry Bank Mill – North West

History and former use
A cotton mill founded in 1784 by Samuel Grey, a merchant/manufacturer based in Manchester. Initially a spinning mill, weaving was added in 1830. The mill buildings were expanded in a series of stages, all retaining the original Georgian style architecture. By the middle of the nineteenth century Quarry Bank Mill was the largest cotton mill in Britain and headquarters of an empire of five mills. The mill stayed in production until 1959.

New use
In 1976 the Quarry Bank Mill Trust was set up to operate the mill as a working museum of the cotton textile industry. The mill and estate (including the apprentice house and Styal village, built to house the mill workers) was given to the National Trust in 1989.

Employment
The mill now employs thirty full-time and sixty part-time staff along with 250 volunteers.

Construction schedule
The main restoration was completed in 1980 – work is continuing.

Financing
Capital works – The National Trust and funds raised by Quarry Bank Mill Trust.

Conservation issues
There is an on-going capital repair programme. Provision of access for approximately 200,000 visitors per annum within a difficult site. Future developments include the restoration and conversion of the gas retort house into an orientation/exhibition space.

Location
Styal, Wilmslow, Cheshire

Listed status
Grade II*

Developer
The National Trust

Architect
Various. Restoration of the mill engine and boiler houses was by S T Walker and Partners

Total floor area
63,000 sq. ft

Ancoats Mills – North West

(Photo: Ian Finlay Architects)

Location
Manchester

Listed status
Conservation area with many listed buildings

History and former use

Manchester was the world's first industrial city. It was here that the industrial revolution came of age, and where the spinning mule and the steam engine, the heart of the British cotton industry, came together for the first time. The area grew piecemeal and today, alongside the mills, can be found Manchester's first municipal housing (Victoria Square), the Daily Express 'black glass' building and the Methodist Women's night shelter (the Derros Building), all buildings of great merit in their own right. At the centre of the area is the landmark building of the Romanesque church of St. Peter's, newly restored externally and acting as a symbol of Ancoats' growing regeneration from its former dereliction (*see Plates 18 & 19*).

There are a number of industrial buildings in the area including those listed below:

Murray's Old Mill (1798), Decker Mill (1802), Redhill Street

Listed Grade II*. The mill fronting the canal on Redhill Street was built in two parts. The original Murray's Old Mill was built specifically to take advantage of the marriage of the spinning mule and steam achieved a year earlier in a neighbouring mill. The early steam power was supplied by Boulton and Watt engines. The Decker Mill was added in 1802 and a larger Boulton and Watt engine was erected.

Sedgwick Mill, 1818–20
(pictured right)

Listed Grade II, this building was designed by James Lowe in association with Sir William Fairburn. Of fireproof construction, except for its timber roof, the building contained an internal engine house.

Ice Plant Building, c1860

Originally built for the warehousing of fruit, vegetables and fish, it had an attached ice making plant from which it acquired its name. The local Italian community became interested in the building because of its ice production facilities and consequently the area became the centre of Manchester's ice-cream manufacture.

Warehouse No.5, corner of Jersey Street and Gunn Street, c1830

A very good example of small-scale development with inset 'taking in' doors and protective rubbing strakes. For many years it was home of Kirkham and Platt printers. Claims that it once housed a street organ factory are being investigated.

Sedgwick New Mill, Redhill Street, 1868

Following the 'cotton famine' of the 1860s and the introduction of larger mules, the more successful cotton firms needed to expand their mills. Houldsworth's of Newton Street moved the whole enterprise to Reddish, creating a company town. McConnel and Kennedy of Ancoats internally reconstructed their existing mills and added the L-shaped New Mill.

Paragon Mill, Jersey Street, 1912
(pictured left)

Listed Grade II*. Built at the same time as the Royal Mill as an extension to Sedgwick Mill. Driven by electric motor from the Corporation mains and still has one of the original motors in situ. Concrete floors are carried on transverse steel beams and cast-iron columns.

Royal Mill, Redhill Street, 1912

Listed Grade II*. Old Mill was demolished and in 1912 the Royal Mill was erected on the site. It received its name following a visit by King George VI in 1942. The construction and power system is exactly as used in the Paragon Mill.

New Little Mill, Jersey Street/Radium Street/Bengal Street, 1908

Listed Grade II, this building replaced an earlier mill of 1820. Constructed in Accrington brick with concrete floors, it is unusual in design for this area, being more like the mills of Bolton and Leigh. It was powered by electricity and is thought to be Manchester's first mill to be run from the Corporation mains system.

Murray's New Mill, Jersey Street, 1804

Listed Grade II*, this was the largest mill on the Murray site, added to complete the typical box formation with its enclosed courtyard.

Fire Proof Mill, Bengal Street and Redhill Street, 1842

Listed Grade II*, these mills were extensions to the Murray's Mills complex and linked by tunnels under Bengal Street. The mill is currently occupied.

Regeneration strategy

A number of groups concerned with the future of Ancoats and surrounding areas have come together and formed a partnership under the auspices of the Eastside Regeneration Executive Partnership Committee, a Manchester City Council SRB initiative which aims to tackle the decline of the area.

The Ancoats Buildings Preservation Trust is an independent charity established in 1995 as a traditional rolling-fund building preservation trust. The Trust works in partnership with the Ancoats Urban Village Company, established to facilitate inward investment and encourage commercial and developer interest in both the historic buildings and the key vacant site new-build opportunities.

The largely forgotten area now has the potential to become a new, vibrant, living quarter of the city. It will become a true Urban Village for the benefit of the existing community attracting new residents and businesses, within five minutes' walk of Manchester city centre.

Regeneration Organisations

Ancoats Buildings Preservation Trust Ltd
Ancoats Urban Village Company Ltd
Eastside Regeneration.

Sources of funding

English Heritage; Manchester City Council; Single Regeneration Budget (SRB); ERDF; ESF; NW Regional Development Agency.

Conservation issues

Ancoats Buildings Preservation Trust Ltd has been established to preserve whatever of the historical, architectural and constructional heritage may exist in and around the Ancoats area of Manchester. Its principal aim is to secure and envelop the key historic buildings and mills. Any land or buildings sold or let will be subject to covenants, conditions and restrictions necessary to ensure their preservation. The Trust has acquired a long lease on one key building, St Peter's Church, and is prepared to act as a 'developer of last resort', taking other semi-derelict buildings into its temporary ownership to undertake refurbishment works to a stage where the buildings have a commercial value on the open market.

Future prospects

Ancoats is set to become one of Britain's first true Urban Villages, demonstrating how formerly neglected urban areas can assist in bringing energy, vibrancy and economic vitality back to cities throughout the country.

(Photo: Ian Finlay Architects)

Castlefield – North West

Location
Manchester

Listed status
Conservation area

History and former use

The Castlefield area of Manchester evolved from a Roman settlement of AD79. From the mid-eighteenth century it became an area of thriving industry and it boasts Britain's first man-made canal – the Bridgewater Canal – and the first passenger railway station, which now houses the Museum of Science and Industry. The network of canals, warehouses, railways and viaducts that dominate the landscape of Castlefield are a legacy of the importance of the area during the Industrial Revolution, however, the decline of industry since the 1950s led to the area becoming a derelict and abandoned wasteland in the heart of the city.

New use

Since the early 1980s, initiatives led by Manchester City Council and Central Manchester Development Corporation (1988–96) have turned the area into a positive working example of urban regeneration for uses including tourism, housing and business. Amongst the many refurbishments and new developments the regenerated industrial buildings include:

Middle Warehouse/Castle Quay

A development to convert a former cotton warehouse, built c1830, (listed Grade II) into forty-four flats, shops, office space, and studios for local radio stations.

Employment
Approximately 100

Developer
Manchester Ship Canal Company

Architects
Frank Stafford (Liverpool)

General contractor
Fairclough (now AMEC)

Total floor area
80,000 sq. ft

Cost
£4.6 million

Sources of funding
£1.6 million City Grant + private finance

Nowhere Bar

A £500,000 conversion of a listed railway arch and former works site into a cafe bar, incorporating modern architecture.

Developers
In House Leisure

Architects
Judge Gill Associates

Eastgate (formerly Gail House)

The conversion of a former rag mop factory into a modern open plan office development. It stands along the original lines of the east gate of the Roman fort.

Employment
Approximately 150 people

Developer
Castlefield Estates

Architects
Stephenson, Somerville, Bell (Manchester)

General contractor
AMEC/Jackson Construction

Construction schedule
Completed July 1992

Total floor area
25,000 sq. ft

Cost
£2.6 million

Sources of funding
£600,000 City Grant + private finance

John Bass (Packers) Warehouse
One of the original ideas was to utilize the John Bass warehouse for a hotel. A great deal of financial consideration has gone into this by the developers, although it is still uncertain as to whether it will indeed be a hotel or offices.

Developer
Castlefield Estates

Architect
OMI Architects

General Contractor
Mansell Construction

Total floor area
25,500 sq. ft

Costs
Phase I – £1.5 million
Phase II – estimated £3 million (not complete)

Dukes'92
Initiated in 1991, the former stable building of the Merchants Warehouse has been extended and converted into a popular waterside café bar. A further extension was completed in 1998. The name comes from its location at the junction of the Duke of Bridgwater's canal and the 92nd lock of the Rochdale canal.

Employment
Approximately forty people

Developer
Castlefield Estates

Architects
Phase I: Stephenson, Somerville, Bell (Manchester) – £300,000
Phase II: OMI Architects – £600,000

General Contractor
Curbishley Construction

Merchants Warehouse
Built in 1827 this is one of the oldest existing warehouses on the canal basin, which has been converted into office space.

Listed status
Grade II

Employment
Approximately 150 people

Developer
Castlefield Estates

Architects
Simpson Associates (Manchester)

Total floor area
39,000 sq. ft

Cost
Phase I – £1.3 million
Phase II – £2.7 million excluding fit-out

Sources of funding
English Heritage – £180,000; European Regional Development Fund – £635,000; + private finance

Community issues
Since the early 1980s the whole area has been transformed. The provision of housing, offices, and leisure has injected new life into the area. (1995 estimated visitors: two million).

Sources of funding
Manchester City Council and Manchester Development Corporation with core funding of £20 million from organizations including: Department of the Environment; European Regional Development Fund; English Heritage; English Partnerships; Millennium Commission. Private sector investment of a further £80 million (to 1996).

Future prospects
Further proposed developments include housing and hotel facilities.

Houldsworth Mill – North West

(Photo: Stockport Metropolitan Borough Council)

Location
Reddish, Stockport, Greater Manchester

Listed status
Grade II*

Developer
The mill is owned by the Heaton and Houldsworth Property Company

Northern Counties (Housing Association) Ltd will purchase and develop floors 1 to 4 of the south mill (125 year lease)

Total floor area
400,000 sq. ft including both wings, the extension and the central core

Cost
Over £8 million

History and former use
Cotton spinning and weaving until mid 1950s. Used as warehouse by mail order company (John Myers) until mid 1970s when sold and split into industrial, commercial and leisure uses. Original construction in 1865; later additions include weaving shed extension to south mill front and additional engine houses to north and south mill. John Myers built large 100,000 sq. ft five-storey rear extension as offices for mail order business on site of north mill pond in late 1960s.

New use
Sixty-eight flats in south mill (floors 1 to 4). Refurbishment of north mill and centre for commercial use including managed workspace and technology training centre. Theme is technology-based office and light industrial use.

Community issues
Proposal to use central engine house and former boiler house for community uses, including café and gallery. Building Preservation Trust set up involving established local community groups and individuals.

Employment
The commercial element of the project will provide employment in refurbished floorspace with potential for 300 to 500 new jobs. The mill contains some existing businesses and they and their jobs will be safeguarded – some businesses will remain in the revamped mill whilst others will be relocated to the extension – any remaining will be given relocation assistance.

Construction schedule
Final completion by September 2000.

Sources of funding
Finance is provided by: Heaton and Houldsworth Property Company; Northern Counties (Housing Association) Ltd; English Partnerships; European Regional Development Fund; Stockport Metropolitan Borough Council.

Conservation issues
The main issues revolve around the changes required to the south mill to facilitate the flat development. These include the need to provide a light well in the south mill, the need to demolish the south engine house and rope race and the need to alter the height of a ground floor extension. All proposed alterations have been discussed with and agreed by English Heritage and Listed Building consent has been obtained for the proposals.

Future prospects
The commercial element will be anchored by: some existing tenants; 40,000 sq. ft of managed workspace to be run by the Council for technology-based and cultural industries; and a centre for IT training run by Ridge Danyers College. Remaining floorspace will be marketed by the owners using the technology theme.

(Photo: Stockport Metropolitan Borough Council)

History and former use

This was the key market area of Victorian Manchester and a major shopping district in the post-war years. When the Arndale Centre was completed in 1981, property values plummeted and the area went into decline. It retained its wholesale trades but many shopfronts were shuttered or became derelict.

Community issues

The Northern Quarter Association was formed in 1993. A voluntary organization, it represents local residents, workers and users as well as promoting the physical, economic, social and cultural development of the area. In 1994 a regeneration study of the area was carried out in conjunction with the City Council, which formed the basis of a regeneration strategy.

New use

The Northern Quarter has now reinvented itself as an area for alternative shopping and experimental businesses. It is a vibrant and diverse area for shopping, music, food, entertainment, fashion, living and being creative. As a result of the bomb in the Arndale Centre in 1996, approximately 120 small businesses relocated to the Northern Quarter and a majority of these have remained. Revival focuses on Oldham Street where many new shops have opened. *The Big Issue* has located its northern office at the corner of Great Ancoats Street and the 1930s *Daily Express* building has been restored and is partly occupied by the Friends Provident. The area has gained a range of new accommodation including housing association developments and loft-style conversions for young urbanites. Several major buildings are re-used:

Smithfield Buildings, Oldham Street
The buildings of Manchester's premier department store of the nineteenth century became vacant in the 1970s. The complex of nine buildings is being developed by Urban Splash to house a fitness centre, shops and apartments (*see Plate 7*).

Developer
Urban Splash

Architect
Stephenson Bell

Quantity Surveyors
Simon Fenton Partnerships

Structural Engineers
Eric Bassett Associates

Sources of funding
Supported by English Partnerships

Manchester Craft Centre, Oak Street
Formerly the fish and poultry market, the Victorian building, which has a huge glass roof, has been converted to provide a complex of two storeys of small studios with a café in the central space.

Afflecks Palace and Arcade, Oldham Street and the Coliseum, Church Street
Have been converted to contain small shops for businesses such as retro clothing, tattooing and body piercing.

Sources of Funding

Over the past three years the Northern Quarter Association has secured: £93,141 of revenue funding from the private and public sector; £30,000 per annum from the Miles Platting, Ancoats and Northern Quarter Single Regeneration Budget; £318,900 of project related funding from private and public sector.

To date approximately £20 million of known private and public sector funding has been attracted into the Northern Quarter for capital projects.

Future prospects

Further redevelopment is planned for the Smithfield Site, which embraces the former wholesale Smithfield Market and surrounding area covering approximately 2.4 hectares. A brief was recently offered with the aim of attracting partners for the development of this site. Potential uses include residential, retail, leisure/hotel, events space, galleries and other mixed uses. Other possibilities include the development of a retail market, perhaps based on fashion and textiles.

Location
Manchester

Listed status
Conservation area

Wigan Pier – North West

Location
Wigan

Listed status
Grade II listed mill within a conservation area

Developer
Wigan Metropolitan Borough Council

Cost
Initial cost of development £4 million

History and former use

A series of canal warehouses and a cotton spinning mill comprise what is known as Wigan Pier. The area was developed when the Liverpool to Wigan section of the Leeds to Liverpool canal was completed in 1777. In 1822 a pier head were erected in the canal basin for loading canal boats with coal, which was brought from local collieries by a wagon road (later the railway). In 1842 the wagon road and pier head was taken over by Winstanley Collieries and it became known as Wigan Pier. Steam engines were introduced to pull coal trucks back from the pier in 1878. During the 1890s brick warehouses were built on the Wallgate side of the canal, and in 1907 the present Trencherfield Mill was built for spinning company William Woods and Son Ltd. Cotton making continued at the mill until 1941–2 when it was used to make munitions. In 1946, following the Second World War, the building was re-equipped with new machinery and at that time approximately 570 people were employed, 80 per cent of them women. In 1964 the mill was acquired by Courtaulds Ltd and the upper storeys of the building are still used by them for the production of household textiles. The pier itself, which had long been disused, was dismantled in 1929 and sold for a scrap value of £34.00.

New use

In 1982 the Wigan Pier Project was launched and the following year Wigan Museum Service took over the engine house. The mill engine was restored to working order and this was opened to the public in 1984 along with the Orwell public house and restaurant, which was housed in one of the brick warehouses. A replica of Wigan Pier was put in place at the same time. Another brick warehouse was used for the heritage centre 'The Way We Were' and a Schools Centre was opened in a stone warehouse that was built in the 1790s. This phase of the project was officially opened by Queen Elizabeth II in 1986.

Community issues

This was an area of low employment, which had once been the hub of cotton, coal and canal industries.

Employment

Forty-three people now work directly for Wigan Pier, with an additional ten people employed as contractors. The upper floors of the mill are leased to Courtaulds textile manufacturers, which provides further employment for the local community. Surrounding buildings have been developed since Wigan Pier. Local people are employed along with over twenty volunteers who act as guides, interpreters, etc.

Construction schedule

Opened April 1986.

Sources of funding

Wigan Metropolitan Borough Council with other grant aid.

Future prospects

Phase II of Wigan Pier is based on the ground floor of Trencherfield Mill. Opie's Museum of Memories houses items from Robert Opie's collection which are displayed as a decade by decade tour of the twentieth century. Public art schemes form part of this Phase II project.

(Photo: Wigan Metropolitan Borough Council)

History and former use

Peter Whitehead built Ilex Mill in 1856 to the best modern standards of natural lighting and fireproofing. The mill has a massive architectural presence overlooking terraces of contemporary workers' housing. Its eastern aspect overlooks a site which is possibly of national importance in the development of the textile industry, from the handlooms of weavers' cottages (listed Grade II), through the water power of Hall Carr Mill (listed Grade II), to the climax of the steam-powered Ilex Mill itself. The mill was used for cotton production until the turn of the century, then for footwear. Large-scale manufacture ended in the mill in 1981. Following a brief spell as a training workshop, it was finally vacated in 1985–6.

New use

A local partnership representing Rossendale Borough Council, Rawtenstall Civic Society, Lancashire Constabulary and the Local Chamber of Commerce has developed proposals for the mill's re-use as part of Rawtenstall. The proposed new uses for the mill include: Town Hall administrative offices; Council Chamber and Members' suite; police custody suite; public hall for community use; tourist information office. Surplus space will be brought up to a good basic standard, which will allow flexibility to meet the needs of occupants who have not yet been identified.

(Photo: Borough of Rossendale)

Community issues

Ilex Mill offers an exciting opportunity for a mixture of vibrant new economic, cultural and social opportunities and will become the heart of the regenerated Rawtenstall town centre.

Sources of funding

Rossendale Borough Council has acquired the building on behalf of the local partnership and secured a funding package of about £4 million from the Heritage Lottery Fund, English Heritage and English Partnerships.

Conservation issues

It is proposed that the project is based on: minimal intervention with as little demolition of the historic fabric as possible; the building retaining as much of the internal open space as possible; keeping in open view the brick arched ceilings; taking full advantage of the potential for enhancement of the outward appearance of the building, particularly on the riverside elevation (e.g. sensitive external lighting).

Location
Rawtenstall, Lancashire

Listed status
Grade II

Total floor area
approximately 11,000 sq. m.

(Photo: Borough of Rossendale)

(Photo: Borough of Rossendale)

India Mill – North West

Location
Darwen, Lancashire

Listed status
Grade II/
Chimney Grade II*

Developer
**Brookhouse
Managed Properties
Ltd.**

Architect
**Campbell Driver
Partnership**

Total floor area
**Approximately
240,000 sq. ft**

(Photo: Brookhouse Managed Properties Ltd.)

History and former use
Eccles Shorrock & Co, cotton spinners, constructed this impressive building between 1859–71. Much of the work, including erection of the massive chimney, was completed in the mid 1860s and machinery was installed in 1871. At its peak in the 1920s, the mill housed almost 100,000 textile spinning machines and employed a significant workforce. The mill began to move towards spinning artificial fibres in 1933, became part of the William Bird Textile Group in 1954, was purchased in 1985 by Carrington Viyella, and closed in 1991.

New use
The building was acquired by Brookhouse Composites Ltd, a leading composite tooling and manufacturing company in the aerospace and automobile sectors. As well as occupying the lower two floors themselves, the company undertook an extensive refurbishment programme to create three business centres: India Mill centre, The Galleries, The Courtyard (*see Plate 24*).

Employment
200+ – expected to rise to between 500 and 1,000.

Financing
Private capital with grant support from English Partnerships.

(Photo: Brookhouse Managed Properties Ltd.)

History and former use

The development of the docks in Liverpool began in the early eighteenth century with the growth of trade with the American colonies and spread of the industrial revolution to Lancashire, Yorkshire and the Midlands. The ever increasing volume of shipping and demand for berthing space eventually led to the development of seven and a half miles of docks and associated warehouses on a breathtaking scale. The period of greatest activity was between 1824–60 when Jesse Hartley was dock engineer. By 1900 Liverpool was the largest port in the world. With the gradual decline of industry and trade towards the mid-twentieth century, many of the magnificent buildings fell into decline. Since the 1980s, with the refurbishment of the Albert Dock, there have been several regeneration projects on the dockside and work continues.

New use

Albert Dock (pictured)

The five-storey warehouses are Grade I listed buildings. Built 1846–8, they were designed by Jesse Hartley and Philip Hardwick. The Dock Traffic Office 1846–7, in the form of a Classical temple, also Grade I listed, forms one external corner of the courtyard. These, along with various smaller buildings in the dockyard, were refurbished during the 1980s to include office space, apartments, a pub, wine bars, shops, craft workshops, Granada TV studios (in the former Dock Traffic Office), the northern outpost of the Tate Gallery, and the Merseyside Maritime Museum. The Tate Gallery has recently undergone major refurbishment. At ground level on the south corner of the Albert Dock, a space that was formerly a TV studio, was fitted out in 1997 by architects Shed KM as a student information centre for Liverpool Hope University College.

Wapping Dock warehouse

Standing south east of the Albert Dock, the Wapping Dock warehouse was built in 1856 to a design by Jesse Hartley, very similar in construction and materials to the Albert Dock. Listed Grade II, the warehouse was refurbished in 1989 to provide 114 residences, from one to four bedrooms in size.

Waterloo Dock warehouse

Built in 1867 by George Fosbery Lyster as a grain store, the warehouse incorporated machinery for raising, storing, turning, ventilating and discharging grain. Beginning in the early 1990s, the building was refurbished by Barratt house builders to provide one-, two-, and three-bedroom apartments. The exterior of the building remains largely intact. The interior has been refurbished to provide typical Barratt homes. Little of the original interior is exposed.

Stanley Dock warehouses

Built in 1848 to the same design and construction (Jesse Hartley) as the Albert Dock and Wapping Dock warehouses, the Stanley Dock warehouses stand at the terminus of the Liverpool and Leeds Canal. The Tobacco Warehouse, which extends along the south front of the dock, is dated 1900. Built of red and blue brick with eleven storeys above a rusticated stone base, it is thought to be the largest in the world. All of the warehouses are currently used for a Sunday market. They have been sold recently to a developer but plans for their re-use are at a very early stage.

Location
Liverpool, Merseyside

Listed status
Various

Liverpool Rope Walks – North West

Location
Liverpool

Listed status
**Conservation area
with listed buildings**

History and former use

The Bold Street and Duke Street area of Liverpool was laid out in the eighteenth century, which was a very wealthy period in the history of Liverpool. Through this area ran a 'rope walk' used in connection with the craft of ropemaking for the sailing ships of the time. It became a fashionable residential area for wealthy merchants, and towards the end of the nineteenth century it was one of the most exclusive shopping areas outside London. Throughout the area there were several warehouses related to the trade of the port of Liverpool. With the decline of the port this area became run down and derelict.

(Photo: Urban Splash)

New use

There is now an initiative to revive the area and make it once again a lively part of the city. The City Council is a leading player in the Liverpool Rope Walks Partnership, which has recently been formed. Meanwhile, regeneration has been continuing with initiatives including:

Concert Square (*pictured left*)
A converted derelict chemical laboratory situated in the core of this quarter. It includes loft apartments, three café-bars, a photographic gallery, nursery and office space fronting a new urban square developed in partnership by Urban Splash and Liverpool City Council.

Liverpool Palace
Nine redundant warehouses in the Slater Street area have been converted by Urban Splash into workspace, offices, studios, specialist shops, and the Baa Bar (*pictured below*). The development is particularly aimed at Liverpool's lively youth culture.

Community issues

New life, vitality and an open space have been brought to a previously run-down area, including the provision of housing in the centre of the city.

Employment

Many jobs have been created in both the construction industry and in the new businesses that are gradually moving into the area. The Liverpool Rope Walks Partnership has engaged an 'employment broker' to encourage opportunities for employment in the area.

Sources of funding

Funding is being sought from both public and private sources.

Conservation issues

A mix of regeneration and new development will ensure a brighter future for the area.

Bass Maltings – Yorkshire & Humberside

History and former use
The maltings were built between 1892 and 1905 and designed by the architect H S Couchman. Made up of eight brick pavilions and a massive central tower, the total frontage amounts to nearly 1,000 feet (*see Plate 16*). The three central pavilions were damaged by fire in the mid 1970s and have been vacant ever since. Other buildings on the site are still at least partially occupied, but there is no wholesale use. The condition of the complex is fair, but certainly deteriorating. Appropriate uses include commercial, residential or mixed.

New use
A working party was set up ten years ago to look at possibilities for the buildings and to encourage new use. To date no appropriate uses have been found.

Community issues
Sleaford is a relatively small town. The sheer size of the site makes sustainable use of the buildings difficult.

Employment
If an appropriate use could be found, employment in the area could be increased.

Future prospects
Action needs to be taken now. Bass Maltings are too important and impressive to lose.

Location
Sleaford, Lincolnshire

Listed status
Grade II*

Total floor area
500,000 sq. ft

Globe Works – Yorkshire & Humberside

(Photo: Allen Tod Architects)

(Photo: Allen Tod Architects)

History and former use
Possibly the world's first purpose-built cutlery factory, c1818. Ad hoc workshop buildings and a courtyard stand behind a Classical façade. Partial damage was caused by industrial unrest in the 1840s. It became a general factory/warehouse until an arson attack in the 1970s, when it was left derelict.

New use
Managed works with leisure and community arts. Uses include workspace, cutlery centre, training area, pub and restaurant.

Construction schedule
1987–8.

Sources of funding
Sheffield City Council; European Regional Development Fund (ERDF); English Tourist Board; English Heritage; Arts Council.

Conservation issues
The aim was to retain as much original fabric as possible after fire damage and dereliction. The stone façades were repaired, timber windows restored and rebuilt off site. Top floor of workshops restored to original design. It was the first significant project in the Kelham Island Conservation Area. A high quality conservation project.

Location
Sheffield

Listed status
Grade II*

Developer
The Leadmill Arts Group

Architect
Allen Tod Architects

General Contractor
Henry Boot Ltd.

Total floor area
Approximately 30,000 sq. ft

Cost
£1.2 million

Templeborough Steelplant (MAGNA) – Yorkshire & Humberside

Location
Rotherham, South Yorkshire

Developer
Magna Trust (company limited by guarantee)

Architect
Chris Wilkinson Associates

Exhibition design
Event Communications

Construction manager
Schal International Management Ltd

Total floor area
34,000 sq. m.

Cost
£37 million

(Photo: Hunting Aerofilms)

History and former use
Steelworks, originally built in 1916, it was converted to Europe's largest electric arc melting shop 1962–5. It was closed in 1993.

New use
Visitor attraction and educational resource themed around the four elements: earth, fire, air and water; and the story of modern steel.

Community issues
The community benefits of the project are considerable. They include the provision of a major new educational resource for the people of the area and the whole of the North of England. The project will act as a catalyst for the transformation of the Templeborough area by regenerating the derelict fabric and lifting the economic profile of the locality.

Employment
Creation of 230 direct/indirect jobs (excluding construction).

Construction schedule
Construction begins early 1999; fully open to the public Easter 2001.

Sources of funding
Millennium Commission 50 per cent matched by: European Regional Development Fund; English Partnerships; Rotherham Metropolitan Borough Council; Stadium Group; sponsorship.

Conservation issues
Preservation of scale and 'feel' of the steelworks; preservation of an electric arc furnace as representation of modern steel production.

Future prospects
Anticipated visitor numbers: 350,000 per annum.

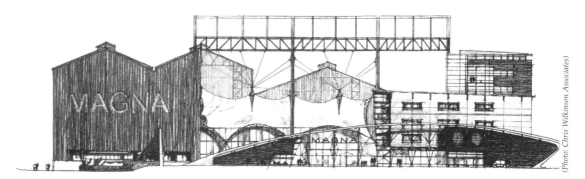
(Photo: Chris Wilkinson Associates)

Bradford Design Exchange – Yorkshire & Humberside

History and former use
Wool merchant's warehouse.

New use
In 1989 Allen Tod Architects took the concept of a Design Exchange to Bradford Metropolitan Council, together with suggested buildings. The concept of studio offices and workshops for designers and artists together with high quality conference and other shared workspace was warmly embraced. It has been very successful in attracting its target market of designers, particularly related to the fabrics industry, architects, graphic and product designers etc. It is regularly used for exhibitions by the Design Council. The project linked together three adjacent Grade II listed buildings.

Employment
Twelve employed at the Design Exchange. Several in various design companies.

Construction schedule
1988–9.

Sources of funding
European Regional Development Fund
English Heritage
City of Bradford Metropolitan Council

Conservation issues
Accessibility to linked split-level structure.
Retention/repair of damaged structure.

Awards
Civic Trust Award.

(Photo: Allen Tod Architects)

Location
**Little Germany,
Bradford,
West Yorkshire**

Listed status
Grade II

Developer
**City of Bradford
Metropolitan Council**

Architect
Allen Tod Architects

General Contractor
Turners

Total floor area
30,000 sq. ft

Cost
£2.1 million

Calder and Hebble Navigation Warehouse – Yorkshire & Humberside

Location:
Wakefield

Listed status
Grade II

History and former use

The Calder and Hebble Navigation Warehouse (*see Plate 6*) fronts the River Calder. Huge for its time, the warehouse was built in 1790, and subsequently altered in 1810, as a grain and storage depot to facilitate trading along the canal system. It is stone built and comprises over 26,000 sq. ft. The building is within the old industrial core of Wakefield, near a number of other traditional mill buildings which are in need of refurbishment and development. To the north of the Navigation Warehouse is the brick-built Rutland Mills complex of 1875, formerly a woollen mill and now an important source of small business units. Next to the complex is the site of the former canal basin and dry dock now filled in. The fourteenth-century Chantry Bridge and Chapel are nearby, east of the main A61 river bridge and adjoining an eighteenth-century pack-horse bridge. To the south of the Navigation Warehouse is the attractive Wakefield Lock, which is the entrance to the canal from the River Calder.

The Warehouse, which is vacant, together with some of the adjoining land and buildings, is owned by British Waterways who are anxious to repair and refurbish the building.

The City of Wakefield Council has established a waterfront partnership, representative of the community, local business and land owners, to steer the regeneration of the entire waterfront area with a strategy based on the creation of a cultural quarter at the southern gateway to the city of Wakefield.

New use

The major focus and attraction will be the refurbished Navigation Warehouse, subject to a detailed feasibility study, to be used as a new gallery for the national collection of sculptures by Wakefield-born Barbara Hepworth. The gallery will be the catalyst and flagship for the regeneration of Wakefield's new Waterfront Quarter. The aim is to refurbish most of the buildings on the site to enable existing businesses to flourish and attract new businesses into the vacant space. There will be some new construction to accommodate shops and offices. The new gallery, together with the canal-based activities and riverside moorings,

will be a major new visitor attraction. The project offers other opportunities including:

Arts workshop and gallery space
Hotel
Residential
Specialist retail
Canal moorings
Workspace – offices
Bars/cafes

Developer

A preferred developer was appointed in April 1998 to work with the waterfront partnership to promote the regeneration of the area.

Costs

The Waterfront Partnership representing the City of Wakefield, English Partnerships, British Waterways, voluntary organisations and the local private sector, has agreed a £40 million strategy to regenerate the site.

Sources of funding

A number of routes to help secure finance into the area have been identified to date:
Property finance company
Investment finance
Heritage Lottery Fund
European Regional Development Fund
English Partnerships
Environmental bodies.

Carlton Mill – Yorkshire & Humberside

History and former use

A mill that was originally powered by water, then by steam. The six-storey stone building stands alongside the River Calder. It was derelict but seen as an important element in the regeneration of the Sowerby Bridge river and canalside areas (*see Plate 2*).

New use

Allen Tod Architects carried out the design, repair and conservation of the structural fabric of the building. The fabric has been secured – external walls, new roof, internal floor and structure. The building has been empty for a number of years but is now being converted into residential accommodation by a private developer.

Community issues

To save an important landmark and listed building until a new economic use could be found.

Construction schedule

Fabric: Autumn 1988 – Spring 1989.

Sources of funding

English Heritage
Calderdale Metropolitan Borough Council.

Conservation issues

Restoration of original fabric (excluding corridors, new slate roof). Exemplary conservation approach. The building was one of three listed derelict buildings that formed the basis of a pioneering 'New Grist' study into the rescue and re-use of important but derelict buildings of the industrial revolution, carried out by Allen Tod with URBED (The Urban and Economic Development Group) for the Civic Trust Regeneration Unit.

(Photo: Allen Tod Architects)

Location
Sowerby Bridge, West Yorkshire

Listed status
Grade II

Developer
Fabric: Calderdale Metropolitan Borough Council

Architect
Fabric: Allen Tod Architects

General Contractor
Fabric: J. Laing

Total floor area
2,300 sq. m.

Cost
Fabric: £250,000

(Photo: Allen Tod Architects)

Dean Clough Mills – Yorkshire & Humberside

(Photo: Dean Clough Ltd.)

Location
Halifax,
West Yorkshire

Total floor area
1.25 million sq. ft

History and former use
Dean Clough is a complex of multi-storey granite buildings in the centre of Halifax. It was built 1840–60 for carpet manufacturer Crossley. By 1860 it was the town's biggest employer. It covered eighteen acres with 5,000 people. In the twentieth century the firm was taken over by Carpets International. The scale of operations was steadily reduced and the mills were closed down in 1983.

New use
Industrial Park. Two hundred firms include: small businesses; major insurance companies; the local VAT office; Calderdale Business Information Centre; cafés/restaurants; art gallery; conference facilities; etc.

Employment
Approximately 1,500.

Developer
The development is privately owned by Sir Ernest Hall who bought Dean Clough because he saw it as an opportunity to create an exciting working environment with supporting cultural, educational and leisure activities.

Financing
Sir Ernest Hall used his own money to buy and develop Dean Clough. He wanted to be free to do things his way, to support tenants as he wished, and to develop the project at a speed that he thought appropriate. It would have been possible for him to apply for an urban development grant or a grant from the European Regional Development Fund, but this would have involved relatively long application times and commitment to a building timetable that would have removed some of his flexibility. He might have raised some private institutional finance, but the project had little security to offer, nor did it offer the rapid returns of normal property development.

Although grants were not applied for, a good relationship was developed with the local authority, to ensure that the scheme was supported from the outset. Details of the amounts spent on the scheme are not available.

Conservation issues
One major building demolished to open up congested core of site. No major interventions into other buildings. Works include mainly repainting, new electrics, plumbing, and insertion of partitioning to create workspaces.

Future prospects
Flexibility has been the keynote of the Dean Clough project. The buildings were large enough to provide a range of different types of space.

East Mill – Yorkshire & Humberside

(Illustration: Allen Tod Architects)

Location
Huddersfield, West Yorkshire

Listed status
Grade II

Developer
University of Huddersfield

Architect
Allen Tod Architects/ Jarvis

General Contractor
Jarvis Construction Ltd.

Total floor area
4,500 sq. m.

Cost
£3.2 million

History and former use
Textile warehouse built c1912.

New use
Education – housing two departments of the University of Huddersfield. The project involves the complete refurbishment of the existing mill and the construction of a new lecture theatre and four-storey extension. The new facility will provide teaching spaces, computer laboratories, studios, administration, research and social spaces.

Community issues
This was part of the development of the University which opened up the canal footpath and led to total regeneration of the area.

Construction schedule
Commenced October 1997.
Completed September 1998.

Sources of funding
U.F.C. Capital Programme.

Conservation issues
A new roof form was applied to create north light. The structure was retained and refurbished with a new-build extension added.

Conservation and regeneration projects in Britain and Ireland   203

Huddersfield Mills – Yorkshire & Humberside

Location
**Huddersfield,
West Yorkshire**

Listed status
Various

History and former use

Stone-built mills once dominated the valleys of this large West Yorkshire town, producing woollen and worsted cloth famed the world over. But changing fashions and cheap foreign competition led the local industry to contract and concentrate on the upper end of the market. Firms closed, others became smaller or introduced new technology to become more efficient. All these factors reduced the space needed by textile companies in traditional buildings. As a result, mills were demolished, became vacant or fell into disrepair as their owners concentrated on business survival.

By the 1980s and 1990s attitudes were starting to change, with a growing realisation that improving and converting mills to new uses could help regenerate the local economy, provide affordable housing and improve the environment. Although smaller than it was, the textile industry continues to be important to the town, and firms have been refurbishing their premises with grant assistance.

New use
Producing the Goods

A number of mill complexes have been converted to provide managed workspace. The local authority, Kirklees Metropolitan Council, operates Gatehouse Enterprise Centre in Lockwood, which has thirty workspace units. Private developers have created similar

schemes at other locations; Holme Mills and Stanley Mills in Milnsbridge were converted with the help of public sector grants.

Owner-occupiers in textiles and other industries have also invested in mill buildings. Under the Urban Programme, which operated in the area between 1987–93, grants were given to improve the external fabric of Albert Mills at Lockwood, Union Mills (*pictured below*), Dale Street Mills, Britannia Mills and Viaduct Mills in Milnsbridge, and Commercial Mills and Turnbridge Mills near the centre of the town.

A seven year programme of Single Regeneration Budget (SRB) funding from 1995 includes £500,000 to be spent on textile mills through feasibility grants, refurbishment grants and stone-cleaning schemes. The strategy is administered by the Council on behalf of the partnership body Huddersfield Pride Ltd. By mid-1998 seven feasibility studies had been completed and five mills refurbished with grant aid: Albert Mills (Lockwood), Savile Mill (Milnsbridge), Rayner's Mill (Turnbridge), Granville Mills and Britannia Mills (Paddock).

Canalside living

The first phase of Crowther Village, alongside the Huddersfield Narrow Canal in Milnsbridge, was completed in 1997. The Grade II listed Union Mill has been converted to thirty-eight residential units, and another seventy-three new dwellings have been built for the North British Housing Association.

The second stage commenced in 1998, with the conversion of the listed Burdett Mill to thirty-three flats for sale. The whole project is being developed by Europa Homes Ltd at a cost of £6 million, supported by grants of £1.95 million from English Partnerships and £50,000 from the Council.

University of Huddersfield

The expansion of the University of Huddersfield's town centre campus is bringing vacant mills into educational use. A £5 million scheme to create teaching accommodation for computing and mathematics in the Grade II listed Firth Street Mills won a Civic Trust Commendation in 1996. The adjoining Larchfield Mill (East Mill) provides space for design, technology and engineering studies

(Photo: Huddersfield Daily Examiner)

following its opening in Autumn 1998, at a cost of £3.2 million.

New opportunities
At July 1998 the following vacant mills were available for acquisition:

Folly Hall Mills *(pictured right)*
Three buildings, including a Grade II* listed mill next to the A616 and the River Colne, 0.5 km from the town centre. Total floor space is 4,650 sq. m. (50,000 sq. ft), and planning permission exists for restaurant, bar and office use.

St George's Warehouse
This Grade II listed former railway warehouse, situated in the heart of the town behind the train station, is served from New North Parade and Fitzwilliam Street. The red brick building has 23,225 sq. m. (250,000 sq. ft) divided into five floors. There is planning permission for a variety of uses including retail, offices and warehousing. Leisure and residential activities could also be considered for this building.

Sources of funding
A number of grant schemes operating in Huddersfield can assist mill improvement and re-use projects: Huddersfield Pride; Mills Feasibility Grants – up to £10,000 or 50 per cent of the cost of the study; Mills Refurbishment Grants – up to £50,000 or 50 per cent of the cost of improvement to the external fabric; PROFILES – gap funding of between £100,000 and £250,000 for employment uses.

English Partnerships Investment Fund

Gap funding of £100,000 or more for employment or residential uses.

Little Germany – Yorkshire & Humberside

Location
**Bradford,
West Yorkshire**

Listed status
**Conservation area
with 85 buildings,
55 of which are
listed**

Cost
£15 million

History and former use

Little Germany is an exceptional area. Standing on the edge of Bradford city centre, it is one of the finest collections of Victorian warehouses in the United Kingdom. It was designated a conservation area in 1973. It was built in a frenetic period of construction between 1855–75 by German and Eastern European merchants and once was the distribution hub of Bradford's textile trade. However, by the early 1980s, half of the floor space was vacant and many of the buildings were derelict.

New use

The process began with stone-cleaning funded by the city council. In 1986 URBED was commissioned to draw up a strategy for the revival of the area. A vision was set out, which highlighted the area's potential for recreation, as a base for innovative companies and designers, and as a place to live. The City Council promoted two flagship schemes, Merchant's House, which provided managed workspace, and the Bradford Design Exchange. This in turn attracted private investment for refurbishing a further fourteen buildings. By 1993, Little Germany had been transformed.

Community issues

Employment was brought to the area. Festival Square was developed as a much needed public open space in the heart of the area. The initial project also sought to overcome barriers to regeneration such as poor environment and parking problems.

Employment

1993: 147 companies employing 3,750 people.

Sources of funding

Public and private investment.

Manningham Mills – Yorkshire & Humberside

History and former use
The Mills were built as silk mills in 1873 by Andrews and Pepper, Bradford architects, for Samuel Cunliffe Lister.

New use
Manufacturing continues in the North Mills, but the future of the South Mills in unclear. Manningham Mills Community Association have use of the ground floor of one wing of the South Mills. Various community events are held in this part of the building. Proposals were put forward in 1996 for a mix of commercial and residential uses. The Association along with the owners (Listers plc), Bradford City Council, and other partners are now looking for sustainable redevelopment of this important building.

Community issues
Manningham Mills Community Association aims to protect and promote the use of the mills for the social, economic and cultural benefit of the multi-cultural community which surrounds it.

Future prospects
This is an important building both architecturally and in particular as a focus for the local community. It is essential that an appropriate sustainable use is found for the building.

Location
Bradford, West Yorkshire

Listed status
Grade II*

Salts Mill – Yorkshire & Humberside

History and former use
In 1853 it opened as a sophisticated, state-of-the-art textile mill employing 3,000 workers on a greenfield site. Titus Salt, who built the mill, also constructed churches, schools and houses in a model village for the workforce. Visitors and the people now living in the village still benefit from Salt's legacy of these attractive buildings (*see Plates 3 & 4*).

New use
When Jonathan Silver purchased Salts Mill in 1987 it was semi-derelict and appeared to have no positive future. The village was in decline. Since then Saltaire has been transformed and now over 1,500 people are employed on the site of Salts Mill by firms which include large, high-tech manufacturing companies like Pace Micro Technology plc and Filtronic Comtek plc. In 1853 Salts Mill was the leading edge of textile industry; it now leads the world in high technology.

The Mill is also well known for its three art galleries devoted to David Hockney. Admission to the art galleries has always been free and the number of works on show has grown to over 300. In addition to the art galleries, the other public spaces include a high quality diner and excellent speciality shops. The mill is open seven days a week from 10am to 6pm. Admission is free.

Employment
Over 2,000 people are employed on the site of Salts Mill.

Conservation issues
The success of combining the above developments in an historic building has helped Salts Mill and the surrounding village of Saltaire win several leading national and European awards.

Location
Saltaire, Shipley, West Yorkshire

Listed status
Grade II*

Salt Warehouse – Yorkshire & Humberside

Location
Sowerby Bridge, West Yorkshire

Listed status
Grade II

Developer
A partnership comprising Sowerby Bridge Wharf Ltd, British Waterways, Calderdale Council, The Salt Warehouse Trust and the 12th Halifax Sea Scouts is jointly developing the site to ensure that their vision is not compromised

Total floor area
Over 50,000 sq. ft will be brought back into productive use

Cost
£600,000 has been committed to the site to date and it is expected that a further £2 million will be invested in the wharf over the next three years

History and former use

The buildings are canalside warehouses, which were designed to allow goods to be loaded and unloaded undercover. The canal basin at Sowerby Bridge (*see Plate 2*) was designed and built during the late eighteenth and early nineteenth centuries as a trans-shipment depot. It sits at the junction of the Calder and Hebble Navigation, the Rochdale Canal and a former turnpike. The carriage of canal-borne goods gradually declined with the introduction of the motorized lorry and effectively came to an end following the nationalization of the waterways in 1948 and the centralization of warehousing facilities at Wakefield. The Rochdale Canal closed in 1952 and the last commercial barge travelled between Wakefield and Sowerby Bridge in 1955 carrying 55 tons of wood pulp. The canal and wharf buildings attracted little attention and no investment until the renewal of interest in canals for leisure use in the 1970s. By this time, years of neglect had left the buildings on the wharf underused.

New use

During the 1960s the 12th Halifax Sea Scouts gradually became established in the canal basin and from 1973 canal boats once again could be found moored on the wharf. Businesses began to establish themselves in the underused buildings and a change in ownership of the wharf allowed a vital new partnership to become established in 1997. The efforts of the partnership have successfully secured funds to carry out the first phase of improvement to the Salt Warehouse and Warehouse No 4. The access into the canal basin has been upgraded and re-setted, views of the canal have been opened up, street lighting installed and more public space has been created near to the canal. Warehouses No 1 and No 2 adjacent to the access road need substantial investment to allow them to become fully occupied. Re-roofing works commenced in summer 1999.

The stimulus for all these works continues to be a belief in the wharf as a working boatyard and a real commitment to the regeneration of the Salt Warehouse and Warehouse No 4. It is essential that these two buildings are brought back into full use if the partnership's vision for the site is to be delivered. The Salt Warehouse is likely to be converted into offices on the upper floors with a café/restaurant and interpretative centre on the ground floor. Warehouse No 4 will be converted into artisan workshop units whilst retaining a business that fits out and hires canal boats on the ground floor.

Community issues

It is essential that the regeneration of the wharf brings real economic benefits for the people of Sowerby Bridge and conserves not just the fantastic historic architectural character of the canal basin. It is also essential that the special work-a-day character of the basin, together with the ancillary businesses, which support boat use, are retained and developed further. Existing small-scale artisan-based industrial uses within the buildings complement this special character.

The area is very special for locals and visitors alike with two pubs, an art gallery, boats, beautiful architecture and ducks providing something for everyone. The improvements that have been carried out have already attracted more visitors to the basin and the town of Sowerby Bridge.

Employment

The partnership has resisted market pressure to develop the wharf into an elitist residential area, which would deprive boaters and locals of the valuable resource and do little to enhance job opportunities in Sowerby Bridge. The town has previously suffered from decline in textile and engineering industries and the canal basin initiative can provide real opportunity to create new jobs in the town.

Financing

The project has attracted support from: Regeneration Through Heritage; English Partnerships; The Sowerby Bridge Forum; English Heritage; and the Heritage Lottery Fund.

Conservation issues

A continually evolving conservation and business plan guide the whole scheme.

Leeds Design Innovation Centre – Yorkshire & Humberside

Redevelopment of Leeds waterfront includes: Granary Wharf where grain warehouses have been converted into design studios; The Calls, a warehouse that now houses a hotel and restaurant; Tetley's Brewery, which still operates as a brewery but new buildings on the Wharf provide a museum and visitor centre. Other refurbished buildings in the area provide housing, restaurants and bars.

History and former use
A concrete-framed grain warehouse built during the 1930s on the banks of the River Aire.

New use
Flexible studio, office and workshop space for designers and design-related businesses around conference facilities and gallery/exhibition space (*see Plate 26*).

Community issues
Initial development was in a run-down area. 100 per cent occupancy kick-started similar workspace projects in the area.

Employment
Office/start up space for twenty-five companies.

Construction schedule
1987–90.

Sources of funding
Commercial mortgage/Urban Development Grant.

Conservation issues
Fabric retained/refurbished. Hoist towers extended, river frontage opened up.

Awards
RIBA Regional Award for Architecture
The Leeds Award for Architecture.

Location
The Calls, Leeds, West Yorkshire

Developer
Yorkshire Design Limited

Architect
Allen Tod Architects

General Contractor
Harrison, Leeds

Total floor area
3,000 sq. m.

Cost
£650,000

(Photo: Allen Tod Architects)

32 The Calls – Yorkshire & Humberside

(Photo: Allen Tod Architects)

(Photo: Allen Tod Architects)

Location
Leeds,
West Yorkshire

Listed status
Grade II

Developer
Johnson Fry
Properties

Architect
Allen Tod Architects

General Contractor
Monk Construction

Total floor area
2,660 sq. m.

Cost
£1.6 million
(excluding pub
fit-out)

Redevelopment of Leeds waterfront includes: Granary Wharf where grain warehouses have been converted into design studios; The Calls, a warehouse that now houses a hotel and restaurant; Tetley's Brewery, which still operates as a brewery but new buildings on the Wharf provide a museum and visitor centre. Other refurbished buildings in the area provide housing, restaurants and bars.

History and former use
A nineteenth-century warehouse on the banks of the River Aire. Derelict for twenty-five years.

New use
A mixed-use development that took advantage of its riverside position, while recognizing and exploiting its listed building qualities. Pub at riverside level, four floors of apartments, and a top floor of open plan offices, now occupied by Allen Tod Architects (*see Plate 23*).

Community issues
Key project in the regeneration of Leeds riverside conservation area.

Employment
Pub: seven.
Offices: thirty.

Construction schedule
1990–1.

Sources of funding
Burner Expansion Scheme.

Conservation issues
The internal structure was completely rebuilt to meet current standards. All apartments, offices and pub provided with south-facing river balconies. Roof trusses were preserved. Windows replaced on two floors with new cast-iron replicas taken from the one remaining original window.

Westwood Mill – Yorkshire & Humberside

History and former use

Westwood Mill is a listed eighteenth-century mill in the village of Linthwaite adjoining the Huddersfield Narrow Canal. It is one of the oldest mills in the valley. A highly attractive stone building, located in a beautiful section of the Colne Valley, it is a feature of the canal towpath. In recent years the mill has become semi-derelict with its large mill pond drained. The canal is currently being restored through Millennium Commission funding and will eventually link through to the Lancashire canals.

New use

The Westwood Mill Development Trust would like to buy and restore this splendid mill, to provide an asset for the local community. The Trust is organizing a feasibility study to assess the viability of turning Westwood Mill into an Environment/Community Centre. The Centre would provide the income to maintain the buildings, at the same time as providing a facility for Colne Valley groups and organizations to meet, and a place where the whole community can become involved.

The main proposal for the use of the buildings is to create a Centre where visitors could see environmental and sustainable ideas put into practice. The Centre would support the principles of Agenda 21 and Permaculture, and reflect the area's local identity whilst encouraging economic diversity and cultural vitality. New uses will include: café, bar and restaurant overlooking the restored mill pond; canal offices and workshop space for businesses which reflect the environmental and economic sustainability of the project's vision; education, training and conference facilities.

Community issues

The Westwood Mill Development Trust was established to promote sustainable regeneration through the restoration and re-use of the mill and to create the much needed employment, education, tourist and leisure facilities. The Trust carried out a community survey to find out the views of local people.

General Contractor

Feasibility study – David Cootey Associates, Huddersfield.

Sources of funding

The Trust has received a grant £25,000 from the Architectural Heritage Fund for a feasibility study.

Conservation issues

The aim is to restore the buildings to a standard that not only preserves the fabric of the buildings in a sensitive way, but also in a manner that maintains the overall character of the site. The restoration will incorporate the latest energy conservation techniques where they are compatible with the historic detail of the structure, and demonstrate good environmental practice in building conservation.

Future prospects

The restoration of the mill and its new activities will create an attractive and stimulating environment for the visitor, and have a strong environmental, practical and educational dimension to complement other attractions in the Colne Valley.

Location
Linthwaite, Huddersfield

Listed status
Grade II

Yorkshire Dance Centre – Yorkshire & Humberside

Location
**Leeds,
West Yorkshire**

Developer
**Yorkshire Dance
Centre Trust**

Architect
Allen Tod Architects

General Contractor
**Ellmores, then
Samuel Armitage for
the Lottery Project**

Total floor area
25,000 sq. ft

Cost
Overall £1 million

(Photo: Allen Tod Architects)

(Photo: Allen Tod Architects)

History and former use
Factory, which had become a sweat-shop for textile manufacturing.

New use
Dance studios including an office suite and café bar.

Community issues
It is recognized as the model for Regional Dance Agencies. The refurbishment of the building has contributed a focus for the cultural development of the Quarry Hill area in Leeds.

Employment
Fifty to seventy.

Construction schedule
1983–96.

Sources of funding
National Lottery Arts Council – £600,000.

Conservation issues
Leeds City Council demanded slate roofs in line with their now discredited 'Leeds look' policy, to the detriment of the client and the building.

Future prospects
Good. The Dance Centre is well established and successful.

Awards
Financial Times/RIBA Community Architecture Gulbenkian Award for workplaces.

(Photo: Etienne Clement Photography)

History and former use

Designed before the Second World War by Hull-based architects Gelder and Kitchen, the building was opened as a working flour mill in 1950 by Rank Hovis. It served as a model for other mills built by the company as part of a reconstruction programme after the Second World War. With a silo capacity of 22,000 tonnes, it was equipped with the most modern and efficient machinery of the time. In 1957 an animal food mill extension was added. The attached warehouse (now demolished) stored 5,000 tonnes and it could dispatch 240 tonnes of grain per hour. At its height the mill employed around 300 people and about 100 were still employed when the company closed the mill in 1981.

New use

The project, scheduled to open in 2000, will transform the building into the largest centre for contemporary visual arts outside London, with exhibition space, associated studios and other cultural facilities. It will not house a permanent collection but will commission new work. It will be at the forefront of contemporary visual arts internationally and is expected to attract about 354,000 visitors a year.

The exciting and innovative design retains much of the imposing brick façade of the building. Concrete grain silos in the centre will be hollowed out and floors added to provide four galleries, lecture theatre and cinema, artists' studios, workshops, shop, riverside café and glass rooftop restaurant, which opens up impressive and panoramic views of the riverscape with its famous Tyne Bridge. The outside of the building will also be used as a screen for videos and still images.

Employment

Estimated to bring £5 million a year into the local economy, more than 500 jobs will be created – 175 directly, 180 indirectly and 148 during construction.

Sources of funding

Arts Council National Lottery Fund: £480,000 feasibility award; £33 million capital grant; £1.5 million a year for five years from 2000 towards running costs. Gateshead Council has pledged £250,000 a year and talks are taking place with Northern Arts.

Conservation issues

Much of the imposing brickwork of the façade will be retained along with the concrete grain silos.

Future prospects

The development is central to the Council's £200 million plan to regenerate the Gateshead area. Alongside the Baltic Centre for Contemporary Art, a new regional music centre is planned in a building designed by Foster and Partners, due to open in 2001. Linking the developments on the Gateshead side of the River Tyne with the newly refurbished Newcastle Quayside will be the Millennium Bridge, to be ready by September 2000. This pedestrian and cycle bridge will operate like a giant eye lid, which opens and turns on a pivot on either side of the river to form an arch under which ships will be able to pass.

Location
Gateshead

Architect
Dominic Williams, Ellis Williams Architects

Total floor area
10,000 sq. m. of space including approximately 3,000 sq. m. of exhibition space

Cost
£46 million

Camperdown Works – Scotland

Location
Lochee, Dundee

History and former use
One of the great 'flagship' mill complexes of Britain that spread over 35 acres and employed 5,000 at its peak. The Cox Brothers pioneered the manufacture of jute cloth in Dundee and invested in stunningly lavish architecture, culminating in the 280 feet high Cox's stack designed by James McLaren & G A Cox. This great polychromatic chimney has been conserved as a beacon for the renewal scheme at Camperdown which was developed after the works closed in 1981.

New use
Sadly it was felt necessary to demolish much of the complex, most of the single-storey sheds being cleared for a cinema, nightclub, megabowl and amusement arcade set round a vast car park. However, the great four-storey High Mill with its cupola at the east end has been converted into flats, and the shell of the calendar mill reworked as a Tesco supermarket. The bleach and dyeworks and jute warehouses have been replaced by new housing. While many striking elements survive, the overall effect of the new Camperdown is confused in terms of access and untidy in its architecture.

Dens Mill – Scotland

Location
Dundee

Developer
Hillcrest Housing Association

Architect
Baxter Clark & Paul Architects

Cost
Upper Works conversion £7.5 million

History and former use
This hillside complex was developed by the Baxter Brothers who became the world's premier linen manufacturers over 1840–90. The Upper Works developed to incorporate a mill, wet spinning mill, calender press, loomsheds and a series of warehouses and foundries. The main range, twenty-four bays long and four storeys plus an attic high was surmounted by a bellcote and spire. The Lower Works consists of four mills, dominated by the Bell Mill with its fine Italianate bellcote.

New uses
The Upper Works were converted into housing with engine house being converted into a dramatic central staircase. New-build housing around the mill is suitably strong in character and large in scale. The landscaping manages to exploit the qualities of the steeply sloping site while retaining both features and the tough atmosphere of its industrial past. The Lower Works buildings contain various retail and wholesale firms.

Dundee Mills – Scotland

History and former use

Dundee developed as a major centre of industry in the nineteenth century, with spinning mills, tanneries, ropeworks and later factories for sweets and marmalade. The mill owners invested in dramatic works typically set on the slopes back from the city centre. Fortunately most of the prime examples have survived, at least in part, despite some comprehensive redevelopment and major road schemes across the city.

New uses

King Street Mill was the first to be converted and is now Jericho House, a rehabilitation hostel. Other conversions include the Logie Works (to housing), North Dudhope Mill (to art studios), Douglas Mill (to business premises), Tay Works (to student accommodation and shopping), Lindsay Street Mill (to housing and leisure use) and Hillside Works (into an Islamic centre). Watson's Bond (*pictured*), a complex of warehouses built c1907, and having an early reinforced concrete structure, have been

converted, in 1996, to flats, a gym and offices, by Hillcrest Housing Association and Scottish Homes, to designs by Geo. Johnston.

Location
Dundee

Verdant Works – Scotland

History and former use

While the modern interpretation centre, Discovery Point, and Captain Scott's RRS *Discovery* are the prime tourist attractions in the city, Dundee Heritage has more recently, in September 1996, opened the Verdant Works as a living textile museum (*see Plate 25*). This compact mill complex dates from 1833 but was largely rebuilt after a fire in 1852. It stopped being used as a textile mill c1895, subsequent trades being curing rabbit skins, producing flock, stuffing furniture and reprocessing non-ferrous metals.

New uses

After closure and purchase by the Dundee Heritage Trust in 1991, Stewart Tod & Partners converted the works into a heritage centre, taking particular care to restore the clocking-in lodge and office block of 1890. More modern displays consider the rise and fall of Dundee's jute industry and living and

working conditions. Machinery was relocated from the Douglas Works to be included in this gallery.

Location
Dundee

Luma Light Factory – Scotland

Location
Glasgow

Listed status
Category B

Developer
Linthouse Housing Association Limited

Architect
Cornelius McClymont

General Contractor
Melville Dundas Limited

Total floor area
Luma Building – 3,580 sq. m.

New-build – 930 sq. m.

Cost
£4,868,627

History and former use

The Luma Factory was designed for the British Luma Co-operative Lamp Company by architect Cornelius Armour. It was built in 1939 to coincide with the Empire Exhibition as the Glasgow headquarters of the first international co-operative factory for the manufacture of electric lamps. It is a famous landmark in the city, one of the few surviving examples of Modern Movement architecture. When in use its special feature was a tall glazed tower, which was illuminated as it was the area where the light bulbs were tested. The factory continued to produce light bulbs until the late 1960s. In the 1970s it changed hands several times and in the early 1980s it was vacated and lay empty.

New use

The factory building was converted to forty-three flats for sale, and three new blocks containing four flats each were built on the site, all of which are rented accommodation.

Construction schedule

June 1993 – Appraisal of site commissioned
June 1995 – Tender accepted
July 1995 – Work started on site
November 1996 – Completion

Sources of funding

Scottish Homes – £1,906,641
Income from sales – £2,299,000
Glasgow Development Agency – £149,155
Glasgow City Council (Conservation) – £40,000
Glasgow City Council (Private sector) – £30,000
European Regional Development Fund – £282,102
Strathclyde Regional Council – £35,000
Private Lender – £125,884

Conservation issues

Radical intervention was required on the existing building. All the interiors were changed except for the tower. The changes were accepted because the building was rapidly falling into a dilapidated condition and was seriously in danger of demolition if alternative measures were not taken. The scheme allowed the tower to be saved and the rest of the building was modified in a sympathetic manner.

Success of the project

Although the cost of conversion was relatively high compared to new-build, the project can be considered a great success. All the flats in the former factory building were sold within two weeks of the show house opening and have proved to be very popular with residents. The building remains a striking landmark on the approach to Glasgow from the airport.

(Photo: Graeme Duncan)

Templeton's Carpet Factory – Scotland

Location
Glasgow

Developer
Scottish Development Agency (now disbanded)

Architect
Charles Robertson & Partners

History and former use
The magnificent building overlooks Glasgow Green. The façade (designed by William Leiper, 1888) which reflects the façade of the Doges' Palace in Venice, vividly advertised the oriental dyed wares that were produced within. Behind the façade was a functional mill designed by mill engineers, Messrs J B Harvey.

New use
Templeton Business Centre.

Community issues
Glasgow was perhaps the first city in Europe to experience the implications of post-industrial decline. In a short space of time more than 20,000 jobs were lost as a result of a decline in the engineering industries. Subsidiary industries suffered equally badly.

Construction schedule
1980–5.

Sources of funding
The factory was renovated as part of the Glasgow East End Project (GEAR), which was the responsibility of the Scottish Development Agency. The project started in 1976 and its area covered 1,600 hectares in the city. The SDA's investment was financed by borrowing, within a limit set by the Scottish Office.

Conservation issues
An early project for the preservation and conversion of an important historic building into a business centre.

Stanley Mills – Scotland

Location
Stanley, Perth

Listed status
Bell Mill, Mid Mill, East Mill (category A), North Range, East Range, and Hydro Electric power station (category B)

Developer
The Phoenix Trust

Architect
Law & Dunbar-Nasmith

General Contractor
B D Trentham

Cost
£5.5 million

History and former use

Described as one of the most complete surviving early cotton mill complexes in the UK, Stanley Mills were founded by George Dempster in association with Sir Richard Arkwright and a group of Perth merchants. The site is on the bend of the River Tay, surrounded by woodland. The land was feuded from the Duke of Atholl to give employment to his Highlanders who were being driven from the hills. The complex comprises buildings ranged round three sides of an irregular courtyard and was originally powered by seven giant water wheels (*see Plate 11*).

Bell Mill, the oldest and most important on the site, was built 1786–7 to the designs of Sir Richard Arkwright. Mid Mill built c.1823–30.

New use

The Bell Mill is to become a Museum of the River Tay, the story of textiles in Tayside and power from water, to be developed by Historic Scotland. The Mid Mill is to be converted by the Phoenix Trust into nine two- or four-bedroomed houses with terraces overlooking the river. The East Mill is to be converted to thirty one- to three-bedroomed flats. An education centre will be operated during the construction phase.

Employment

Up to 125 during construction. One to three permanent; ten to twenty in total.

Construction schedule

September 1998 – Spring 2001.

Sources of funding

National Heritage Memorial Fund
Historic Scotland
Architectural Heritage Fund (loan)
Phoenix Trust funds.

Conservation issues

A listed building, where the relationship of the building to its setting adjacent to the River Tay is of great importance.

The Linthouse Engine Shop – Scotland

(Photo: Scottish Maritime Museum)

Location
Scottish Maritime Museum, Irvine, Ayrshire (formerly Govan, Glasgow)

Listed status
Category A

Architect for reconstruction
Irvine Development Corporation

General Contractor for reconstruction
Mowlem Construction Ltd

Total floor area
40,000 sq. ft

History and former use

The former engine manufacturing shop was originally one of the workshops of the Linthouse shipyard owned by Alexander Stephen & Sons, and was located in Govan, Glasgow on the south side of the River Clyde. It was built in 1872 to the design of John Frederick Spencer, a naval architect who had worked with Brunel. It was extended and altered more than once during the following 100 years of its working life and finally, when threatened with demolition for industrial redevelopment, it was removed for preservation in the latter part of the 1980s. It is a magnificent example of Victorian civil engineering, constructed of huge iron castings, Russian pine, steel and glass. Dismantling took place in 1988 and reconstruction was completed in 1991. It is thought that the dismantling and rebuilding of the engine shop is the largest project of its type that has been undertaken in Britain.

New use

The engine shop is awaiting redevelopment as the main exhibition halls and visitor facilities for the Scottish Maritime Museum. The building is an outstanding feature within a redevelopment scheme, which includes local authority housing. This has won numerous awards including the 1998 Regeneration of Scotland Award.

Financing

For relocation and reconstruction – Scottish Maritime Museum, Historic Scotland, National Heritage Memorial fund, Irvine Development Corporation, Strathclyde Regional Development Fund.

Conservation issues

Development of the site must be sympathetic to the building. No internal building work can be fixed to, or obstruct the view of, the internal structural features. A conservation plan has been produced for the building.

(Photo: Scottish Maritime Museum)

New Lanark Mills – Scotland

Location
South Lanarkshire

Listed status
**Category A
in an outstanding
conservation area**

Developer
**New Lanark
Conservation Trust
(Registered Scottish
Charity)**

Architect
**David Willis of
Crichton, Willis &
Galloway**

General Contractor
**Various – main
contracts have been
carried out by John
Laing (Scotland)**

Total floor area
**approximately
250,000 sq. ft**

Cost
**approximately
£20 million**

History and former use
New Lanark Mills is a water-powered cotton manufacturing settlement which was established in 1785 and largely completed by 1820. It became famous as a model community under the enlightened management of social pioneer Robert Owen. The cotton mills continued in production until 1968.

New use
The mill buildings have been put to various new uses: visitor facilities – gift shop, café, exhibitions including the 'dark ride'; hotel and self-catering accommodation; commercial lets – office, retail, workshop space; hydro-electric generation using original lade, waterways and turbine.

Employment
Visitor centre, hotel, conservation trust – 100 seasonal and casual staff. Other businesses – approximately fifty staff.

Financing
Public Agency Partnerships – Historic Scotland, Lanarkshire Development Agency, European Regional Development Fund (via Strathclyde European Partnership), South Lanarkshire Council, plus revenue income generated through the activities listed above. In 1996 £1.8 million was granted from the Heritage Lottery Fund towards the refurbishment of Mill One into the New Lanark Mill Hotel.

Conservation issues
New Lanark is an outstanding conservation area, a nominated World Heritage Site and, together with the Falls of Clyde, is listed in the Inventory of Gardens and Designed Landscapes.

Future prospects
The Trust will continue to work towards the aim of restoring and revitalizing the entire village as a living working community.

Awards
In 1997 the Trust gained Best Practice Award from the British Urban Regeneration Association.

Conway Mill – Northern Ireland

History and former use

Former flax spinning complex on the east side of Conway Street, a short distance from the Falls Road. It is suggested that the original mill, along with some of the buildings, was constructed in the early 1840s, and the new engine and boiler houses were built in the 1890s. In the 1900s the weaving sheds were demolished to make way for a second spinning mill on Conway Street. The mill ceased operation around 1970.

New use

The complex is now owned by a community organization and has been subdivided into a range of units which are let for community and commercial use. With no public assistance, except during a brief initial period, the building has housed many innovative projects and created jobs for hundreds of people over a fourteen-year period. It is used for social, educational, community functions and houses a community based print shop, office space for the West Belfast Taxi Association, craft workshops, accommodation for small service and light industries. There is a gym, snooker hall and crèche. There are now proposals for the development of these facilities to provide accommodation for businesses, student and visitor accommodation, theatre, museum, craft workshops, café/restaurant, and extended leisure facilities.

Community issues

The mill is situated on the borders of three areas of great social need. Out of a population of 15,000 people, at least 1,700 are unemployed – equivalent to an estimated 36 per cent unemployment rate (compared to 16.5 per cent B.U.A.). The area has a higher than average youth population.

Employment

Eighty people are currently working in the mill. There is the potential for more than doubling that number.

Construction schedule

There will be a three-phase programme of work – the initial phase taking eighteen months to two years to complete.

Financing

Applications for grant aid are being made to the Heritage Lottery Fund, International Fund for Ireland, Making Belfast Work, and European structural funds.

Conservation issues

It is intended that as many buildings are preserved on the site as possible.

Future prospects

Redevelopment of the mill could trigger major redevelopment of the area on both sides of the interface wall between the Falls and Shankill.

Location
Belfast

Listed status
Not yet listed but recommended for listing at Grade II

Developer
Conway Street Community Enterprises Project Ltd – the community organization that owns the mill

Total floor area
1,000,000 sq. ft

Cost
First phase approximately £1,800,000

Stewart's Mill – Northern Ireland

Location
**Coalisland,
County Tyrone**

Architect
**McKeown & Shields,
Coalisland**

General Contractor
**Donaghmore
Construction
Edendork,
Dungannon**

Total floor area
**1,000 sq. m.
+ car parking**

Cost
**£815,000
including
landscaping, water
feature and car
parking**

History and former use
Situated at the head of a canal, the mill was built in 1907 by Robert Stewart and Son Ltd as a corn mill to process grain. The town's electricity was generated at the mill between 1918–35. It became disused in 1978. As its name implies, Coalisland is a unique 'island' of the nineteenth-century industrial revolution in Ireland. Its prosperity was based on canals, pottery, coal, textiles and manufacturing.

New use
Now known as The Corn Mill, it has been converted for a variety of uses, including on the second floor a Heritage Centre with an exhibition of Coalisland's industrial heritage, opened in June 1993 by Mary Robinson, President of Ireland. The ground floor is tenanted by the Southern Education and Library Board and the first floor accommodates community uses including mother and toddler, arts and crafts, senior citizens, language classes. The second floor depicts the unique industrial heritage of the Coalisland area by a variety of interpretative techniques. On the third floor is a performance area used for music, drama, dancing, conferences, meetings, exhibitions.

During the first week of July each year, the Coalisland International Music Festival, which won the British Airways Tourism Award for the best outdoor event of 1996, is centred around the mill. Hundreds of musicians, dancers and singers from all over Europe join with the best musicians from throughout Ireland to bring an extravaganza of multicultural entertainment to the Coalisland area.

Community issues
As the traditional industries of Coalisland declined, the town itself began to decay and became an area of great urban deprivation. With a population of 4,000, the town's two electoral wards are classed as disadvantaged.

In 1981 the Coalisland and District Development Association was formed by the local people in order to halt the further decline of the town. Funds were raised to purchase a disused weaving factory and provide workspace and training. Their efforts were successful and in 1991 the Association was awarded the first Community Regeneration and Improvement Special Projects Scheme (CRISP), whose objective was 'to remove dereliction from the town'. This scheme was jointly funded by the International Fund for Ireland and the Department of the Environment for Northern Ireland. Stewart's Mill was a major part of that regeneration as it was situated in the centre of the town.

Developer
The regeneration of the building and regeneration of Coalisland was inspired and carried out by the Coalisland and District Development Association with support from the International Fund for Ireland and the Department of the Environment (NI).

Sources of funding
Fully funded by the the International Fund for Ireland and the Department of the Environment (NI) as part of the regeneration of Coalisland, through the Community Regeneration and Improvement Special Projects Scheme.

Conservation issues
The building gives character to the centre of the town and is the flagship of a wider heritage and conservation plan, which hopes to include the opening of a coal mine as a visitor attraction and the reopening of Coalisland Canal.

Award
The project won the British Urban Regeneration Association Best Practice Award 1996 in recognition of its outstanding contribution to urban regeneration.

Temple Bar Warehouses – Republic of Ireland

Location
Dublin

Listed status
Various

Total area
30 acres

History and former use
The Temple Bar area of Dublin on the south bank of the River Liffey contains a network of narrow streets extending from Trinity College and eighteenth-century parliament buildings in the east to City Hall and Christ Church Cathedral in the west. It contains many warehouses. The area had fallen into decline along with other similar areas on both sides of the river.

New use
Until 1987 the area was subject to proposals for massive clearance and redevelopment. With the assistance of the European Regional Development Fund from 1991, a less drastic approach was encouraged. A competition was devised to produce a design guide for the area, encouraging minimal demolition and imaginative refurbishment. As a result, many warehouses have been refurbished for housing and commercial uses.

Community issues
Great efforts are being made to improve housing conditions and reduce homelessness in Dublin. This is reflected in schemes such as Focus Point at Stanhope Green.

Sources of funding
European Regional Development Fund
Private finance.

Future prospects
The Temple Bar scheme is just one initiative that is continuing in the regeneration of the Quays area of Dublin. The banks of the River Liffey are set to return to the lively state that they enjoyed in the eighteenth century.

Index

Page numbers in **bold** refer to Figures